About the editor

Srila Roy is a lecturer in sociology at the University of Nottingham. She completed her undergraduate studies at the University of Delhi and her graduate work at the University of Warwick. Her research/teaching interests include post-colonial feminism, social movements, violence and conflict, and memory, emotions and trauma studies – many of which take as their starting point the contemporary political history of India and South Asia. She is the author of *Remembering Revolution: Gender, Violence and Subjectivity in India's Naxalbari Movement* (Oxford University Press, 2012). She serves on the executive committee of the Feminist and Women's Studies Association, UK.

New South Asian feminisms

Paradoxes and possibilities

EDITED BY SRILA ROY

Zed Books

LONDON | NEW YORK

New South Asian feminisms: Paradoxes and possibilities was first published in 2012 by Zed Books Ltd, 7 Cynthia Street, London N1 9JF, UK and Room 400, 175 Fifth Avenue, New York, NY 10010, USA

www.zedbooks.co.uk

Editorial copyright © Srila Roy 2012
Copyright in this collection © Zed Books 2012

The right of Srila Roy to be identified as the editor of this work has been asserted by her in accordance with the Copyright, Designs and Patents Act, 1988

Set in OurType Arnhem and Monotype Futura by Ewan Smith, London
Index: ed.emery@thefreeuniversity.net
Cover design: www.alice-marwick.co.uk
Printed and bound by CPI Group (UK) Ltd, Croydon, CRO 4YY

Distributed in the USA exclusively by Palgrave Macmillan, a division of St Martin's Press, LLC, 175 Fifth Avenue, New York, NY 10010, USA

A catalogue record for this book is available from the British Library
Library of Congress Cataloging in Publication Data available

ISBN 978 1 78032 190 5 hb
ISBN 978 1 78032 189 9 pb

Contents

Acknowledgements

My biggest thanks go to the contributors of this volume, without whose passion, willingness and deep sense of responsibility, this book would not have been possible. Their innovative and inspiring pieces of work form the crux of this project. This book would not have come to fruition without the encouragement and enthusiasm of Jakob Hortsmann, who found its rightful home at Zed Books. As the first editor that I have ever worked with, he set the bar high in ways that the rest of the team at Zed Books, especially Tamsine O'Riordan, more than fulfilled. My thanks to everyone at Zed whom I worked with subsequently for their support and accommodation in what proved to be fairly exceptional circumstances for me. True to her word, Malathi de Alwis stuck through this book as its 'consultant', from proposal to finished product. My thanks to her and Nivedita Menon for commenting on many key ideas and themes presented, especially in the introduction. Finally, my thanks to Shirin M. Rai for writing the foreword to this book with little hesitation and true belief in its significance and value.

Foreword

SHIRIN M. RAI

In editing *New South Asian feminisms*, Srila Roy has put together an excellent volume that explores several important themes of gender and politics. This volume will be an innovative, thoughtful and challenging contribution to the literature on South Asian feminisms at a time of great change in this region. As neoliberal economic regimes integrate South Asian economies ever more closely into the global economic order, women are facing increasing challenges in the labour market, the domestic spheres and in the organization of resistance to the downward pressures on the economy. As a 2010 UN report notes, 'on the whole, women still fall short of men in the region in their employment rates, pay and job opportunities. Most employed women in Asia-Pacific are in vulnerable employment – broadly defined as self-employed or own-account workers and contributing family workers' (UN 2010: 5). This vulnerability is increasing with the lengthening of migratory chains, in which women are a growing category of labour – low-paid, open to abuse, and yet contributing enormously to the remittances that increase the national income. In particular, global care chains are channelling women's labour into domestic work, 'where the isolated nature of household work in unfamiliar and harsh conditions, combined with inadequate local labour laws, put domestic workers in particular at greater risk to verbal, physical and sexual abuse' (ibid.: 6).

At the same time, we are also witnessing a political reshaping – both discursive and institutional – in this region. On the one hand there is a hardening of discursive borders – the language of *hindutva*, Islamophobia and Islamization are becoming predominant in public spaces as never before. At the same time the discourse of security is being appropriated by states to limit the freedom of ordinary citizens as well as mobilized political movements; terror talk is replacing dialogue, as unstable borders become sources of increasing state mobilizations of physical force, which is then legitimized in the name of security. With this reshaping of political landscapes, women's movements and groups have been mobilizing for change but with different strategies and outcomes. An engagement with the state has been a feature of many women's groups and NGOs, and has brought with it some rich rewards in terms of institutional arrangements and practices – allotted positions for women in political institutions at different levels, the establishment of women's national machineries, the introduction of women's studies syllabi and centres in higher education institutions, for example. However, despite all these successes, gender representation continues to be skewed heavily in favour of men, with women making up only 18.2 per cent of representatives in national legislatures in Asia (ibid.: 8). Violence against women also continues to be a growing concern in the age of neoliberal growth – women face high levels of domestic violence in the changing landscape of work. They are also vulnerable to violence in areas of political conflict, with rape being used to traumatize communities. With formal and informal discriminations underpinning legal systems in the region, challenging these political issues has been difficult. So, while there are significant challenges to gender equality, there have also been growing concerns about the strategies that are being employed to address these. In particular, and of particular concern to this volume, is the issue of the engagement of women's groups with the state – the growing NGO-ization of the women's movement in the context of the backlash that is attendant upon the relatively few but highly visible political gains that women's movements have been able to secure. An overarching concern is the nature of the women's movement, and, as Roy notes, the very category of 'woman', the subject of feminist politics, is being reviewed and rethought. The questions that Roy puts to the contributors of this volume are important:

- How is the increased mediation of a variety of agents transforming the very character and the broader field of women's activism in contemporary South Asia?
- How are feminist politics being reconfigured in this context?
- And how does this wider terrain affect the production and transmission of feminist politics and knowledges, especially across a perceived generational divide?

The issue of the generational divide within women's movements is a salient one as we move from the early political mobilizations of the 1970s, which focused on violence against women and on women's legal rights, to the identity-based interest in the discursive recognition of difference among women. The Shona saying goes 'paths are made from walking'. As feminists we are also walking on paths made by feet that struggled to forge new directions. That these paths are not smooth, have led us into cul-de-sacs on occasions and have been rather rough at times does not of course mean that we reject them, forget them or refuse to recognize their importance. We continue to reshape these paths to freedom. However, I worry about what I would call the bane of 'presentism' that is evident in our critiques; I worry that we continue to focus on the present at the expense of our past struggles, that by insisting that all phenomena and events ought to be seen with reference to the present gives a normative priority to the present, and the past is seen as something to be progressively overcome. Losing our histories can only be a delegitimization and disempowering of ourselves. So, addressing the issue of a generational divide makes this volume a timely and urgent one.

A second important theme that Roy identifies for this volume is that of structure and agency. Starting from a position where feminism and transformation of social relations were inextricably tied in South Asia, we now often approach the world out there as an object of study rather than as a social space that we all inhabit. While in the 1970s and the 1980s feminists worried about being co-opted by the state if they engaged with structures of power, the 1990s saw a reversal of this position – feminist engagement became increasingly part of the institutional fold. Whether it was NGOS or the state in its different forms – women's machineries, for example – or indeed international political and economic institutions such as the UN or the World Bank, we engaged with all these. If the vocabularies of difference kept us apart, then the learning of the vocabularies of power also posed questions for us. What is also worrying is that the language of politics is transforming into the language of expertise – feminist theorization and empirical research are becoming fodder for reports, governmental and non-governmental; the distance that such research demands is creating new silences. Expertise, while generating a demand for feminist research, is also creating some roadblocks on the way to interdisciplinary and creative politics on the ground. Some of the chapters in this book focus on these themes of how structures of power and the agential moments and actors interact – imperfectly, in fractured ways – and these chapters also open up new challenges for women's movements in the region. In particular the chapters address issues of work, law, sexual politics and subjectivities, feminist movements and state power, which one welcomes. I hope that the readers will engage productively with this collection of excellent essays.

Reference

UN (2010) *The World's Women 2010: Trends and Statistics*, New York: Department of Economic and Social Affairs, United Nations, unstats. un.org/unsd/demographic/products/Worldswomen/WW_full%20 report_BW.pdf, accessed 14 August 2012.

Introduction: paradoxes and possibilities

SRILA ROY[1]

Current assessments of feminism and women's movements tend to begin on a grim note. The present is imbued in such evaluations with a sense of urgency, even crisis, while feminism is understood as being lost or as having passed away (see Walby 2011 for a recent summary). Such uncertainty is propelled, if anything, by the many achievements of feminist initiatives observable in the unprecedented visibility afforded to 'woman' and gender in national and transnational discourses alike. That the face of global poverty is consistently the Third World woman is surely a marker of feminist success, especially in the 'developing' world (see John 2005). In South Asia – where the essays in this volume are located – such forms of success are perceived in more ambiguous terms. For many, the new-found visibility of gender in the discourses and practices of the state and international development signals, if anything, the successful 'co-option' of feminist achievements and ends by a variety of non- and anti-feminist forces (Tharu and Niranjana 1994; Chaudhuri 2004; Menon 2004, 2009; Gangoli 2007; De Alwis 2009; Karim 2011). 'Co-option' itself has repeatedly proved inadequate to the task of describing the complexities of the present in which gender and 'woman' have gained unprecedented political patronage just as women's movements have become institutionalized and housed in 'the conservatism of neoliberal policies' (Sangari 2007: 50). Much like the 'double entanglement' that McRobbie (2009) finds characteristic of 'postfeminism' in the West, feminist goals of agency and empowerment are being, it is argued, resignified (as economic efficiency, for instance) rather than outright rejected. While the spaces in which feminist activism can take place have enormously expanded, these are increasingly associated with practices of professionalization, managerialism and bureaucratization, or 'NGO-ization'. NGOs dominate feminist mobilizations in many of these countries that have seen the emergence of the NGO as a 'shadow state' (Karim 2011) in the face of 'failed' nation-states, as detailed below. Even when the state has been responsive to women's needs, its liberal legal impulse has served to strengthen rather than subvert conservative and patriarchal ideologies.

The liberal inheritance of women's movements, most manifest in their privileging of 'woman' as a rights-bearing subject to be protected by the state, is consequently seen to have come to its logical conclusion (Menon 2004; Madhok 2010). The presumed transparency of this subject, unmarked by community, caste or religious affiliations, has, moreover, lent to majoritarian and essentializing impulses *within* women's movements as well as to fierce identity-based politics and cleavages (see Sunder Rajan 2003). Globalization, privatization, (neo) liberalization, and increased and excessively militarized ethnic and religious nationalisms and violence are fundamentally transforming the terrain upon which feminists must wage their struggles, as well as the nature and form of such struggles. The future, it seems, has never been more uncertain (John 2005).

Feminist loss and hope

As with routine declarations of the 'death' of feminism in the West, feminist assessments of contemporary challenges outside its borders, as in South Asia, are marked by the affective force of loss, despair and foreboding (see Roy 2009). Laments over feminism's passing in an observable 'ageing' of the women's movement, as well as calls for the return to a more 'truly political' past, are not unheard of in such a context (John 2002; Menon 2004; De Alwis 2009). Across the region – as attested to in this volume – fears of the threat of 'co-option' are also generationally articulated. Young women are positioned on this terrain increasingly in terms of 'apathy, consumerism, and the appeal of conservative forces' (Nazneen and Sultan, this volume), factors used to explain their lack of identification with women's organizations and feminist issues and the consequent demise of feminism. Political pessimism inevitably emerges as the only response to the large-scale transformations and challenges to feminist politics in these countries (or indeed elsewhere; see Dean 2010).

Overtly pessimistic accounts of feminism's fragmentation, decline and even death preclude the hard task of empirically discerning and characterizing the *specificity* of feminist organizing and practice today. A rejection of current critiques of feminism's decline (in 'NGO-ization' and other processes) does not automatically imply a celebratory assertion of its revival; it provides, as Dean (ibid.) notes in his recent mapping of contemporary British feminism, 'an opportunity for detailed critical analysis, not simply celebration'. As evidenced in the current volume, there are rich and complex empirical instances of feminist mobilization in contemporary South Asia that emerge

2

unexpectedly and are associated with new subjects such as younger women and sexual subalterns – to use Ratna Kapur's (2005) coinage – with contradictory political effects. Such new feminist spaces and subjects – some of which have been enabled by the governmentalities of the state, development and international funding – are poorly understood by generationally motivated and/or leftist accounts of feminism's passing.[2] They are also not 'new' in any straightforward sense. Dean (2010) argues that celebratory narratives of feminism tend to overestimate their newness in much the same way as narratives of loss exaggerate their decline. The complex process of continuity and change across decades that he identifies in the British context resonates in the South Asian one.

The idea for this volume emerged from the impetus to explore, both theoretically and empirically, some of the wider changes to feminist mobilizing in South Asia engendered by the external and internal formations of power described above. Some of these have been analysed in recent mappings of South Asian feminism today (Azim et al. 2009; Loomba and Lukose 2012), even as cross-regional reflections remain scarce. What has been less remarked upon is that these are also interesting and not merely crisis-ridden times for feminist activism in South Asia, configured by the paradoxes and possibilities inherent in globalization and economic liberalization. The region is witness to new developments in contemporary feminist politics and not simply to the passing of feminism, as we once knew it. Through serious theoretical consideration, the essays map the empirical developments in South Asian feminist politics today in ways that go beyond the latter's production through the modality of crisis and/or decline alone. The volume's title, *New South Asian Feminisms*, signifies these new developments on the changing terrain of feminist organizing in South Asia and in its diaspora.

Set against the challenges of the present and motivated not by rampant pessimism or unqualified optimism, the volume provides an original exploration of the current state of South Asian feminist politics. Through 'thick' ethnographic description and sustained theoretical reflection, individual chapters explore the social realities of this contemporary feminism, its subject agents, emergent spaces of mobilization, and the paradoxes and possibilities inherent in its origin and actualization in the local and everyday. In showing how emergent feminist articulations are contending with key contemporary concerns (the neoliberal state, politicized religion and secularism, neoliberal development, political conflict, and new modes of governance and regulation in tandem with new assertions of rights and identities), the essays present ways of (re)thinking the feminist political for the predicaments of the present, globally.

The essays focus on four broad themes, which the rest of the introduction will highlight in terms of existing debates and perspectives. The first outlines feminisms in South Asia or 'South Asian feminisms', an unwieldy category that requires justification and elaboration given national and regional disparities, besides the unease with which 'feminism' has translated into local contexts. The volume's mapping of contemporary feminist political articulations as they intersect with established and 'newer' social movements such as sex workers' movements, nationalist and labour struggles, and struggles against 'ordinary' and 'extraordinary' forms of violence, also serves to expand preconceptions of the feminist political.

The second theme that the essays explore is that of the institutionalization of feminist politics in a number of sites such as the state and the law, and especially in the complexities of NGO practice. In considering and theoretically reworking the implications of 'mainstreaming' women's issues in projects and agendas of developmentalism and good governance, the essays draw out the implications of feminist politics in the context of its institutionalization.

Violence is a third theme that unites several of the interventions here presented, which is not surprising given the bloody histories of nearly all of the countries under consideration, as well as the specifically gendered nature of such violence. Together, they continue a long tradition of feminist theorizations of and resistance to violence in moments of rupture and relative stability, drawing on established sites such as the law but also newer, virtual ones.

This brings us to a final theme, which is that new modes of feminist intervention and activity, as well as a new generation of feminists, are discernible in a variety of local sites. Some of these, such as those centred on sexuality and violence, are also attached to 'younger' and middle-class feminist subjectivities in ways that have not been fully considered.[3] A generational paradigm which pits those feminists who constituted the vanguard of autonomous women's movements in the 1970s against those who are today part of a 'professionalized' academic and/or NGO culture has also made it difficult to recognize young women's activism as sufficiently feminist, if at all. The volume addresses, in this manner, a more general area of neglect within the study of social movements to do with generational divide, besides challenging, like recent interventions (Harris 2004; Aune and Redfern

2010; Dean 2009), globally pervasive accounts of the deradicalization of feminist politics located in the political apathy of younger women.

South Asian feminisms

'South Asia' and 'feminism' are both complex categories, not amenable to easy definition. Post-colonial South Asia, which today includes the nation-states of Bangladesh, India, Maldives, Nepal, Pakistan, Sri Lanka and, most recently, Afghanistan, is continuously overshadowed by regionalism, geopolitics and ethnic strife, making it difficult to speak of as a singular region. This is in spite of the fact that it shares interlocking geographical and historical, as well as cultural, legacies and is part of the daily global traffic of people, goods and ideas. The traditional hegemony exercised by India, whether through economic imperialism or political manoeuvring (as with the 1971 Bangladesh Liberation War and more recently through 'peacekeeping' in Sri Lanka), besides, of course, the long-standing India–Pakistan stand-off, renders possibilities for a common or pan-South Asian identity largely impossible.

For the lives and identities of women of the region, there is more that unites than separates. It has been well documented that the 'woman's question' came to be central to nation-making processes in British South Asia (Jayawardena 1986; Chatterjee 1989; Sangari and Vaid 1989; Mani 1989; De Alwis 2002; Rouse 2004). While colonial powers judged the ability of colonies to self-govern on the basis of this question, (male) nationalist elites sought to define the nation via authentic cultural identity and difference from the West, secured through the presence of women, 'the embodiment of that difference' (Niranjana 2007: 212). Nation-making as well as national identity was premised, in other words, on national culture to which women were exclusively aligned. Normative (middle-class) femininity came to stand in for the nation with specific consequences for 'real' women who had to negotiate this symbolic burden within and outside the home. Like the formation of the nation-states of India and Pakistan, the later creation of Bangladesh relied on the mobilization of Bengali womanhood (as against Muslim womanhood) for the consolidation of national cultural identity (Azim et al. 2009). The history of mass rapes that accompanied the birth of Bangladesh was consequently domesticated in the discursive transformation of the raped woman into a war heroine or *birangona* (Mookherjee 2008; see also Saikia 2011). Post-independence definitions of authentic cultural identity continue to be inscribed and asserted on the backs of women. Globalization of the region has renewed anxieties around the loss of cultural identity

5

and sovereignty that are routinely manifest in the increased and invariably violent regulation of women's bodies (Oza 2006).

The colonial legacy and identification of women with national culture have also entailed, in post-colonial South Asia as elsewhere (John 2004; Niranjana 2007; Madhok 2010; Roces 2010; Al-Ali 2002 on Egypt), a dismissal of feminism on the grounds of cultural inauthenticity or Westernization. A dichotomy between 'indigenous culture' and 'Western culture' is effectively shored up every time questions of gender relations and women's rights are raised in ways that are not at play when it comes to other political demands. In the context of the growing Islamization of countries like Pakistan, Zia (2009) has recently shown how a 'moderate' Islamic feminism is being offered as a cultural and political defence against Western, liberal and culturally alien feminisms; schisms that have become more naturalized post-9/11. Indeed, feminist critiques of the Enlightenment project emerging in the afterlife of the 'civilizational discourses' of 9/11 have aligned feminism almost exclusively with secular, Western liberalism, with which women's pious and religious identities are being counterposed, as critically discussed in Dhaliwal and Patel's contribution to this volume.

Given, then, what Al-Ali (2002: 10) in the context of the women's movement in Egypt calls the 'culturalisation' of political, especially women's issues, South Asian feminists – like their Middle Eastern counterparts – have been sceptical of rejecting the label 'feminism' on the grounds of 'purity' and 'authenticity' (see John 2004). This is not to say that feminism has travelled to this part of the world with relative ease, and there is a long (post-)colonial history of disidentification with feminism among women (summarized in Chaudhuri 2004). Niranjana (2007: 210) remarks how in the South Asian context activists and academics alike have been more comfortable with the use of 'the women's question (in historical contexts) and the women's movement (with reference to more contemporary formations)' than with feminism invariably associated with Westernization. The charge of Westernization and elitism (which often go together) still constitutes grounds for easy dismissal when it comes to 'newer' expressions of feminist politics in the subcontinent, as in the case of urban middle-class feminist politics in India, as Mitra-Kahn's chapter in this volume shows.

Notwithstanding continuing complexities around the use of the term feminism, what is undeniable and perhaps even singular to the region is the long history of women's mobilizations and feminist activism. What further marks the singularity of women's movements in South Asia is their alliances with other democratic struggles, starting with anti-colonial movements, and continuing, post-independence, with struggles around war and militarization, against religious and right-wing fundamentalisms, state repression, sexual violence, and being generally embedded in concerns of both recognition and redistribution (for important overviews, see Jayawardena 1986; Kumar 1993; Ray 1999; Rouse 1988, 2004). In being understood through the prism of class, caste, community and religion, gender has always been intersectional for feminist theorization, while feminist politics has invariably been articulated as alliance- and issue-based rather than strictly or solely around identity. Academic research has been nourished by activism and organizing on the ground in ways that are also, perhaps, unique to the South Asian context.[4]

Ongoing processes of democratization of the state coupled with the pressures of globalization, changing discourses and practices of development, and neoliberal agendas and market-based state reform have dramatically altered the conditions under which feminist and other political struggles unfold in South Asia today. Nearly all countries have had to contend, in more recent times, with the reconfiguration of the state and civil society in tandem with neoliberal economic policies that are deepening existing inequalities (Sangari 2007). Changes in women's mobilizations in countries like India and Bangladesh have closely paralleled transformations in the post-colonial developmental state from, broadly speaking, nationalism to neoliberalism, as Rai (2008) puts it. In Sri Lanka and Nepal, in contrast, militarized ethnic and class-based conflicts have posed additional challenges. The entry of religious fundamentalisms into the political mainstream, which was initially peculiar to some nation-states like Pakistan, has now come to define others, as the region is itself reconfigured as per the cartographies of a global 'war on terror'. It is upon such a changing political field that feminist struggles 'have shaped themselves and engaged with various formations of power' (Azim et al. 2009).

In so doing, contemporary feminist mobilizations are expanding existing ideas of the feminist political at a time when it risks being depoliticized and packaged into 'gender equality'. Several of the contributions to this volume attest to this expansion, whether in terms of new areas of feminist intervention or in expanding ideas of 'feminism' and 'activism' in conjunction with a range of social movements, state mechanisms and civil-society-based or informal 'grassroots' initiatives. Some of these have been enabled by the particular governmental and non-governmental technologies engendered by the opening up of the economy and globalization, even as these processes have created new categories and 'docile subjects' of/for the governance agenda.[5] Menon (2009: 105) draws out a key paradox of such an agenda, which relates to its tendency to stabilize and thereby domesticate 'gender' and sexuality *and* to radicalize the same in unexpected ways: 'government programmes can produce new solidarities among women drawn into them, and radicalize women hitherto unexposed to public activity despite the fact that this is not the goal of such programmes'.

Svati Shah's chapter, along with recent work on the Indian sex industry (Kotiswaran 2011a, 2011b), brings out these tensions in mapping the transformation of the 'prostitute' into the 'sex worker' with the advent of HIV/AIDs prevention and control in India. While the sex worker emerged as a distinct category of governance within the global landscape, it also enabled the politicization of existing subjectivities and the creation of new ones observable in the rise of sex workers' movements in India (see Gooptu 2000). Shah shows how intersecting histories of prostitution, feminism and pornography have shaped the current US-led and highly coercive abolitionist policy that tends to conflate prostitution with human trafficking. In foregrounding US discourse and practice in shaping South Asian complexities around sex work and human trafficking, Shah exemplifies the need to locate and understand the local in relation to wider, transnational processes and global discourses of gender and race. Her intervention, like that of Dhaliwal and Patel, reminds us of the need to go beyond an engagement with South Asia as nation, geopolitical entity or locale, given its imbrication in multiple and cross-cutting histories and contemporary struggles (see Sinha 2012).

Even as contributors map the widening of 'feminisms' in contemporary times, they remain mindful of its continuous regulation and foreclosure. Religion has recently emerged as a contentious site upon which feminist ideas are thought of as being discursively expanded (to new understandings of agency and subjectivity; Mahmood 2005) or foreclosed. Growing feminist interest in religion is also prompted by changes on the ground, such as the resurgence of religious-based political movements in South Asia (see Bhasin et al. 1994 and Basu and Jeffery 1998), or the shift from multiculturalism to multi-faithism in the UK, with specific implications for South Asian women. Set in the latter unfolding context, Sukhwant Dhaliwal and Pragna Patel (this volume) argue *not* for a greater accommodation of women's religious identities but for a renewed feminist focus on and commitment to secularism. Such a commitment has, of course, been at the heart of South Asian feminism, but not unproblematically, as in the case of India, where secular feminist values were seen to be harbouring majoritarian ones (see Sunder Rajan 2003).[6] Dhaliwal and Patel's urgent plea to uphold secular public policy spaces in the contemporary UK is informed by the complexities of a post-9/11 world in which 'feminism and secularism are being used as part of an assimilationist pressure' on ethnic minorities. The contemporary context should not result, they argue, in the defensive repudiation of secularism but in a clearer understanding of the ways in which the institutionalization of religion could be bad for ethnic minority women, in particular. Written by two long-standing activists, this chapter brings in another dimension of the region, its vibrant diaspora and the role that South Asian women in Britain have played in resisting the 'patriarchal racism' (Brah 1996) of the state (see Wilson 2006).

Feminism institutionalized

It is striking how, across the North–South divide, the eighties and nineties mark the embedding of feminism in institutions of the state, governance and civil society, thereby endowing it with a more formal, stable and, some would argue, less visible or even apolitical form. For some, this 'maturing' of feminism in governmental and non-governmental institutionalization signifies an abdication of its autonomy and radicality. The 'broad antistatism' (Sunder Rajan 2003: 31) that characterizes feminist debates in South Asia makes, in any case, the question of forming alliances with the state extremely problematic.[7] Feminist reservations have been borne out not only in the case of legal reform that has exponentially increased the powers of the state (Menon 2004) but also in the backlash against the visibility of women in politics and public life more generally. Mayaram (2002: 405) documents the specificity of a 'South Asian [feminist] backlash' with respect to 'the feminization and democratization of the rural public sphere' in India via legislative changes such as the introduction of reservations (quota systems) and the involvement of rural women in state-led development programmes.[8] The latter underscored the limits of politicizing rural women under the rubric of a state that employed progressive feminist language to further its own interests (such as population control) besides those of international agencies (Saheli 1991; see also Madhok and Rai 2012).

As a number of chapters detail, the institutionalization of feminist movements in 'NGO-ization' is a locus of anxieties similar to those that have been documented elsewhere (Lang 1997; Alvarez 1998; Jad 2007; Al-Ali and Pratt 2009), including the relegation of autonomy and agency to global funding imperatives, professionalization and manage-rialism, and a move away from mass-based political struggles, broader coalitions and structural critique to neoliberal modes of governance (Sangari 2007). As the 'empowerment' of Third World women came to monopolize transnational development rhetoric, several 'autonomous' and grassroots women's organizations transformed into NGOs given access to funds and resources for the sake of survival. Notwithstanding the imbrication of grassroots NGOs in wider and increasingly neoliberal economic processes, particular local fields (in a Bourdieuean sense; see Ray 1999) and historical moments complicate uniform assessments of their purpose and effects. While Ruwanpura (2007) critiques NGOs in Sri Lanka for development-oriented projects that fail to consider and thereby reinforce the gender politics of ethno-nationalisms, Jafar (2007) upholds the effective force of Pakistani feminist NGOs in coun-tering the rising tide of religious fundamentalisms, urging, thereby, a reconsideration of 'NGO' as a unified category.

Bangladesh is paradigmatic of the 'neoliberal turn' in development discourse (Madhok 2010) exemplified in the management of poverty through a microfinance industry to which poor women are key. In a scathing critique of the optimism surrounding microfinance opera-tions in transforming poor women's lives, Karim (2011) shows how NGOs have emerged as a 'shadow state' in rural Bangladesh, alloca-ting themselves forms of sovereignty reserved for states in providing essential services and employment (see also, for a recent summary, Chowdhury 2011). Given the production of gendered neoliberal subjects through the governmentalities exercised by NGOs, Karim (2011: 204) is not surprisingly led to conclude that 'real' political change can come only from social movements 'that sit apart from the developmental sector' or from imperatives that are not driven by the compulsions of funding, as has been argued in the Indian context (Menon 2004).

Sharp divides of this kind – between 'NGO-ized' feminisms and 'autonomous' or social-movement-based ones – tend to undermine what Alvarez (1998) calls the hybrid nature of most feminist NGOs or the performative character of development itself (Sharma 2008). Interrogating this performativity entails moving beyond a considera-tion of whether developmental projects succeed or fail (and are 'good' or 'bad') to consider what they mean in practice and 'how they are brought to life through everyday actions and interactions' (ibid.: xix). In India, for instance, NGOs and governmental practices around AIDS prevention have promoted the rights of sexual minorities in ways that older women's organizations that tended to view issues of sexuality as 'Western' and alien to an Indian context never managed (Menon 2008). Still, it has become possible for some Indian feminists to evade the challenges of the burgeoning sexuality rights movement by seeing it as an offshoot of neoliberal globalization, as noted and critiqued by Mary John (2009).

Feminist organizing in this part of the world, as elsewhere, is also marked by a multiplicity which has rendered the label of 'movement', let alone that of feminism, inadequate to capture all that falls within its ambit. This multiplicity (reflected in the title of this volume in its use of 'feminisms') has also emerged as a locus of concern in the face of the growing diversification and diffusion of feminist aims and agendas. The ideal of autonomy, key to the shaping of normative visions of feminist organizing and change and not in South Asia alone (see, in the context of Latin America, Alvarez 1998, and for Britain, Dean 2010), is rendered less stable in the face of the blurring of the boundaries between the state, civil society and the market. Against the need to recover a pure 'autonomous' feminism, contributors to this volume emphasize the hybridity and heterogeneity that are pervasive to feminist organizing and its distinct legacies in South Asian countries. Several of the chapters (see especially Ahmad; Basu; Nazneen and Sultan) track the organizational lives of feminist interventions and campaigns; ones that counter easy oppositions between statist and anti-statist feminist practices, governmental and non-governmental modes of regulation, and revolutionary and reformist political strategies. They open up, in this manner, a wider discursive domain for imagining and actualizing feminist interventions that go beyond established polarities.

The on-the-ground politics of 'NGO-ization' in Bangladesh that is the focus of the contribution by Sohela Nazneen and Maheen Sultan makes evident its transformation of the feminist field as a whole, from demanding the professionalization and even corporatization of women's organizations to assisting smaller, local ones through an increase in resources. NGO-ization, in their text, emerges as a heterogeneous practice, malleable in the hands of different women's organizations with varying levels of capital, compromise and costs (see also Chowdhury 2011). It is productive not merely of new modes of mobilization but also of new 'professionalized' subjectivities, new temporalities ('pre-' and 'post-'NGO-ization), and new risks and vulnerabilities in ways that are not uniformly experienced or negotiated. The constant negotiation by development and social movement actors on the ground renders 'NGO-ization' a dynamic if ambivalent process against its theorization as a 'final, fixed and irreversible moment' and that of the feminist professional as a 'sell-out' (Murdock 2003: 525; see also Markowitz and Tice 2002; Jenkins 2009; Roy 2011).

Sadaf Ahmad's rich and detailed analysis of an Alliance Against Sexual Harassment or AASHA in Pakistan addresses the uses of the law and the state for the fulfilment of feminist ends, in a wider context of growing feminist scepticism with the 'scandal of the state' (Sunder Rajan 2003). Most significant was the way in which this campaign drew, on the one hand, on donor-aided and state-focused interventions and, on the other, non-funded and civil-society-based ones, circumventing, in this manner, the inherent weaknesses of both institutionalized and anti-statist approaches. Likewise, Srimati Basu's chapter considers the distinct spaces for intervening in everyday marital trouble and domestic violence in urban India as opened up by the women's movements' engagement with the state on questions of family and violence. In spite of differing ideological and political commitments, Basu unearths remarkable similarities in the strategic solutions put forth by politically affiliated and autonomous women's groups to 'mediate' and support women through marital breakdowns. In the case of both anti-sexual harassment legislation in Pakistan and that of marriage mediation in India, time-worn oppositions between revolution and reform are countered in the manner in which social change was visualized and enacted in context-specific ways. These ethnographies are, in Basu's words, 'a reminder of the importance of the contingent and contextual in activist engagements with law, marriage and violence'.

Witnessing and resisting violence

The gendered nature of violence, trauma and witnessing has been at the heart of feminist theorizing and mobilizing in South Asia. This has included violence of a 'spectacular' variety, as in the originary violence of Partition (Menon and Bhasin 1998; Butalia 2000), communal pogroms in India (Sarkar 2002; Chatterji and Mehta 2007) and 'ethnic cleansing' in Sri Lanka (De Mel 2001, 2007), and the more routine forms of gender-based violence and inequalities that structure public and intimate spaces alike, constituting, for many, a continuum (Pandey 2006; Coomaraswamy and Fonseka 2005; Roy 2008; Desai 2009). The feminist endeavour has not merely been to make the gendered nature of such violence visible but also to fundamentally alter, through sustained activism and thought, our understanding of what violence is. In the context of the partition of British India, for instance, the use of women's bodies to enact forms of violence against the other (men/families/communities/nation) provided new purchase on the relation between the nation and gender, and on how gendered violence actively produces nation-states and its citizen-subjects (on Bangladesh, see Mookherjee 2008; on India, Das 1995, 2007; on Pakistan, Ghani 2009).

Ethnographies and activism around violence in South Asia have repeatedly laid bare the inadequacy of theorizing gender-based violence as the exercise of male power or sexual desire alone given its historical enactment in allegories of nation and community belonging. In India and Pakistan, large-scale public protests took place in the seventies and eighties around issues of gender violence but also as part of a wider politically repressive climate during which the state itself was called to account (see Kumar 1993 on India and Rouse 1988 on Pakistan; see also Ahmad, this volume). In Sri Lanka and more recently in Maoist Nepal, ethnic and class-based armed conflict have forced feminists to move beyond images of women as forever victimized and marginalized by war and militarization to 'empowered' images of women as armed combatants and mothers of soldiers/martyrs (De Alwis and Jayawardena 1998; De Mel 2001 on Sri Lanka; Manchanda 2004 on Nepal; see also Roy 2009).[9] Such a new repertoire of gendered imagery has shaken established understandings of violence and war as being always and only bad for women (Rajasingham-Senanayake 2004).[10]

Across the region, the more *everyday* forms of violence that women face – and that is the focus of several chapters – are understood, even in legal discourse, in terms of the modesty, 'honour' and 'purity' that women's bodies are seen to bear and risk losing. In an age of unprecedented economic and cultural globalization, women face newer forms of coercive control as they enter previously male-dominated public spaces as waged labourers (Siddiqi 2010), developmental workers (as in the case of the developmental worker Bhanwari Devi in India; see Mayaram 2002, Madhok and Rai 2012) or even as emancipated middle-class women (see Oza 2006 and Mitra-Kahn, this volume). The systematic violence that has emerged against women in this new economic order resonates with Dhaliwal and Patel's rationalization of the UK government's 'faith agenda' as partly a way of controlling women who seem to have had it 'too good'.

Drawing on rich feminist theorizations of violence emerging from/ on the region (De Alwis and Jayawardena 1998; Kannabiran and Kannabiran 2002; Chatterjee et al. 2009), individual essays turn to the complexity and adequacy of feminist responses to violence, documenting, in some instances, new modalities of collective witnessing and resistance. At the heart of the Indian urban cyberfeminist Blank Noise project is, Trishima Mitra-Kahn (this volume) tells us, an emphasis on moving beyond shame and victimhood to engage in 'public confrontation' with street sexual harassment with female victims (re)interpellated as 'action heroes'. Urban middle-class women are in this manner not merely asserting women's right to public space (see also Phadke et al. 2011) but are also testing the limits of what counts as feminist agency and activism, as I go on to explain. Locating women's agential capacities in particular configurations of constraint and visibility, Rebecca Walker's chapter on feminist peace activism in eastern Sri Lanka provides a thoroughgoing material basis on which normative paradigms of peace-building and conflict resolution must be grounded. These must take into account, Walker insists, the increased vulnerabilities of women in wartime situations that are in danger of being eschewed in an opposition between 'suffering' and 'resilience' that even feminists have employed. At the same time, and much like Mitra-Kahn, Walker's intimate ethnography pushes beyond the received convention of what counts as feminist activism in moments of conflict, particularly at a time when feminist peace activism and women's movements are said to be in decline in Sri Lanka (De Alwis 2009).

A new generation of feminists: spaces and practices of 'young' feminists

Generational paradigms have come to dominate feminist research and writing in the Anglo-American context. The use and dominance of the 'wave metaphor' has been interpreted as setting up the history of feminism's recent past in terms of an inter-generational family feud. Young women or 'third wave' feminists are positioned in such a narrative as refusing to inherit the legacies of their feminist foremothers in carving out a feminism that is distinct from if not oppositional to 'second wave feminism' (Adkins 2004 and Dean 2009 for the UK context; and Weigman 2000 and Purvis 2004 for the US). While Roces and Edwards (2010) note, in their recent large-scale mapping of women's movements across Asia, that this periodization of women's movements is limited to the Anglo-American context, it is fair to say that feminist history-writing is indeed periodized in some contexts. In India, for instance, the use of the wave metaphor is not unknown (Madhok 2010), with some noting a 'generational gap, if not actual conflict' (Sunder Rajan 2003: 31) among Indian feminists over the issue of whether or not to ally with the state. The generational shift in feminist movements in Bangladesh is, as Nazneen and Sultan note in their contribution to this volume, strongly linked to the process of NGO-ization which began much earlier than in neighbouring countries. Elsewhere in the region, younger women are overwhelmingly seen as the subjects of a professionalized, NGO-ized feminism, as affirmed in the appellation of a 'temporary, careerist, "nine-to-five feminis[t]"' (De Alwis 2009: 86; see also Menon 2004). Speaking of Sri Lanka, De Alwis (2009) maps, again in a generational mode, the manner in which feminists have shifted from refusing the ideologies of the state and militants to making requests or demands of the state, which are indistinguishable from projects of governance.

Responses such as these are not surprising given the non-funded, non-party, voluntary and autonomous mode in which feminists have traditionally mobilized and politically intervened in these countries. 'Autonomous politics' still provide a strong normative idea of what feminist politics ought to look like, against which contemporary manifestations are measured and invariably fall short. Against such generational narratives of decline and loss, many of the essays uphold the vibrancy and radicalism of contemporary feminist politics associated, moreover, with a newer generation of 'younger women'. The discussions by Mitra-Kahn and Nazneen and Sultan explicitly take up and explore the activism, identities and affections of 'young' South Asian feminists.

In Bangladesh, for instance, young feminists grew up in a context wherein the development paradigm was already ubiquitous, informing 'professionalized' modes of engaging women's rights as well as adopting more professionalized feminist subjectivities. While such professionalism is the cornerstone of critiques by 'older feminists', Nazneen and Sultan usefully point to the pressures of time and money that make remuneration so essential for younger women, implicitly critiquing, thereby, a metropolitan feminism rooted in ideals of voluntarism (that are inherently gendered; Jenkins 2009; see also Roy 2011). That young, especially urban and middle-class women (as opposed to lower-middle-class women from small towns) are not joining established women's groups in contemporary Bangladesh does not mean a lack of political will. Other campaigns and movements have been able to channel their support, especially through the political reinvention of cyberspace.

The dynamics of urban cyberfeminist activism in India are the explicit focus of Mitra-Kahn's chapter. The subject of such a new form of feminist praxis is not merely young but urban and middle-class, a decidedly unusual creature in the Indian feminist landscape. Mitra-Kahn offers her reflections on the hybrid activist spaces comprised of 'offline' street activism and 'online' campaigning in India as a conscious countering of the assumption that young middle-class women are apathetic towards feminist politics. In different ways, these chapters show how globalization and the different configurations that it made possible, such as the opening up of the media and Internet technologies, have created spaces for young women to politically intervene in ways that might not have been possible for previous generations. New feminist subjectivities are discernible upon such a terrain but not as easily reducible to a 'co-opted' neoliberal subject as is generally assumed.

In the South Asian context, a generational paradigm is also inflected with anxieties around class/caste, and an enforced divide between material and cultural concerns. Class politics have always been at the heart of feminist politics in the region, largely ascribable to the leftist heritage of women's movements in the 'Third World' (Rouse 1988). Women's movements in India and Pakistan have tended to draw their leadership from the ranks of the urban and educated but have privileged the language and aspirations of a socialist feminism in taking as their subject poor rural women. As Mary John (1996) has noted of Indian feminism (and Mitra-Kahn discusses in her chapter), this was one of the primary ways in which it could establish its legitimacy and Indianness against routine declarations of feminism as elite, Western and therefore irrelevant to the concerns and struggles of the majority (on Pakistan, see Rouse 1988). Unlike middle-class feminists of a previous generation, young Indian women are articulating a feminist politics that is neither defensive about its borrowing from Western feminist repertoires or, indeed, about its middle-class and urban location. Mitra-Kahn points, however, to their reflexivity with respect to 'multiple markers of privilege', and activist efforts to transgress a caste/class-infused digital divide. Class-based anxieties continue to haunt urban expressions of young women's activism, as was witnessed in the reactions to the SlutWalk marches that took place in the Indian metropolises of Delhi and Kolkata during 2011/12. Queer feminist politics in India is equally subject to dismissal on grounds of privilege, elitism and cultural inauthenticity, even as many lesbian support groups are consciously non-elite, even working-class and lower-caste.[11]

Not all these new forms of feminist mobilization are middle-class, as is often assumed, as the chapters on sex workers' movements (Shah), subnationalist struggles (Sen) and those around violence against women (Basu) and violence more generally (Walker) show. Debarati Sen turns to poor Nepali women plantation workers, the backbone of Darjeeling's economy, who are caught in between a subnationalist struggle pitted against the Indian state and labour activism for rights and protection from the state. The 'multiple marginalities' of these women as well as their political action belie easy taxonomies of 'recognition' and 'redistribution' given the imbrication of the material and the affective, the cultural and economic in everyday life. Just as an ethnonationalist discourse uses images of women as good workers to fuel its political ambitions, women appropriate the politics of recognition for the 'redistribution of power and resources within the plantation hierarchy'. A subnationalist movement that responds to some but not all of women's needs (and silences others) is thereby reinvented in women's activism, engendering in them new capacities.

Finally, such feminist and sexual politics are also not straightforwardly 'new'. While sex workers' movements in India are, as Shah's chapter shows, a recent visible entrant on the feminist scene, they reiterate established modes of engaging issues of rights and making political demands via the law. The 'young' feminist subjectivities that Nazneen and Sultan and Mitra-Kahn's chapters explore are products of multiple forces, just as the forms of activism they are involved in creatively reconfigure existing tropes and orientations of feminist struggles in the region (see Ram 2008). 'Never has a time for intergenerational dialogue seemed more apropos,' Mitra-Kahn concludes.

Conclusion

The activism of younger women poses critical challenges to global declarations of feminism's passing and death that resonate in the South Asian context. Bringing us back to the tensions of pessimism and optimism that we started with, these discussions eschew both extremes in providing a nuanced consideration of the everyday forms of activism women are involved in, which are not straightforwardly the measure of feminist 'success' or 'failure'. The comparative South Asian perspective also acts as a check on tendencies towards oversimplification and generalization (Basu and Jeffery 1998). It complicates, for instance, the dominant tropes of women's movements in the region as being always and only elite and upper-caste by unpacking the intersections of gender, caste and class in feminist mobilizations around nationalism, development, sexuality, religion and violence. The politicization if not racialization of religion in the diaspora that lead Dhaliwal and Patel to reassert feminism's secular credentials undermines easy ideas of South Asia as ridden with religious crisis in opposition to a secular and stable West. Specific political fields have informed particular processes of 'NGO-ization' with distinct, at times unintended, effects in ways that recent theorizations of neoliberal development that inevitably see it as a tool of domination might benefit from considering. In an instance of the many similarities uncovered in feminist activism in the region, the essays point to the productive and not merely repressive capacity of local development organizations as they draw on the multiple legacies and languages of women's movements in different locales. The feminist past is itself rendered heterogeneous, mired in histories of colonialism, nationalism, nation-building and development, which make any proclamations of autonomy and authenticity difficult (John 2009). Feminist assessments of loss and achievement in the present have equally to be cognizant of such a hybrid history that informs the manner in which feminist ideas have travelled and come to be varyingly institutionalized or marginalized (Berry 2003).

In analysing the traffic of ideas and the production of subjectivities in South Asia, the essays point towards the inadequacy of existing conceptual tools and the need for a new lexicon. As already indicated, conceptual and empirical expectations of political radicality and autonomous agency might be inadequate to capture and make sense of a rapidly changing socio-political context in which freedom and subjection increasingly intersect. Analytic distinctions between institutionalized and non-institutionalized and civil and political spaces are also not sufficient for the hybrid manifestations of feminist activism in the present. Works located elsewhere, such as in Europe and Latin America, have already made significant headway in bridging these analytic divides, and are thus drawn on in the explorations in this volume (Alvarez 1998; Genz 2006; Dean 2010; Al-Ali and Pratt 2009). They also reflect the two distinct bodies of scholarship that the essays as well as this introduction draw on and speak to – namely, political theory and development studies. With respect to the former, commentators argue against the problematic delineation of the idea of political 'radicality' within certain assumed spaces and subjects (Dean 2009). Dean proposes, instead, a reinvigorating of the signifier 'radical' by associating it with a host of political practices not ordinarily viewed as such in being defined as moderate, conservative and/or co-opted. An emphasis on the performative and political force of radicality is also implicit in recent (feminist) ethnographies of developmental programmes. These map the production of unruly, politicized, even feminist subjects and not simply docile governmentalized ones in developmental spaces (Berry 2003; Moodie 2007; Sharma 2008). Together, they suggest the inadequacy of theorizing political subjectivity and agency as occurring entirely outside the structures of power, be they formations of the state, capital or development. Harris (2004) notes how young women activists in the contemporary West seek new kinds of political engagement and affective communities even as these remain embedded within – and not outside or transgressive of – particular regimes of power. For these and other reasons, the 'new' forms of feminist activism being engaged in by young women, subaltern women and queer women the world over are often not recognizable as such but are, as a number of recent commentators passionately show, no less socio-politically engaged for that reason; they are embedded *and* transformative.

Instead of seeking to recover or reclaim a truly transformatory feminist politics (as is often the current impulse), the essays turn to the kind of future or idea of the future that these discursive and affective economies open up for post-colonial and transnational feminism today. What emerges, however, is not a utopian future but a very concrete space for feminist political engagement, embroiled in the messiness of the (neo)liberalizing imperatives of the state, rights discourses, religious and secular spaces, nationalisms and developmentalism, conflict and peace. It is our hope that the new empirical developments in feminist activism that they map and the new theoretical challenges that these pose will prompt a rethinking and re-evaluation of established understandings of feminist politics, its spaces and subjects, at a moment of transformation, if not of crisis, in contemporary South Asia.

Notes

1 Many thanks to Nivedita Menon, Malathi de Alwis and especially to Srimati Basu for critical readings and comments on this introduction.

2 For a critique of left feminist declarations of feminism's passing such as that found in Nancy Fraser (2009), see Eschle and Maiguashca (2011).

3 This collection was also meant to include a very important intervention by Niluka Gunawardena on the slow recognition of disabled women by young South Asian feminists.

4 The conscious links between the women's movement and women's studies in India is one im-

mediate example. The link between theory and practice was institutionalized in the very establishment of women's studies in India such that 'research' was not conceived of as an end in itself but as politically committed from the start, as a form of outreach or as 'action research' (John 2002). Ritu Menon (2011: xxi), in an introduction to a recent collection of memoirs of the Indian women's movement, remarks how the 'Indian Association for Women's Studies (IAWS) ... must be the only academic body in the country that has a very large non-academic, activist membership'.

5 Menon (2009) defines the

concept of governance in distinction from the old model of 'government' 'as something carried on by the state, and to make "civil society organizations" (which have come to be understood as NGOs) responsible for basic necessities such as health, education and water'. Here she alludes to a broader understanding of development agencies as centrally implicated in the processes and politics of governmentality, especially in the context of neoliberal economic organization.

6 Increasingly, secularism or its denial has become a critical factor in the self-definition of the modern nation-state in South Asia, with Pakistan defined as an Islamic state and Sri Lanka and Bangladesh privileging the dominant religion. Only Nepal has recently affirmed its secular nature.

7 Indian feminism did not, however, have the explicit anti-statism of its Pakistani counterpart, holding the state accountable and also working with the state (see Chakravarti 2007; Sangari 2007). In the face of the rise of the Hindu right and changes in the state with the consolidation of a neoliberal economic regime, its relation to the state is a more vexed one today.

8 Mayaram (2002) is here referring to the women's quotas that were introduced by the Indian state in the early nineties as a result of which about a million women in rural India now serve as elected heads. She also refers to the landmark women's development programme in the northern state of Rajasthan which mobilized poor rural women in the service of grassroots development, and was abruptly disbanded.

9 The need to move beyond images of women as homogeneously powerless and victimized 'to conceptualize women as benefactors, supporters or even perpetrators of violence' (Al-Ali and Pratt 2009: 12) has been stressed in other transnational feminist explorations, as in the context of the Middle East recently.

10 South Asian women's agency *in* violence, whether through their involvement in armed insurgencies or in the violent ideologies and manifestations of religious politics, has forced an urgent reconsideration of the erstwhile emphasis on victimhood (see Butalia and Sarkar 1995; Basu and Jeffrey 1998; De Mel 2007; Sen 2007). An older, now classic oral history of women in armed struggle is Stree (1989). For a more recent account see Roy (2012).

11 On the development of lesbian politics in India, see Basu (2006); Achuthan et al. (2007); Bacchetta (2002) and Dave (2010). There are today approximately nine organizations and eight newsletters that work and publish on lesbian and bisexual women's issues in the country. On the class dynamics of India's queer movement, see Gupta (2005), and on working-class lesbians in India, see Sharma (2006).

References

Achuthan, A., R. Biswas and A. K. Dhar (2007) *Lesbian Standpoint*, Kolkata: Sanhati.

Adkins, L. (2004) 'Passing on feminism: from consciousness to reflexivity?', *European Journal of Women's Studies*, 11(4): 427–44.

Al-Ali, N. (2002) 'Women's movements in the Middle East: case studies of Egypt and Turkey', Working paper, Geneva: United Nations Research Institute for Social Development.

Al-Ali, N. and N. Pratt (2009) 'Introduction', in N. Al-Ali and N. Pratt, *Women and War in the Middle East: Transnational Perspectives*, London and New York: Zed Books.

Alvarez, S. (1998) 'Advocating feminism: Latin American feminist NGO "boom"', www.mtholyoke. edu/acad/latam/schomburg-moreno/alvarez.html, accessed January 2009.

Aune, K. and C. Redfern (2010) *Reclaiming the F Word: The new feminist movement*, London and New York: Zed Books.

Azim, F., N. Menon and D. M. Siddiqi (2009) 'Negotiating new terrains: South Asian feminisms', *Feminist Review*, 91: 1–8.

Bacchetta, P. (2002) 'Rescaling transnational "queerdom": lesbian and "lesbian" identitary-positionalities in Delhi in the 1980s', *Antipode*, 947: 973.

Basu, A. R. (2006) 'Lesbianism in Kolkata', Sappho for Equality Research Papers Series no. 1, Kolkata: Sappho.

Basu, A. and P. Jeffery (eds) (1998) *Appropriating Gender: Women's activism and politicized religion in South Asia*, London and New York: Routledge.

Berry, K. (2003) 'Developing women: the traffic in ideas about women and their needs in Kangra, India', in K. Sivaramakrishnan and A. Agrawal (eds), *Regional Modernities: The cultural politics of development in India*, Stanford, CA: Stanford University Press.

Bhasin, K., R. Menon and N. S. Khan (eds) (1994) *Against All Odds: Essays on Women, Religion and Development in India and Pakistan*, New Delhi: Kali for Women.

Brah, A. (1996) *Cartographies of Diaspora: Contesting Identities*, London: Routledge.

Butalia, U. (2000) *The Other Side of Silence. Voices from the Partition of India*, London: C. Hurst and Co.

Butalia, U. and T. Sarkar (eds) (1995) *Women and the Hindu Right: A collection of essays*, Delhi: Kali for Women.

Chakravarti, U. (2007) 'The "burdens" of nationalism: some thoughts on South Asian feminists and the nation state', in N. de Mel and S. Thiruchandran (eds), *At the Cutting Edge: Essays in honour of Kumari Jayawardena*, New Delhi: Women Unlimited.

Chatterjee, P. (1989) 'The nationalist resolution of the women's question', in K. Sangari and S. Vaid (eds), *Recasting Women: Essays in Indian colonial history*, Delhi: Kali.

Chatterjee, P., M. Desai and P. Roy (eds) (2009) *States of Trauma: Gender and violence in South Asia*, New Delhi: Zubaan.

Chatterji, R. and D. Mehta (2007) *Living with Violence: An Anthropology of Events and Everyday Life*, New Delhi: Routledge.

Chaudhuri, M. (2004) 'Introduction', in M. Chaudhuri (ed.), *Feminism in India*, New Delhi: Kali for Women and Women Unlimited.

Chowdhury, E. H. (2011) *Transnationalism Reversed: Women Organizing against Gendered Violence in Bangladesh*, SUNY Press.

Coomaraswamy, R. and D. Fonseka (eds) (2005) *Peace Work: Women, Armed Conflict and Negotiation*, Women Unlimited.

Das, V. (1995) *Critical Events: An Anthropological Perspective on Contemporary India*, New Delhi: Oxford University Press.

— (2007) *Life and Words: Violence and the Descent into the Ordinary*,

Berkeley: University of California Press.

Dave, N. (2010) 'To render real the imagined: an ethnographic history of the lesbian community in India', *Signs: Journal of Women in Culture and Society*, 35(3): 595–620.

De Alwis, M. (2002) 'The changing role of women in Sri Lankan Society', *Social Research*, 69(3).

— (2009) 'Interrogating the "political": feminist peace activism in Sri Lanka', *Feminist Review*, 91: 81–93.

De Alwis, M. and K. Jayawardena (eds) (1998) *Embodied Violence: Communalising Women's Sexuality in South Asia*, New Delhi: Kali for Women.

De Mel, N. (2001) *Women and the Nation's Narrative: Gender and nationalism in twentieth century Sri Lanka*, Lanham, MD: Rowman and Littlefield.

— (2007) *Militarizing Sri Lanka. Popular Culture, Memory and Narrative in the Armed Conflict*, New Delhi: Sage.

Dean, J. (2008) 'Feminist purism and the question of "radicality" in contemporary political theory', *Contemporary Political Theory*, 7: 280–301.

— (2009) 'Who's afraid of third wave feminism?: on the uses of the "third wave" in British feminist politics', *International Feminist Journal of Politics*, 11(3): 334–52.

— (2010) *Rethinking Contemporary Feminist Politics*, Basingstoke: Palgrave Macmillan.

Desai, M. (2009) 'A history of violence: gender power and the making of the 2002 pogrom in Gujarat', in P. Chatterjee, M. Desai and P. Roy (eds), *States of Trauma: Gender and violence in South Asia*, New Delhi: Zubaan.

Eschle, C. and B. Maiguashca (2011) 'Feminism in/against globalised neoliberalism: rethinking feminism, the left and transformative politics', Presentation for the 2nd European Conference on Politics and Gender, Central European University, Budapest, 13–15 January.

Fraser, N. (2009) 'Feminism, capitalism and the cunning of history', *New Left Review*, 56: 97–117.

Gangoli, G. (2007) *Indian Feminisms: Law, patriarchies and violence in India*, Aldershot: Ashgate.

Genz, S. (2006) 'Third Way/ve: The politics of postfeminism', *Feminist Theory*, 7(3): 333–53.

Ghani, A. (2009) 'Abducted identities: Pakistan, its partition and its abducted women', in P. Chatterjee, M. Desai and P. Roy (eds), *States of Trauma: Gender and violence in South Asia*, New Delhi: Zubaan.

Gooptu, N. (2000) 'Sex workers in Calcutta and the dynamics of collective action: political activism, community identity and group behaviour', WIDER Working Papers 185, May.

Gupta, A. (2005) '"Englishpur ki Kothi": class dynamics in the queer movement in India', in A. Narrain and G. Bhan (eds), *Because I Have a Voice: Queer Politics in India*, New Delhi: Yoda Press.

Harris, A. (2004) *Future Girl: Young Women in the Twenty-first Century*, New York and London: Routledge.

Hemmings, C. (2011) *Why Stories Matter: The Political Grammar of Feminist Theory*, Durham, NC: Duke University Press.

Jad, I. (2007) 'The NGO-isation of Arab women's movements', in A. Cornwall et al. (eds), *Feminisms*

in Development, London and New
York: Zed Books, pp. 177–90.

Jafar, A. (2007) 'Engaging funda-
mentalism: the case of women's
NGOs in Pakistan', Social
Problems, 54(3): 256–73.

Jayawardena, K. (1986) Feminism and
Nationalism in the Third World,
London: Zed Books.

Jenkins, K. (2009) '"We have a lot
of goodwill, but we still need to
eat …": valuing women's long
term voluntarism in community
development in Lima', Voluntas,
20: 15–34.

John, M. E. (1996) Discrepant Disloca-
tions: Feminism, Theory, and
Postcolonial Histories, Berkeley:
University of California Press.

— (2002) 'Women's studies:
legacies and futures' in L. Sarkar,
K. Sharma and L. Kasturi (eds),
Between Tradition, Counter Tradi-
tion and Heresy: Contributions in
Honour of Vina Mazumdar, Noida:
Rainbow Publishers.

— (2004) 'Gender and development
in India, 1970s–90s: some reflections on the constitutive role of
contexts', in M. Chaudhuri (ed.),
Feminism in India, New Delhi: Kali
for Women & Women Unlimited.

— (2005) 'Feminism, poverty and
the emergent social order', in
R. Ray and M. F. Katzenstein
(eds), Social Movements in India:
Poverty, power, and politics,
Oxford: Rowman and Littlefield.

— (2009) 'Reframing globalisation:
perspectives from the women's
movement', Economic and Political
Weekly, 44(10): 47–8.

Kannabiran, K. and V. Kannabiran
(2002) De-Eroticizing Assault:
Essays on Modesty, Honour and
Power, Kolkata: Stree.

Kapur, R. (2005) Erotic Justice: Law
and the New Politics of Post-
colonialism, London: Glass House
Press.

Karim, L. (2011) Microfinance and
Its Discontents: Women in Debt in
Bangladesh, Minneapolis: Univer-
sity of Minnesota Press.

Kotiswaran, P. (2011a) Dangerous
Sex, Invisible Labor: Sex Work and
the Law in India, Princeton, NJ:
Princeton University Press.

— (ed.) (2011b) Reader on Sex Work,
New Delhi: Women Unlimited.

Kumar, R. (1993) The History of Doing,
New Delhi: Kali for Women.

Lang, S. (1997) 'The NGOization
of feminism', in J. W. Scott,
C. Kaplan and D. Keates (eds),
Transitions, Environments, Transla-
tions: Feminisms in International
Politics, New York: Routledge.

Loomba, A. and R. A. Lukose (eds)
(2012) South Asian Feminisms,
Durham, NC: Duke University
Press.

McRobbie, A. (2009) The Aftermath
of Feminism: Gender, Culture and
Social Change, London: Sage.

Madhok, S. (2010) 'Rights talk and
the feminist movement in India',
in M. Roces and L. Edwards (eds),
Women's Movements in Asia: Feminisms and Transnational Activism,
London: Routledge

Madhok, S. and S. M. Rai (2012)
'Agency, injury, and transgressive
politics in neoliberal times',
Signs, 37(3).

Mahmood, S. (2005) Politics of
Piety: The Islamic revival and the
feminist subject, Princeton, NJ,
and Oxford: Princeton University
Press.

Manchanda, R. (2004) 'Maoist
Insurgency in Nepal: radicalising
gendered narratives', Cultural
Dynamics, 16(2/3): 237–58.

Mani, L. (1989) 'Contentious
traditions: the debate on sati in

colonial India', in K. Sangari and S. Vaid (eds), *Recasting Women: Essays in Indian colonial history*, New Delhi: Kali for Women.

Markowitz, L. and K. Tice (2002) 'Paradoxes of professionalization: parallel dilemmas in women's organizations in the Americas', *Gender & Society*, 16(6): 941–58.

Mayaram, S. (2002) 'New modes of violence: the backlash against women in the Panchayat system', in K. Kapadia (ed.), *The Violence of Development: The Politics of Identity, Gender and Social Inequalities in India*, New Delhi: Kali for Women.

Menon, N. (2004) *Recovering Subversion: Feminist Politics Beyond the Law*, Delhi: Permanent Black.

— (2008) 'Introduction', in N. Menon (ed.), *Sexualities*, London: Zed Books.

— (2009) 'Sexuality, caste, governmentality: contests over "gender" in India', *Feminist Review*, 91: 94–112.

Menon, R. (ed.) (2011) *Making a Difference: Memoirs from the Women's Movement in India*, Delhi: Women Unlimited.

Menon, R. and K. Bhasin (1998) *Borders and Boundaries: Women in India's Partition*, New Delhi: Kali for Women.

Moodie, M. (2007) 'Enter microcredit: a new culture of women's empowerment in Rajasthan?', *American Ethnologist*, 35(3): 454–65.

Mookherjee, N. (2008) 'Gendered embodiments: mapping the body-politic of the raped woman and the nation in Bangladesh', *Feminist Review*, 88(1): 36–53.

Murdock, D. (2003) 'That stubborn "doing good?" question: ethical/epistemological concerns in the study of NGOs', *Ethnos*, 68(4): 507–32.

Niranjana, T. (2007) 'Feminism and cultural studies in Asia', *Interventions*, 9(2): 209–18.

Oza, R. (2006) *The Making of Neoliberal India*, New York: Routledge.

Pandey, G. (2006) *Routine Violence: Nations, Fragments, Histories*, New Delhi: Permanent Black.

Phadke, S., S. Khan and S. Ranade (2011) *Why Loiter? Women and Risk on Mumbai Streets*, Penguin Books India.

Purvis, J. (2004) 'Grrrls and women together in the third wave: embracing the challenges of intergenerational feminism(s)', *NWSA Journal*, 16(3): 93–123.

Rai, S. (2008) *The Gender Politics of Development*, London and New York: Zed Books.

Rajasingham-Senanayake, D. (2001) 'Ambivalent empowerment: the tragedy of Tamil women in conflict', in R. Manchanda (ed.), *Women, War, and Peace in South Asia: Beyond victimhood to agency*, New Delhi and Thousand Oaks, CA: Sage Publications.

— (2004) 'Between reality and representation: women's agency in war and post-conflict Sri Lanka', *Cultural Dynamics*, 16(2/3): 141–68.

Ram, K. (2008) '"A new consciousness must come": affectivity and movement in Tamil Dalit women's activist engagement with cosmopolitan modernity', in P. Werbner (ed.), *Anthropology and Cosmopolitanism: Rooted, Feminist and Vernacular Perspectives*, Oxford: Berg.

Ray, R. (1999) *Fields of Protest: Women's Movements in India*, New Delhi: Kali for Women.

Roces, M. (2010) 'Asian feminisms:

women's movements from an Asian perspective', in M. Roces and L. Edwards (eds), *Women's Movements in Asia: Feminisms and Transnational Activism*, London: Routledge.

Roces, R. and L. Edwards (eds) (2010) *Women's Movements in Asia: Feminisms and Transnational Activism*, London: Routledge.

Rouse, S. (1988) 'Women's movement in Pakistan: state, class, gender', *Women Living under Muslim Laws*, Dossier 3, www.wluml.org/fr/node/241, accessed September 2011.

— (2004) *Shifting Body Politics: Gender, Nation and State in Pakistan*, New Delhi: Women Unlimited.

Roy, S. (2008) 'The grey zone: the "ordinary" violence of extraordinary times', *Journal of the Royal Anthropological Institute*, 14(2): 314–30.

— (2009) 'Melancholic politics and the politics of melancholia: the Indian women's movement', *Feminist Theory*, 10(3): 341–57.

— (2011) 'Politics, passion and professionalization in contemporary Indian feminism', *Sociology*, 45(4): 587–602.

— (2012) *Remembering Revolution: Gender, Violence and Subjectivity in India's Naxalbari Movement*, Delhi: Oxford University Press.

Ruwanpura, K. (2007) 'Awareness and action: the ethno-gender dynamics of Sri Lankan NGOs', *Gender, Place & Culture*, 14(3): 317–33.

Saheli (1991) *Development for Whom? A Critique of Women's Development Programs*, A report on the development programme in Rajasthan with a specific focus on the Ajmer district.

Saikia, Y. (2011) *Women, War, and the Making of Bangladesh: Remembering 1971*, Durham, NC: Duke University Press.

Sangari, K. (2007) 'Shaping pressures and symbolic horizons: the women's movement in India', in N. de Mel and S. Thiruchandran (eds), *At the Cutting Edge: Essays in honour of Kumari Jayawardena*, New Delhi: Women Unlimited.

Sangari, K. and S. Vaid (eds) (1989) *Recasting Women: Essays in Indian Colonial History*, New Delhi: Kali for Women.

Sarkar, T. (2002) 'Semiotics of terror: Muslim children and women in Hindu Rashtra', Economic and Political Weekly Commentary, sacw.insaf.net/DC/CommunalismCollection/ArticlesArchive/TanikaSarkarJUL02.html, accessed January 2006.

Sen, A. (2007) *Shiv Sena Women: Violence and Communalism in a Bombay Slum*, London: C. Hurst and Co.

Sharma, A. (2008) *Logics of Empowerment: Development, Gender, and Governance in Neoliberal India*, Minneapolis: University of Minnesota Press.

Sharma, M. (2006) *Loving Women: Being Lesbian in Underprivileged India*, Minneapolis, MN: Yoda Press.

Siddiqi, D. (2010) 'Do Bangladeshi factory workers need saving? Sisterhood in the post-sweatshop era', *Feminist Review*, 91: 154–74.

Sinha, M. (2012) 'A global perspective on gender: what's South Asia got to do with it?', in A. Loomba and R. A. Lukose (eds), *South Asian Feminisms*, Durham, NC: Duke University Press.

Stree Shakti Sanghatana (1989) *'We were making history ...': Life stories of women in the Telangana People's Struggle*, London: Zed Books.

Sunder Rajan, R. (2003) *The Scandal of the State: Women, Law and Citizenship in India*, Durham, NC, and London/New Delhi: Duke University Press/Permanent Black.

Tharu, S. and T. Niranjana (1994) 'Problems for a contemporary theory of gender', *Social Scientist*, 22(3/4): 93–117.

Walby, S. (2011) *The Future of Feminism*, Polity Press.

Weigman, R. (2000) 'Feminism's apocalyptic futures', *New Literary History*, 31: 805–25.

Wilson, A. (2006) *Dreams, Questions, Struggles: South Asian Women in Britain*, London: Pluto Press.

Zia, A. S. (2009) 'The reinvention of feminism in Pakistan', *Feminist Review*, 91: 29–46.

1 | Sex workers' rights and women's movements in India: a very brief genealogy

SVATI P. SHAH[1]

Since the mid-1990s, international interest in prostitution has become increasingly consolidated within the discourse on human trafficking. Trafficking is the dominant metaphor and analytic frame for understanding sexual commerce, particularly for the majority of Western governments (with notable exceptions, e.g. New Zealand) and for the majority of multilateral development agencies and financial institutions. While the official discourse on sexual commerce has become entwined with the idea of human trafficking, sex workers' rights movements have also emerged the world over, tracing their recent histories back to the early days of grassroots AIDS activism and the development of the funded HIV/AIDS services sector. The internationalized rise in institutionalized interests in prostitution, particularly among international organizations and governmental agencies seeking to intervene in how sexual commerce is currently defined and regulated, has been produced in no small part through the idea of sexual commerce in the global South, and specifically through the idea that there is little capacity for local response to prostitution in the global South. In this exploratory piece, I situate the internationalized discourse on sexual commerce within India, and specifically within Indian feminist and HIV/AIDS movements, in order to offer a brief genealogy of the current proliferation of interest in prostitution in India. In sketching this genealogy, I discuss the ways in which this interest has become meaningfully interpolated within internationalized discourses on sexual commerce. The contemporary moment is a significant one, owing to the internationalization of abolitionist anti-prostitution analyses and policies, and their effects.

Feminism and sex work

A marker for the politics of sex work anywhere is the discursive distinction between 'feminist movements' and 'sex worker movements', a distinction that raises the question of whether, and why, these movements are discrete. To be sure, sex worker movements have evolved distinctly from 'feminist' (or 'women's') movements, an evolution that signals the theoretical and strategic tensions between them, to be sure, but tensions that are never a priori. Over the course of the twentieth century, people who sell sexual services were represented by various social movements as, at best, evidence of historically consistent and/or continuous social and political inequality. At worst, social movements of all stripes have treated sex workers as either abject victims, or as immoral pariahs. The consolidation of an independent set of organizations seeking to represent the perspectives of sex workers per se is relatively new, the ancient guilds of prostitutes mentioned in the *Arthashastras* notwithstanding.

The route to a contemporary rights-based sex workers' movement that has international linkages must be traced through the discourse of sex work among women's movements over the course of the twentieth century. Women's movements have been among the most vocal about prostitution for three major reasons: first, because the iconic subject of prostitution is discursively produced as a *female* seller of sexual services; secondly, because prostitution was held up as evidence of the existence of gender-based social hierarchies early in the development of a contemporary feminist political and theoretical framework; and thirdly, because, with the consolidation of prostitution as a distinct and discrete commercial practice during the late nineteenth century, female sellers of sexual services came to be understood by feminist reformers as inhabiting the ultimate allegory of all women's ('un') worth. This last point has had profound implications for prostitution as a career since the late nineteenth century in India.

While the transaction of sexual services for money has been presented by some feminists as an indication of the reduction of women's bodies to a singular, objectified image and function, anti-abolitionist sex workers' organizations and advocates have forcefully argued against this perspective. The conflation of prostitution with the summary objectification of women is one way in which women's movements institutionalized in government have precluded the inclusion of sex workers as feminists in those movements. According to this formulation, female sex workers can be apprehended only as victims of systematic patriarchal oppression, and are therefore either symbolic of that oppression, or serve as participants in perpetuating that oppression on other women. Some feminists have extrapolated this equation between prostitution and gender inequality to argue for the abolition of all sexual commerce. The feminist abolitionist position on sex work has tended to conflate prostitution, human trafficking and violence. The idea that all these concepts are indelibly similar, linked and co-constitutive has driven much of the policy debate on prostitution and human trafficking since the late 1990s, and has informed legal responses to prostitution in the USA, Sweden, Cambodia, South Korea and, most recently, Taiwan, where prostitution has become increasingly criminalized.

The impasses between feminist and sex worker movements have been addressed many times in the past decade, such that there is no longer as clear a categorical division between 'feminists' and 'sex workers'[2] as there has been historically. It has therefore become more and more crucial over time to specify to *which* political category of feminists and sex workers one is referring when describing the polarities of the debate on prostitution. At the same time, the alliances that are being built between sex worker, feminist, and lesbian, gay, bisexual, transsexual, queer (LGBTQ) movements around the world are resulting in shifts in perceptions of sex workers as being only, or primarily, biological women. Shifting these perceptions has also entailed disrupting the notion of a helpless woman or girl who needs rescuing from the universalized horrors of prostitution, a notion that has rested at the centre of the production of a gendered victim/rescuer dyad within the abolitionist discourse, in which the victims are always girls and young women. Critics of abolitionism as a unilateral approach to prostitution have argued against this, not because women and girls are never victimized by sex industries, but because the notion of victimization as a universal truth of prostitution hampers both efforts to offer real assistance to sex workers in distress,[3] and to discern the complex and varied realities of selling sexual services.

'The woman question'

By assuming a position of sympathy with the unfree and oppressed womanhood of India, the colonial mind was able to transform this figure of the Indian woman into a sign of the inherently oppressive and unfree nature of the entire cultural tradition of a country. (Chatterjee [1993: 118])

The contemporary politics of sex work in India has grown out of a complex discourse on gender and nationalism in the region. India's 'unfreedom' was evidenced by the status of its women, according to its colonial rulers, until India's independence in 1947. Sati was the ostensible focus of this discourse during colonialism as the ultimate metaphor for women's worth. However, the discourse on sati alone cannot account for the ways in which the perceived status of women was used to rationalize the colonial project. The regulation of women's sexuality formed a core framework for colonialist discourses on Indian women. The debates on the age of marriage during the 1880s, along with the discussion of the representation of Indian women via criticisms of Katherine Mayo's book *Mother India* (Mayo 1927), revolved around the ways in which women in India were victimized through regimes of power that controlled and commoditized female sexuality. The distance from child bride to prostitute, it seems, was relatively short in these debates.

> Singling out Brahmin men and their laws for moral condemnation, [Katherine] Mayo also refused to make a distinction between the well-being of high- or low-caste women, insisting that in India, women were universally oppressed. Most shocking of all: she correlated prostitution with Hindu religious practice, alleging that high-caste wives with impotent husbands were sent to temples to be impregnated by priests, that young girls were bequeathed to priests as devadasis (whom she interpreted as prostitutes), and that the Indian widow 'not seldom falls' into prostitution. (Albinia 2005: 429)

If the idea of female prostitution in India serves as an allegory for India within the internationally hegemonic anti-trafficking framework, it is because this idea has helped to produce the rhetoric of Indian sociality for more than a century.

Trafficking and prostitution

While a complete discussion of the history and critiques of the discourse on human trafficking is far beyond the scope of this chapter, a discussion of the intersections between sex worker and feminist movements entails reviewing some of the critiques of human trafficking for two reasons. First, because human trafficking and prostitution are now being used as nearly interchangeable terms by humanitarian activists and lawmakers in western Europe and the USA, a semantic and political development that emerges from late-nineteenth-century concerns about 'white slavery' (Walkowitz 1992). This has had important consequences for how sex work is governed in the global South, and particularly in Asia, where US international policy on trafficking/prostitution has compelled some governments, e.g. in South Korea and Cambodia, to institute laws that seek to abolish prostitution altogether. Sex workers in those countries were summarily criminalized overnight, taken to prisons and remand homes, and stripped of their livelihoods

(Globe News 2011; Thrupkaew 2009). Secondly, because the debate about legalizing, criminalizing or decriminalizing prostitution within national and international fora has been framed by the challenge of crafting appropriate state-sponsored solutions to address human trafficking, it becomes necessary to elaborate a brief genealogy of the globally hegemonic discourse on trafficking/prostitution, and the ways in which this discourse is linked with the histories of anti-prostitution and anti-pornography work within US feminism.

The challenge of the discourse on prostitution and human trafficking has been both compounded and produced by the ideological cast imbued in the terms 'prostitution', 'trafficking' and 'sex work'. The definition of trafficking itself has been disputed among feminists on ideological grounds; feminists seeking the abolition of prostitution altogether have argued that, because prostitution is equivalent to violence against women, trafficking and prostitution are also equivalent terms. Non-abolitionist advocates have responded by insisting that the term 'human trafficking' should cover the forced movement of people across borders and long distances for any labour, and should not be primarily linked with prostitution.[4] The current definition, contained within the 'Palermo Protocol',[5] was a compromise between many different actors, but it does succeed in defining human trafficking according to the conditions by which people are transported for work, and not solely by the work for which they are transported, although the practice of anti-trafficking work still belies many of the long-standing disputes in definitions and emphases (Doezema 2002). Given the history of discourses of prostitution and trafficking, it is important to recall that the interest in and resources for anti-trafficking work did not emerge out of a vacuum, nor from an overbearing US governmental policy that was somehow apprehended globally. The contemporary international anti-trafficking development industry is the result of a complex interplay between and among the priorities of various social movements, and between those of social movements and governments.

History and feminism

In order to understand the current state of affairs surrounding the politics of sexual commerce in India, it is important to understand the role of policies originating from the USA in shaping the international discourse on sex-work-as-trafficking. The US government has been influential in asserting the conflation of prostitution and trafficking through its support of organizations domestically and internationally that espouse and work within this framework. This governmental priority has been built over time, in part through the convergence of the interests of the government in controlling illegal migration across all international borders, including human trafficking, and those of feminists in the USA who opposed prostitution, many of whom had earlier opposed pornography. In addition to offering a contemporary model for liberal feminist collaboration with the state, US feminist anti-pornography activists consolidated their positions on violence, gender and consent in an analysis of pornography that equated it with harm. Following the feminist debates on pornography in the 1980s, these positions re-emerged within the context of the discussion on 'forced' versus 'voluntary' sex work during the 1990s. The categories 'forced' and 'voluntary' were deployed during the debates on pornography, and have since been deployed in debates on the language that distinguishes 'trafficking' and sexual commerce in international human rights instruments. The assertion of these categories can be found in many key UN documents, including General Recommendation 19 of the Convention on the Elimination of All Forms of Discrimination Against Women (CEDAW) and the Declaration on the Elimination of Violence Against Women, and in position papers and statements issued by the United Nations Special Rapporteur on Violence Against Women, as well as being found in the anti-trafficking protocol (the Palermo Protocol) itself.

Sex workers' rights advocates have come to question the utility of the emphasis on 'forced' versus 'chosen' prostitution in furthering a progressive position on sex work within these debates. In particular, non-abolitionist advocates have argued that making this distinction leads to constituting two classes of sex workers: one, a 'forced' class that deserves legal protection, and another, a 'voluntary' class that does not. Jo Doezema has observed, 'No international agreement condemns the abuse of human rights of sex workers who were not "forced"' (Doezema 1998: 34). She cites two main reasons for this. The first is that, although prostitution is generally criminalized in law, there is no one clear response to 'voluntary' prostitution from feminists. The second is that, in respecting the right to self-determination for sex workers' rights organizations to lobby for themselves, it is more feasible, in the terms of international law, to gain support for a negative rights claim: e.g. that a woman should be free from coerced prostitution, rather than arguing for a positive rights claim, e.g. the right to sell sexual services, while challenging the structures, institutions and people that may violate sex workers' human rights.

The notion of two 'classes' of sex workers, as structured, for example, by the historically tenacious forced–voluntary dichotomy, can be used as an interpretive lens for thinking through the myriad ways in which sex workers are dyadically categorized as deserving/undeserving, moral/immoral and powerful/disempowered. The differential representation of sex workers in the global North and the global South is a critical vector for discerning the formation of these dyads and dichotomies in the discourse on sexual commerce. Considering the North/South politics of the discourse on prostitution provides an opportunity to reflect on the ways in which prostitution is, and has been, a racialized discourse, and to geopolitically situate the issues presented in this chapter.

Force, choice and race (and caste)

Historian Philippa Levine offers one trajectory for the racialization of prostitution, through the history of British colonialism in India. Discussing the nineteenth-century rise in official concerns about British soldiers having relationships with 'native' women in the colonies, including soldiers cohabiting with local women and having children with them, Levine argues that soldiers were encouraged to become clients of sex workers instead, a move which may have given rise to the brothel system in many places, including Bombay. Official concerns about white soldiers having sexual relationships with non-white women in the colonies coincided with the entrenchment of allopathic medicine, public health and humanitarian social work around this time. Given this nexus of emergent discourses,

> The prostitute fulfilled a role as the most degraded of women, a polluted and despised wretch removed from decency but nonetheless providing a 'necessary' outlet. As masculine and feminine roles became more sharply defined in the nineteenth century and as fears of VD grew, the prostitute as a social problem acquired greater urgency. Weighted down with a confused medico-moral baggage tied to long-standing conceptions about gender, class, and race, prostitution symbolized difference. As such, it could also serve to yoke 'lesser' populations to ideas of sexual disorder, offering a veritable commentary on the savagery and barbarism of colonized peoples. (Levine 2003: 179)

The idea that sex workers in the British colonies represent that which is degraded, savage and barbaric dovetails with Chandra Mohanty's argument in her famous essay 'Under Western eyes', first drafted during the early years of American 'second wave' feminism, on the cusp of the fissure in US feminism over pornography. Mohanty argues that the beginning of second-wave feminism in the West, e.g. from the late 1960s and early 1970s in the USA and the UK, was laced with the belief that women in the global South did not enjoy the same rights, freedoms or social movements that were available to women in the West. Mohanty argued that 'third world women' were constructed as 'a homogeneous powerless group often located as implicit *victims* of particular socio-economic systems' (Mohanty 1991: 57). The contemporary abolitionist rhetoric of forced prostitution draws a critique that consolidates both Levine's historicized argument about sexual disorder and degradation, and post-colonial feminist arguments on the homogeneity of victimization with which women in the global South were cast. It does this by primarily locating forced prostitution, and its attendant remedies (including 'rescue' and 'rehabilitation'), as embodied by economically impoverished women in the global South, and by poor and working-class women of colour living in global North countries. This is not to say that sex workers are never forced to participate in prostitution anywhere, nor is it to say that force is not a relevant term for describing what some sex workers experience during the course of their working lives. It is to say that the iconicity of forced sex work has been produced by a powerful nexus of historical forces, and has come to serve as the prevailing 'common sense' about women in the global South and women of colour in the West who sell sexual services. This potentially occludes the politics of force and choice in sexual commerce.

The iconicity of female sex workers from the global South, and of women of colour in the West, includes a victim narrative of having been abducted and sold into the industry, or having 'no choice' but to enter prostitution because of poverty. The latter narrative has given rise to an anthropomorphic sense of poverty, when advocates argue, for example, that poverty 'traffics' women and girls into prostitution (Shah 2007). In the internationalized discourse on prostitution and human trafficking, 'forced prostitutes' are usually portrayed as helpless, unwitting and non-Western, and are often attached to certain iconic stories, such as being sold into prostitution by extremely impoverished patriarchal families, while 'voluntary sex workers', if they are represented in the debate at all, are presented as unrepentant, agentative, immoral and Western. The iconic image of the 'Western' (read: global North) sex worker embodies the epitome of Western libertarian sexual mores and privilege, and makes a 'free choice' to enter the trade. This image of a white Western sex worker effectively structures non-white, non-Western sex workers as its opposite and other. Each image renders the other's legibility within the larger framework as it currently stands.

This notion of forced prostitution resonates with the major strains of the abolitionist anti-trafficking position that asserts a narrative of prostitution and trafficked women in which all female sex workers in the global South are thought to have had some rural and impoverished point of origin, having little or no real agency in their trading sex for monetary and other material resources. In the contemporary Indian context, this narrative has provided the ballast for 'rescue' efforts directed at female sex workers working in red light districts in major cities (Kristoff 2011). 'Rescuing' sex workers involves their compulsory transfer by police and non-governmental organizations to government or privately funded rehabilitation facilities. This practice has been criticized for separating women from what may have become extended networks of financial and emotional support, and for detaining women without due process. In Cambodia, for example, 'rehabilitation' facilities for sex workers have been shown to be little more than prisons where sex workers are held without formal charge (Human Rights Watch 2010).

Abolitionist anti-trafficking advocates have ultimately achieved a measure of success in promoting 'rescue' as a mainstay intervention for prostitution by arguing that eliminating prostitution as trafficking means eliminating another avenue by which migrants may cross international borders illegally. This has effectively empowered governments to further regulate the movement of impoverished labourers across international borders (Chapkis 2003). This critique may be effectively contextualized, in part, by critiques of the implementation of 'free trade' agreements since the early 1990s. Some of these critiques have included the argument that an unstated consequence of these agreements has been to further delimit the migration of people across international borders, while encouraging the migration of capital, a situation that has led to the production of wealth for some, and a much more tenuous situation for millions of poor migrant workers.[6]

Migration and HIV/AIDS

Alongside feminist debates on pornography, the advent of HIV/AIDS – by which I mean the advent of the virus and the syndrome, the activism that they spawned, and the public and private funding streams that emerged through AIDS-related activism – had a profound impact on the ways in which sex work, and sex worker activism, was organized in India. Discourses on HIV prevention largely centred on female sex workers in the global South, and eventually necessitated a convergence between sexuality-based social movements and feminist movements, as sex workers and their advocates reacted to sex workers being 'spoken for' (as 'vectors', primarily) rather than being understood as subjects themselves within the epidemic.

Until the advent of HIV/AIDS, female prostitution was subject to social stigma and state-sponsored regulations that categorized prostitutes as lacking honour and respectability, as criminals, and as vectors of sexually transmitted diseases (STDs). Although several STDs are potentially fatal without proper treatment, linking prostitution with incurable HIV infection facilitated profound changes in discourses on prostitution. The most significant of these was the shift from seeing female sex workers as morally and physically suspect, to casting women selling sex as potentially among the most vulnerable groups for becoming HIV infected (Whiteford and Manderson 2000; Roy 2001; Veeraraghavan and Singh 1999; Agarwal and Jana 1999; Kunte et al. 1999; Chatterjee 1999), and, therefore, as potential vectors of a fatal STD (Treichler 1999). Hypotheses about the high rate of infection and HIV transmission in brothels and red light districts in the global South entered into an already vigorous debate about sexuality and bodily autonomy. These debates grew to encompass questions about the physical and socio-political implications of women and girls selling sexual services to men, and eventually became interpolated into broader questions on the polarities of female agency and powerlessness (Vance 1984; Duggan and Hunter 1995; Brown 1995).

Historically, politically and economically, marginalized migrating subjects have been central to public health discourses on the spread and prevention of communicable disease. However, discourses on 'migration' per se have been primarily produced within the purview of the policies and politics of economic development and labour. In other words, public health discourses have traditionally used an understanding of migration as theorized by economics and sociology. Given the relevance of discourses on HIV/AIDS in producing knowledge about poverty and mobility as gendered phenomena (e.g. Farmer 1992), public health discourses with respect to HIV in India bear examination, not only for their role in constituting the contemporary category of 'prostitute', but also for their importance in using and shaping theories of migration. This is particularly useful in discerning which groups are labelled as 'migrants' and which are not, regardless of where, how much or why they may move from place to place.

The categories 'migrant', 'truck driver' and 'prostitute' populate numerous public health studies conducted in Asia and sub-Saharan Africa. While populations of both truck drivers and sex workers in

India are overwhelmingly constituted by people who have migrated from their place of origin in search of work, the ascription of 'migrant' was kept separate from that of 'prostitute' or 'sex worker' in public health literatures on HIV/AIDS produced in the 1980s and 1990s. For example, of the then potential spread of HIV in India, P. Pais wrote, 'As in Africa, infection has been mainly by heterosexual intercourse, with commercial sex workers, long distance truck drivers and migrant labor serving as vehicles of spread' (Pais 1996). For Pais, as for most other epidemiological researchers into the spread of HIV in India, 'migrant labour' and 'sex workers' were distinct categories. However, the majority of sex workers in India have, at some point in their working lives, migrated for work, or are active migrants currently. In addition, many people throughout India, migrant or otherwise, sell sexual services in more episodic modes and do not identify themselves as 'sex workers' or 'prostitutes' per se. Placed in relation to the discursive distinction between 'migrants' and 'sex workers', these observations raise the question of how this distinction operates in constituting 'migrant' and 'sex worker' subjectivity vis-à-vis the reiteration of gendered norms which vest men and maleness with mobility, and women and femaleness as something separate from the ability and necessity to move for economic survival.

The growth of a sex workers' movement

The tendency to turn towards the state for protection, rather than questioning state power to regulate and discipline, is one that [Wendy] Brown sees as especially problematic for feminism. She notes women have particular cause for greeting such politics with caution. Historically, the argument that women require protection by and from men has been critical in legitimating women's exclusion from some spheres of human endeavor and confinement within others. Operating simultaneously to link 'femininity' to privileged races and classes ... protection codes are also markers and vehicles of such divisions among women. Protection codes are thus key technologies in regulating privileged women as well as intensifying the vulnerability and degradation of those on the unprotected side of the constructed divide between light and dark, wives and prostitutes, good girls and bad ones. (Doezema 2001: 20)

Jo Doezema's argument here summarizes some of the core issues at stake in the spaces between abolitionist feminist and sex worker organizations. Abolitionists' reliance on a strategy which centres on codifying liberal states' legal protection of women has come at the cost of 'legitimating women's exclusion from some spheres of human endeavor and confinement within others'. Studying this strategy shows that the rhetorical foundation of violence against women is the basis on which remedies for that violence are conceived – embodied for abolitionists as prostitution per se. Primary among these remedies is the criminalization of prostitution and the 'rescue' of people, thought of largely or mainly as women and girls, who sell sexual services. This strategy has found favour with governments, and has spawned anti-trafficking work as a growth sector in international development work. One reason for this, in addition to the appeal for governments of committed feminist activists working to help curb illegal cross-border migration, is the symbolic value of anti-trafficking work. In a political environment in which feminists of all stripes have made significant gains, such that governments can now be held publicly accountable, to a degree, for their efforts to ensure legal rights, protections and access to opportunities for women, supporting anti-trafficking programmes fits the bill almost perfectly. Supporting anti-trafficking work has, in effect, become a proxy for governments showing their commitment to women, and to the notion of gender equality, because of the symbolic value that anti-trafficking work has attained for feminism. By support-ing an agenda that is 'feminist', governments may argue that they are supporting the expansion of the rights of women, without accounting for the multiplicity of feminist positions, while fulfilling other goals, including stronger border controls and more police regulation of vis-ible, urban sex work.

At the same time, consolidated sex workers' organizations have entered the fray, and, in several countries, have initiated a process by which governments have had to recognize an array of positions on these issues. The advent of HIV/AIDS led to numerous political developments, including the rise of patient-led health activism in the USA, and the rise of sex worker organizing in countries like India. Organizations like SANGRAM in southern Maharashtra and the Durbar Mahila Samanwaya Committee (DMSC) in Calcutta emerged in the 1990s, in the wake of HIV/AIDS, and, like their Western activist coun-terparts, were drawing connections between HIV and other concerns, including migration, livelihood, housing and access to basic public services. These organizations grew from HIV prevention outreach projects formed by non-sex-worker activists, in the early 1990s, to organizations that had sex-worker-led initiatives, and legions of sex worker advocates and peer educators, by the early 2000s. One of the most recent of these initiatives is the Karnataka Sex Workers' Union in Bangalore, which won recognition as a union from the national New Trade Union Initiative. Their mission statement identifies the spaces for intervention that the dominant discourse on prostitution has contributed to producing.

> KSWU [Karnataka Sex Workers' Union] strives to get sex work recognised as dignified labour, campaigns for decriminalisation of sex work and demands labour rights that are guaranteed to all other workers. KSWU defends the rights of sex workers and resists violence, oppression and exploitation by the police, goondas, government agencies and others. KSWU advocate for fair working conditions and social entitlements including voting rights, health services, housing, access to public distribution system [ration card], savings-credit and loan facilities, retirement benefits, Provident Fund, Employees State Insurance, insurance, education for sex workers' children and full social security.[7]

Autonomous feminism

The integration of queer women, Dalit women and sex workers in the 2006 conference for National Autonomous Women's Movements in Calcutta, India, illustrates some of the tensions regarding prostitution within Indian women's movements, and how one aspect of the autonomous feminist movement in India is negotiating these tensions. The conference statement, entitled 'Challenging divisiveness, affirming diversities', read, in part:

> We believe that as women, we share common interests and goals, and hence come together in our collective struggles. But caste, nation, class, religion, ethnicity, sexuality, ability or disability are deeply rooted social constructs which create multiple identities for many of us. Consequently, the politics of identity throws up several contradictions, yet we remain committed to recognizing and respecting these 'diversities' even as we seek justice for the inequities that result from them. In particular, we seek support for the struggles of women who are made further vulnerable by specific facets of their identities – as adivasis, dalits, poor and working class, religious minorities, lesbian, bisexual, transgendered, sex workers, disabled, and women of other socially marginalised groups. We believe as women we must have the right to make choices about our lives, our bodies, our sexuality and our relationships. We also recognise that these choices are not unchanging. We commit to creating the space for different choices to be recognised and evolving the supportive structures that can make all of these choices

a meaningful reality. We reiterate our commitment to continue our efforts to realise these expressions of our politics and struggle, and to support the struggles of all who seek justice, with a vision that remains autonomous of the discourse of dominant powers and politics.[8]

While there is a growing sense that sex workers' and feminist organizations must continue to recognize their overlapping constituencies and concerns in order to build alliances with one another, there also remains an entrenched sense of political difference between sex worker movements and the mainstream women's movement in many countries. In India, some of these tensions have been mitigated by alliances that have been taking shape since the early 2000s. The idea of sex work as labour, and as a practice that is not only relevant to women, or to violence against women, has been taken up by Indian autonomous feminist groups, and by academics and film-makers, as well as sectors of the labour movement. Prior to this period, sex work and sex workers' organizing in India were distinct from feminist organizing, which was focused on the rise of Hindu nationalism and privatization throughout the 1990s, as well as anti-violence campaigns, and campaigns in alliance with left and civil liberties groups that pressured the judiciary and other sectors of the state on a broad range of issues. The rise of HIV/AIDS-related activism, as well as sexuality-related activism in the 2000s, also facilitated the rise of Indian feminist engagements with sex work. While some groups pressed for the criminalization of sex work as a means to protect people selling sexual services, others began to argue for the decriminalization of sex work in India. Alliances with individual organizations representing, respectively, LGBTQ people, hijras and sex workers, e.g. through the coalitions that have been working towards the decriminalization of homosexuality in India, have also led to some feminist organizations arguing for the decriminalization of sexual commerce in particular.

Conclusion

In this chapter, I have discussed the intersecting histories of pornography, prostitution and feminism, and the theoretical and strategic implications these histories have for contemporary sex workers' social movements. The historical examples I have discussed here have focused on the USA and India. While I have emphasized developments that can be used to derive a generalized historical framing for the development of sex-work-related movements, these histories cannot be universalized to every national context in the global North and South. Rather, these histories help to contextualize the international policy initiatives on sex work and human trafficking sponsored by the US government over the past decade.[9] By the same token, the history of the development of sex worker organizing in India cannot easily be applied to other global South countries. However, India offers a national context for sexuality-based activism which has formed an exemplary model for defining international 'best practice' guidelines for HIV prevention, as well as offering an array of organizational positions on sex work in a global South country, while having a historically entrenched and rich tradition of social movements, including those that are now major actors in the changing discourse on sex work there.

In evoking, and aiming to contextualize, these histories and concepts, this chapter raises more questions than it resolves. These questions include the future of sex worker organizing, and the alliances that this work will spawn. The question of the nature of sex workers' movement rests at the centre of this debate – what constitutes, for example, sex-worker-led organizing? How much of the sex workers' rights movement is sex-worker-led? What does this mean, and where, and how, is it important? What racialized, North/South dynamics is the movement itself producing or perpetuating as it exists today? These questions frame challenges for constructing a more critical, democratic, post-abolitionist discourse on sex work, as well as outlining challenges for generating new analytics for the productive tensions between sexuality and geopolitics, and new ways in which feminist movements might engage these tensions.

Notes

1 Thanks to Creating Resources for Empowerment and Action (CREA), for which a draft of this chapter was originally prepared, and to Veronica Magar and Srilatha Batliwala for their comments on the earlier draft.

2 This impasse and its aftermath have been productively discussed in many different venues, including Nagle (1997).

3 A 2007 report by the Global Alliance Against Trafficking in Women (GAATW), entitled 'Collateral damage', extends this critique by describing ways in which women and girls have been themselves victimized by anti-trafficking measures that are conceived through an abolitionist framing (www.gaatw. org/Collateral%20Damage.../single file_CollateralDamage).

4 A classic analysis of the contemporary trafficking discourse in the late 1990s can be found in Chapkis (2003).

5 The full title is 'Protocol to prevent, suppress and punish trafficking in persons, especially women and children, supplementing the United Nations Convention Against Transnational Organized Crime'.

It can be found at untreaty.un.org/English/TreatyEvent2003/Texts/treaty2E.pdf. This protocol contains the foundational definition for human trafficking used in all subsequent international conventions.

6 Examples of these critiques include: Harvey (2007 [1982]); Ong (1999); and Breman (1996).

7 kswu.blogspot.com, accessed 1 December 2011.

8 www.sacw.net/Wmov/TowardsaPoliticsofJustice.html.

9 This is the condition that, under the President's Emergency Plan for Aid Relief (PEPFAR), recipients of USAID grants are still required to sign. The condition states that grant recipients do not consider prostitution a livelihood option. See www.genderhealth.org/loyaltyoath.php.

References

Agarwal, A., S. Jana et al. (1999) 'The prevalence of HIV in female sex workers in Manipur, India', *Journal of Communicable Diseases*, 31(1): 23–8.

Albinia, A. (2005) 'Womanhood laid bare: how Katherine Mayo and Manoda Devi challenged Indian public morality', in *Bare Acts: Sarai Reader 2005*, New Delhi: Sarai, pp. 428–35.

Bernstein, E. (2007) *Temporarily Yours: Intimacy, Authenticity, and the Commerce of Sex*, Chicago, IL: University of Chicago Press.

Breman, J. (1996) *Footloose Labour: Working in India's Informal Economy*, Cambridge: Cambridge University Press.

Brown, W. (1995) *States of Injury: Power and Freedom in Late Modernity*, Princeton, NJ: Princeton University Press.

Chapkis, W. (2003) 'Trafficking, migration, and the law:

protecting innocents, punishing immigrants', *Gender & Society*, 17(6): 923–37.

Chatterjee, N. (1999) 'AIDS-related information exposure in the mass media and discussion within social networks among married women in Bombay, India', *AIDS Care*, 11(4): 443–6.

Chatterjee, P. (1993) 'The nation and its women', in *The Nation and Its Fragments: Colonial and Postcolonial Histories*, Princeton, NJ: Princeton University Press, pp. 116–34.

Doezema, J. (1998) 'Forced to choose: beyond the voluntary v. forced prostitution dichotomy', in K. Kempadoo and J. Doezema (eds), *Global Sex Workers: Rights, Resistance, and Redefinition*, New York: Routledge, pp. 34–50.

— (2001) 'Ouch! Western feminists' "wounded attachment" to the "third world prostitute"', *Feminist Review*, 67: 16–38.

— (2002) 'Who gets to choose? Coercion, consent, and the UN Trafficking Protocol', *Gender & Development*, 10(1): 20–7.

Duggan, L. and N. Hunter (1995) *Sex Wars: Sexual Dissent and Political Culture*, New York: Routledge.

Farmer, P. (1992) *AIDS and Accusation: Haiti and the Geography of Blame*, Berkeley: University of California Press.

Globe News (2011) 'South Korean sex worker protests', 17 May, www.plri.org/resource/south-korean-sex-worker-protests.

Harvey, D. (2007 [1982]) *The Limits to Capital*, New York: Verso.

Human Rights Watch (2010) *Off the Streets: Arbitrary Detention and Other Abuses against Sex Workers in Cambodia*, 19 July, www.hrw.org/reports/2010/07/19/streets.

Kristoff, N. (2011) 'Raiding a brothel in India', *New York Times*, 25 May, www.nytimes.com/2011/05/26/opinion/26kristof.html.

Kunte, A. et al. (1999) 'HIV seroprevalence and awareness about AIDS among pregnant women in rural areas of Pune district, Maharashtra, India', *Indian Journal of Medical Research*, 110: 115–22.

Levine, P. (2003) *Prostitution, Race, and Politics: Policing Venereal Disease in the British Empire*, New York: Routledge.

Mayo, K. (1927) *Mother India*, London: Jonathan Cape.

Mohanty, C. T. (1991) 'Under Western eyes: feminist scholarship and colonial discourses', in C. T. Mohanty, A. Russo and L. Torres (eds), *Third World Women and the Politics of Feminism*, Bloomington: Indiana University Press, pp. 51–80.

Nagle, J. (ed.) (1997) *Whores and Other Feminists*, New York: Routledge.

Ong, A. (1999) *Flexible Citizenship: The Cultural Logics of Transnationality*, Durham, NC: Duke University Press.

Pais, P. (1996) 'HIV and India: looking into the abyss', *Tropical Medicine & International Health*, 1(3): 295–304.

Roy, D. (2001) *Community Action on HIV for Indian NGOs*, New Delhi: Voluntary Health Association of India.

Shah, S. (2007) 'Distinguishing poverty and trafficking: lessons from field research in Mumbai', *Georgetown Journal on Poverty Law and Policy*, 9(1): 441–54.

Thrupkaew, N. (2009) 'The crusade against sex trafficking', *The Nation*, 16 September, www.thenation.com/article/crusade-against-sex-trafficking.

Treichler, P. A. (1999) *How to Have Theory in an Epidemic: Cultural Chronicles of AIDS*, Durham, NC: Duke University Press.

Vance, C. (ed.) (1984) *Pleasure and Danger: Exploring Female Sexuality*, Boston, MA: Routledge and Kegan Paul.

Veeraraghavan, V. and S. Singh (eds) (1999) *HIV and AIDS: An Interdisciplinary Approach to Prevention and Management*, New Delhi: Mosaic Books.

Walkowitz, J. (1992) *City of Dreadful Delight: Narratives of Sexual Danger in Late-Victorian London*, Chicago, IL: University of Chicago Press.

Whiteford, L. M. and L. Manderson (eds) (2000) *Global Health Policy, Local Realities: The Fallacy of the Level Playing Field*, Boulder, CO: Lynne Rienner.

2 | AASHA's approach to instituting sexual harassment legislation in Pakistan

SADAF AHMAD

The government of Pakistan passed two pieces of legislation in early 2010. One – an amendment to Section 509 of the Pakistan Penal Code (PPC) – defined sexual harassment and made it a crime in Pakistan. The other made the development of self-regulatory mechanisms to deal with instances of sexual harassment mandatory for all organizations. These laws were the culmination of ten years of activism by AASHA (Alliance Against Sexual Harassment) – an alliance of like-minded individuals, affiliated with different organizations, who came together to work on the development, drafting and implementation of these laws.

Work on gender issues in Pakistan has largely been taken up by NGOs through donor-funded projects since the early 1990s. This dominant trend has been interspersed by civil society activists coming together to engage in short-term radical[1] activism around specific issues. But AASHA's approach – what its members believed was the most effective way of getting sexual harassment legislation passed – was deliberately designed to circumvent what it saw as the weaknesses of foreign donor-funded projects and institutions as well as the radical and usually anti-state approach taken up by civil society activists. AASHA members' cognizance of the extent to which the strategies adopted by others had been effective in meeting their respective goals – particularly in the arena of law-making – thus played a significant role in their configuration of their own strategies.

The success of AASHA's strategies confirms their usefulness and underscores the process through which such change can be brought about effectively. AASHA's strategies also play a critical role in challenging conventional understandings of feminist action in which the latter is neatly organized into discrete and dichotomous categories; the alliance's fluid and multi-stranded politics are illustrative of the multiplicity of feminist organizing, are difficult to categorize, and hence undermine the utility of organizing feminist action in such a way. This chapter will draw upon AASHA's strategies in order to expand upon this idea, but it will first provide an overview of the manner in which work on women's issues has been and continues to be done in Pakistan. Familiarity with this context is necessary to understand the manner in which AASHA's strategies were different.

Work on women's issues in Pakistan: an overview of the strategies

It is a fallacy to assume that women's strategies to institute change fit one pattern or that all women have a similar conception of how change needs to be instituted or what improvement even means (Gangoli 2007). An overview of Pakistani women's activities over time illustrates this multiplicity even as it highlights – as it does in other parts of the world (Alvarez 1998) – the important role the socio-political climate plays in determining the nature of their action.

Social welfare and radical politics Pakistani women took up a social welfare approach after 1947, when the newly formed country was in a state of crisis, trying to deal with basic issues in the wake of a very violent partition. A number of women's organizations committed to social welfare work came into being during that time and enjoyed state patronage as they opened schools and colleges for women, developed women's skills through establishing industrial homes, and worked on women's health issues (Mumtaz and Shaheed 1987).

The relationship between the nature of women's work and the socio-political climate was also clearly visible during General Zia-ul-Haq's military dictatorship (1977–88), a period when changes began being instituted under the rubric of Islamization (Jilani 1994; Rouse 2006a and b). Women, for instance, were banned from participating in spectator sports in 1982. Single women were no longer able to serve abroad via the Foreign Service according to another policy implemented in 1983 (Khan 2004a; Mumtaz and Shaheed 1987). However, the most damaging of Zia's policies was the introduction of the Hudood Ordinance, which sought to 'define and regulate women's morality' (Khan 2004a: xiii; Zia 2004). The Hudood Ordinance was based on the government's interpretation of Islamic law and was especially harmful for women through its Zina Ordinance, which made consensual sex outside marriage a criminal, punishable offence (Raja 2006). It was also problematic because it made no distinction between rape and pre/extramarital sex. This meant that if a woman was unable to prove that she had been raped she was charged with the 'crime' of engaging in pre/extramarital sex, was imprisoned and lashed a hundred times (Gardezi 2004; Khan 2004a; Saigol 2004).

It was therefore during Zia's time that women – who had largely if not solely engaged in social welfare and development work until then – changed their approach and began to openly challenge the government's policies and endeavours that threatened their rights of equal citizenship. Feeling the need for a platform from which they could act, a group of upper-middle- and upper-class women, some already members of different organizations, came together and formed the Women's Action Forum (WAF). WAF was unique in its anti-state approach, one that set it aside from women's organizations that had dominated the scene until then and which had sought accommodation within the state or worked within a development paradigm (Rouse 2006b).

WAF was initially a 'lobbying cum-pressure group' (Rouse 1988: 7). For instance, on learning that Dr Israr, a member of the Council of Islamic Ideology, was making very controversial statements on a television programme called *Al-Huda*,[2] women immediately gathered outside the Pakistan Television office in Karachi to protest. Ultimately, after a prolonged battle over many months, Dr Israr was removed from television and the programme was shut down (Khan and Saigol 2004; Mumtaz and Shaheed 1987). However, WAF became more diversified over time and began organizing consciousness-raising seminars and workshops around issues such as those of women's legal rights and health. Protests about specific issues, which included but were not limited to the Hudood Ordinance, continued. Thus the activities that took place during the 1980s, and which were largely undertaken through WAF's platform, were a combination of acts – 'pickets, demonstrations, processions, media campaigns, awareness workshops and seminars' that primarily took place in direct response to the regressive and harmful environment women found themselves in (Khan 2004b: 5).

A number of positive outcomes are linked with the women's movement of the 1980s (Rouse 1988). Yet the more diverse a group, the more potential for debate and disagreement. It is in this context that some writers highlight the differences, such as those of agenda and approach, which existed between the different chapters of WAF. WAF Karachi, for instance, dealt with broader human rights and had seminars open to both men and women. WAF Lahore, known for being the most radical chapter, dealt only with women's issues and never allowed men to participate in any of its events. Tensions sometimes arose between members desiring 'militant' action and those who were not so inclined. Discussions also took place between different members regarding the approach they should take with the government. This meant 'waffling on whether or not to recognize Zia's regime as legitimate, whether to direct attacks against it or to appeal to it' (ibid.: 9). These points of dissension, along with other factors, such as whether to frame their arguments and work within a religious or a secular human rights framework, their inability to engage in strong networking and partnership-building, and a lack of personal connection and sense of solidarity among the women who worked together, have been frequently highlighted to explain why WAF did not become more popular and more successful in achieving its goals (Gardezi 2004; Khan and Saigol 2004; Zia 2004).

The development paradigm The need for radical politics declined after Zia's death in 1988 and an institutionalization of the woman's movement in the form of NGO-ization came to dominate the terrain of feminist politics in Pakistan. Development and 'rights' discourse began permeating women's work and began influencing their modus operandi. Many feminists opened up their own NGOs while others began working in the development sector by joining international organizations such as Oxfam, Action Aid, etc. They continued engaging in radical politics whenever they felt the need for such action. Dozens of civil society organizations and NGOs, for instance, came together to rally for the repeal of the Zina Ordinance when General Pervez Musharraf (1999–2008) brought up the issue for discussion. However, many of the activities that feminists now engage in take the form of funded projects that largely take place within the arena of development.

A similar trend has been witnessed in other parts of the world. Most Indian women's organizations worked independently in the 1980s but very few of them were not the recipients of aid from government or foreign donors by the 1990s (Gangoli 2007). Decreased social welfare from their respective governments in the 1970s in combination with heavy funding from USAID – in what has been portrayed as an attempt to support and strengthen the grass roots and civil society with the larger goal of strengthening democracy – have resulted in the proliferation of NGOs working on women's issues in the Arab world (Jad 2008). Funding for development projects has also been made available to nations such as Afghanistan for the larger goal of facilitating international security (Kandiyoti 2008).

Accepting donor funding for specific projects or for the sustenance of their organizations, or working on gender issues within the context of international development organizations, can lead to a range of difficulties. One of these is the problem of coming up with a 'principled feminist response' whereby many women feel that they can no longer question what may be 'imperial meddling' in local affairs (Fisher 1997; Kandiyoti 2008: 192). Another is their no longer engaging in a critical interrogation of their work, its politics and the effectiveness of 'simplistic "magic bullet" solutions' (Win 2008: 85) in which the power structures prevalent within society remain untouched (Mukhopadhyay 2008; Woodford-Berger 2008). Furthermore, work done through development organizations has also been accused of analytical simplicity whereby the impact of mediating factors such as those of class or ethnicity on women's experiences is not recognized and whereby 'men' and 'women' are construed as monolithic and oppositional categories who can never form alliances and work together (Woodford-Berger 2008). Feminist critique of development work also focuses on its top-down approach and its ineffectiveness because of a lack of local ownership (Kandiyoti 2008; Tsikata 2008). More specifically, donor agencies have been accused of specifying the agenda for local communities, what Menon refers to as co-option (2004: 220).

Local NGOs, often focusing on specific women's issues, have been the subject of much of the same critique as above. Other factors that have been held responsible for limiting the amount of genuine transformation NGOs can inculcate within communities include the competition between NGOs to secure donor funds or to receive recognition at national and international fora which may get in the way of their cooperating over issues (Jad 2008). There is an abundance of literature that manifests its writers' concerns with the 'bureaucratization, NGO-ization, and "technification" of the women's movement' (Molyneux 2008: 234) and a shared belief that change 'can only come from political initiatives that are not driven by the compulsions of funding' (Menon 2004: 222).

The point of highlighting these issues is not to suggest that all development work is besieged by these problems or that donor-funded development work has not made a difference or does not have the potential to make a difference in women's lives. The purpose is to draw attention to some of the constraints and limitations of development work as identified by development practitioners across the world, particularly as these concerns are equally applicable to the Pakistani context (Zia 2009: 29). It was AASHA members' cognizance of these concerns, based on their experience with and examination of the dominant development paradigm, their assessment of the activist approach and a close look at how each had worked to formulate and amend laws, which fed into their configuring their approach, as will be illustrated below.

AASHA – an alliance against sexual harassment[3]

Sexual harassment is a phenomenon that is seen all around the world and it is particularly prevalent in Pakistan. According to a situational analysis of sexual harassment at the workplace conducted by AASHA (2002), 58 per cent of nurses, 91 per cent of domestic workers and 93 per cent of women working in both private and public sector organizations claim to have experienced some form of sexual harassment. Ninety-two per cent of the women also spoke of experiencing severe sexual harassment while using public transport. Prior research highlights the high frequency of sexual harassment in vans, a common means of public transport for women from low-income groups (Brohi 1998). Research undertaken among young women from higher-income groups reveals that although these women did not face sexual harassment in spaces such as vans and at bus stops – spaces that were not a part of their daily experiences – they were equally vulnerable to sexual harassment and faced it in their homes, their friends' and relatives' homes, in marketplaces and in their educational institutes. The perpetrators included their Qur'ān teachers, friends, peers, teachers, servants, cousins, uncles and strangers (Malik 2009). Although Pakistani women may differ in their understanding of why sexual harassment occurs and what the solution is, it is not an exaggeration to say that most Pakistani women have faced sexual harassment in some form or other and to varying degrees during their lifetime. It was one such case that led to AASHA's formation.

AASHA's story began in 1997 when eleven women working in the United Nations Development Programme (UNDP) Islamabad drew upon their organization's sexual harassment policy to file a complaint against a man occupying a senior management position in the organization (Ahmad 2001). The main lesson for one of these women, Dr Fouzia Saeed, was that 'it doesn't matter how much courage victims of sexual harassment are willing to display. They cannot fight the behaviour unless and until there are policies and an awareness of those policies in place.'

Sexual harassment is a form of abuse that has been naturalized, i.e. deemed to be one of those things that 'just is' by society at large. It also never received attention from civil society or from donor agencies. This silence on sexual harassment has occurred in a context where no legislation specifically addressing this issue existed prior to 2010. Pro-equality and anti-discriminatory provisions do exist in the Constitution of Pakistan (Articles 25, 26 and 27 in particular), and the PPC also provided protection from discrimination and harassment, but these provisions were rather general. Section 509 of the PPC, for instance (prior to its amendment), stated that anyone who 'insults the modesty of any woman' should be punished. The vagueness of the term 'modesty' contributed to the limited implementation of the law, and its dependence upon social attitudes and its interpretation by law-enforcing agencies contributed to its limited effectiveness.

It is in this larger context that Fouzia Saeed utilized the lessons she had learnt while fighting the sexual harassment case in UNDP, combined them with her lifelong experience of activism and what she had learned from years spent working with development organizations, and set up AASHA in 2001. Volunteer-based and non-hierarchical, AASHA was established on the premise that no one organization had the resources to handle an issue of this scope. An alliance, its members claimed, provided a broad geographical spread and also allowed the diverse strengths of different organizations to be utilized to meet their goal. The goal was getting sexual harassment legislation passed.

Those who have studied laws and their effectiveness in different parts of the world make the point that laws, on their own, may not be an effective deterrent to crime as they do not challenge the power structures within a society (Fisher 1997; Rajan 2003). AASHA members were aware that sexual harassment had deep roots in their society, recognized that laws could not bring about attitudinal change or challenge patriarchal structures, and knew that the presence of the latter was likely to curb the effectiveness of the laws once they were passed. However, they were equally aware that tackling the roots of the issue – the strategies for which were different and more long-term – was beyond their scope and the resources that were available to them. The decision to deal with the issue at symptom level was thus made deliberately and in full cognizance of its limitations, but also its advantages. They had seen how legislation was a prerequisite for harassers to be made accountable for their behaviour and how it had its own role – which fulfilled its own set of needs – to play. They also believed that it was a more productive alternative to not taking any steps at all in a context where crimes against women are rampant, an argument that one hears from feminists across the world (Gangoli 2007).

AASHA's efforts significantly contributed to the government of Pakistan passing an amendment to Section 509 of the PPC in January 2010, making sexual harassment in any location a crime in Pakistan. This amendment clearly defined sexual harassment and the different forms it could take. The government of Pakistan also passed a law called the

'Protection Against Harassment of Women at Workplace Act 2010' in March 2010, making the development of self-regulatory mechanisms to deal with instances of sexual harassment through adopting the Code of Conduct mandatory for all organizations, be they public or private. This Code defines sexual harassment, informs employees of the avenues they can take if they face sexual harassment and outlines the responsibilities of the management in following the Code – which include but are not limited to displaying it, spreading awareness about it and establishing a three-member inquiry committee to deal with instances of sexual harassment by following particular procedures.[4] Any management that fails to get the Code instituted within their organization or does not establish a three-member committee can be taken to court and fined. Mechanisms are also laid out for people to seek redress through an ombudsperson established for this purpose if they feel that the dynamics in their organization are not conducive to their getting justice.

AASHA engaged in an intense two-year process characterized by strategic lobbying and crisis management before the legislation mentioned above was unanimously passed. The process itself had many steps: the bills first had to go through and be approved by the relevant ministries, then the cabinet, followed by the National Assembly (NA) and then finally the Senate. Some of the key strategies they utilized in this process, from drafting the bills to facilitating their implementation – and which highlight the manner in which their approach was different to the ones mentioned earlier – are given below.

The formulation, passage and implementation of the sexual harassment legislation

Inclusive politics I: a bottom-up approach One of the common concerns analysts and practitioners have with legislation is the extent to which it can capture the complexity of the phenomenon and the diversity of people's experiences. Getting information about the scope of the problem and educating themselves on the forms and dynamics of sexual harassment on the ground was thus one of the first steps AASHA members took. They understood that a top-down approach – the imposition of a law – would be effective only if it was shaped by a bottom-up approach whereby the law was shaped on the basis of how the issue manifested itself and was experienced by people. One of the ways in which this was done was through research among women who they learned were particularly vulnerable in the workplace. Their research among domestic workers, office workers in both the public and private sectors, nurses, saleswomen and women working in factories and brick kilns revealed the extent to which they faced sexual harassment and allowed them to gain an in-depth understanding of their experiences and the dynamics of the phenomenon.

AASHA also increased their understanding of the issue and strengthened their alliances with working women by organizing annual working women's assemblies from 2002, each assembly taking place on 22 December.[5] Working women from diverse occupations were provided with an opportunity to share their experiences with each other, and these assemblies quickly became a space for them to bond and affirm their experiences. The assemblies also highlighted the visibility of working women as a constituency and became an opportunity to bring in strategic partners so that they could learn about the issue and begin owning it.

The Code of Conduct for Gender Justice that AASHA developed was signed and became a bill at the end of a long process in which it was discussed and commented upon by a variety of regional and international players. However, soon realizing that the government would not be ready to seriously discuss the bill if it were presented in cabinet, AASHA changed its strategy and began getting the Code passed in the private sector. More than three hundred organizations – such as Shell Petroleum, Awari Hotels, Attock Oil Refinery, the Jang media group – had adopted the Code by 2008. AASHA also introduced the annual AASHA awards for those organizations that were assessed to be the most gender friendly in terms of adopting the Code, setting up the prescribed mechanisms, etc. The public recognition these companies received reinforced their commitment to the Code and acted as an incentive to others to follow in their footsteps. Networks were strengthened and support was garnered. This process continued until the elections of February 2008, at which point AASHA members agreed that the time had come to give the Code legal standing in order to take it nationwide.

Inclusive politics II: building ownership AASHA members wanted both the bills to be owned by the state and by the different segments of society in order to increase the chances of their implementation. Representatives of some of these segments – which included the police and other law-enforcing agencies, labour unions, the Chamber of Commerce, local councils, employers, like-minded parliamentarians, media activists and members of civil society – were invited to attend the AASHA assemblies, and others were brought on board through intense lobbying. AASHA deliberately focused on target groups that covered a vast spectrum of society because they believed that it was only through the ownership and combined efforts of all stakeholders that the bills could be passed and implemented later on. This overall strategy paid off in concrete ways in a range of sectors.

The media, which through its numerous private channels enjoys a lot of power when it comes to shaping public opinion in Pakistan, was one such sector and played a critical role in giving the issue a very positive space. The Jang group, for instance – which includes a range of television channels and newspapers – had adopted the Code itself and continuously facilitated this process because of a sense of ownership. It, along with other television channels, began free biannual campaigns to raise public awareness of the issue. AASHA members made regular appearances on these programmes and began using them to spread awareness about the issue of sexual harassment, the nature of the bills and what their passage would mean in practical terms if they became law.

Networking and building ownership of the issue among ministerial staff such as clerks and security guards also facilitated the process. The security guards, for instance, were particularly helpful in helping AASHA members locate senators so that they could undertake last-minute lobbying before a Senate session began, telling them where different people were at that particular moment or which routes they usually took from their offices.

AASHA also utilized the ownership various parliamentarians and senators developed by requesting them to undertake specific tasks that were appropriate to their individual skills and level of authority. Some people thus helped them secure passes to attend the NA and Senate sessions. Others were relied upon to make speeches and explain the bill or defend it within these and other fora. Supporting parliamentarians and senators also manifested their ownership of the bill by engaging in last-minute lobbying within the NA or the Senate once the sessions had begun. This lobbying was done by women belonging to different political parties and represented the cross-party ownership that AASHA had been successful in inculcating. Ultimately, their ownership was manifest in the way both the bills were passed unanimously, with all political parties supporting it.

Keeping an eye on the goal 'Alliances are always made at some cost, because they are made with those who share some, but not all, political goals; and while many can agree on the need for such alliances, it is much more difficult to agree on the point at which compromise becomes defeat' (Cornwall et al. 2008: 15). AASHA was not willing to compromise on anything that reduced its effectiveness in reaching its goal. It thus parted ways with some civil society organizations that were not like minded in its first year; the latter's interest in self-credit or their upholding a very different approach to instigating change was found to jeopardize the process and got in the way of their working on the issue.

Keeping to the most effective path sometimes created awkward situations – for instance, on the occasion when one woman cabinet member became very enthusiastic about the idea of the bill and volunteered to introduce it in cabinet as a private member bill. Private member bills are easier to table but their rate of success is as low as 1–2 per cent according to the research AASHA had conducted. They wanted to introduce it as a government bill, which was much more difficult and time consuming to organize, but which significantly increased its chances of becoming a law. Finesse and diplomacy were required to keep to their path and still keep the support of this politician.

It is also important to mention that AASHA's work was not donor funded at this stage. AASHA members' prior experience of working on donor-funded projects meant that they were aware that women's groups 'lack autonomy from the compulsions of getting and retaining funding' (Menon 2004: 220). This autonomy was essential for them given the nature of their work, which took place in a context that was marked by ambiguity and crisis management and where flexibility in changing one's strategy according to the needs of the moment was critical. '[T]op-down managerial blueprints (which also include the blueprints for "bottom-up" participatory approaches)', on the other hand, often include 'limited timeframes and specification of outcomes' that often give rise to contradictions when the modus operandi they prefer clash with 'the strategies of political actors on the ground' (Kandiyoti 2008: 194). AASHA members were determined to stay away from confining blueprints to specifics and in general to avoid any path that they believed would limit their effectiveness in meeting their goal.

Controlling the content of the bills Accounts of Indian women's experiences of reporting rape and sexual harassment reveal how sexist laws can be harmful for women (Gangoli 2007). The rape laws in India illustrate how the process of relying upon the law can often end up serving the interests of those in power and reinforce the patriarchal status quo. For instance, a lot of emphasis is given to a woman's 'morality' or lack thereof to strengthen the case for whether or not she was attacked (Menon 2004). Such arguments serve to reinforce the good woman/bad woman divide and police women's sexuality, which is necessary for the continuation of a patrilineal social order (Saeed 2001). French feminists' success in attaining legal reform that gave women some access to contraception in the 1960s and 1970s also illustrates the manner in which laws can both reinforce and perpetuate patriarchal hegemony; their success was heavily dependent upon their deliberately linking the idea of family planning with stronger families, which would then lead to a stronger nation (Jenson 1996).

AASHA members were aware of this issue from the history of law-making in Pakistan and most recently witnessed it in the Women's Protection Act of 2006. General Pervez Musharraf initiated a discussion on the Zina Ordinance in 2002 and instructed the National Commission on the Status of Women[6] and the Council of Islamic Ideology to analyse it. Their recommendations ultimately led to the creation of the Women's Protection Act in 2006, a step that the civil society organizations, which had been asking for the repeal of the Ordinance, were not fully satisfied with. But the religious trappings of the Ordinance in conjunction with the religious parties' activism, which framed opposition to the Ordinance on the grounds that it was unIslamic, significantly reduced the probability of it being repealed and a compromise was sought. Thus while the Women's Protection Act – which now came under the aegis of the PPC and not the Hudood Ordinance – includes checks and balances to curb the abuses that took place under the Zina Ordinance and separates rape from sex outside of marriage, the latter, deemed 'fornication' in the PPC, remains a crime. The hegemonic ideology permeating society regarding people's sexuality and normative sexual conduct remained untouched and the structures within which people are meant to live within society were reinforced.

Laws can thus reinforce social structures by emphasizing certain discourses through their content. Wanting to minimize damage to the content of the bills in this context, AASHA members made a point of sitting through all the government meetings in which the two bills were discussed. Although the bills were 'government bills', i.e. tabled by the government, AASHA's involvement in the entire process and its role in organizing many of these meetings from the very beginning resulted in an impression being created that all negotiations had to be undertaken with its members. AASHA members kept a tight control over the content of the bills and were able to divert most of the changes that they thought would have resulted in the bills becoming less effective in practice. On some points there had to be compromise, however. Many within the ministries, for instance, reacted to the term 'sexual' in the 'sexual harassment policy' that AASHA first drafted in 2002. That is the main reason the name was altered to the Code of Conduct for Gender Justice. It was a compromise that allowed the process to move forward and gave AASHA members more negotiating power when it came to resisting changes in the actual content of the Code, and later in the content of the bills.

Flexible framing WAF members have engaged in much debate regarding how to frame arguments when speaking of change and the pros and cons of using a secular versus religious framework (Mumtaz and Shaheed 1987; Rouse 2006a). AASHA members did not limit themselves to using any one kind of framework while lobbying. The nature of their activist approach meant their meeting people from a range of backgrounds, and they altered their framework accordingly, often using a combination of frameworks simultaneously. They thus chose to build upon the rights that they already had in the Constitution and presented their bills as loyal to the spirit of the Constitution each time they presented their case to the Law Ministry. They spoke of the Baloch nationalists always taking a secular stance historically when they spoke to them and succeeded in breaking the alliance they had formed with the religious political parties who were critical of the bill at a particular point. They spoke of the issue of sexual harassment as an employee–management and human resource issue and highlighted the importance of changing the organizational culture to make the environment more dignified when they approached people in the private sector. This strategy increased the number of social segments they were able to successfully reach out to and built ownership among different kinds of people. This ownership was clearly manifest when the bills were supported by parliamentarians and senators – both men and women – in public fora; they used arguments that resonated with them, be they Islamic (e.g. Islam teaches equality), secular/development oriented (e.g. freedom from intimidation is necessary for the country's progress) or based in structures that already existed (e.g. the laws are merely specifying what already exists in the Constitution so why the debate?).

Breaking through the glass wall AASHA's strategy of working with the government to the extent that it broke through the invisible glass wall that exists between the state and civil society is one of the unique features of its approach and sets it apart from other organizations, which have always maintained the distinction between the two spheres. AASHA's engagement with the government – which was marked by patience, persistence and non-confrontation – challenged this divide and took the form of its members organizing each procedural step but making the Ministry of Women's Development (MoWD) the host on each occasion, writing speeches on sexual harassment for various politicians, briefing them with updates before their television appearances, and providing them with written notes and points before NA and Senate sessions so that the chosen parliamentarians and senators would know what points to raise if the bill was challenged on any front. They also assessed the bills for various political actors on more than one occasion. If their file (containing the bills) became stuck in any ministry because the minister in question had not read it or commented upon it despite (AASHA-instigated) reminders by their staff, AASHA members were known to provide them with comments. Fouzia Saeed recalls that 'we would tell them that we've written these notes, why don't you see if you can use them ...'

AASHA members' constant engagement with the different levels of the government machinery to discover the status of their file or learn the nature of the next steps they would have to take meant that, as Aqsa Khan, an active AASHA member, explained:

> the system began working the other way around. We would be the ones giving them [the politicians] the information. We would say 'you have to sign this and send this off to ... this is what's coming on the agenda on Tuesday ... these are the people who are likely to raise these objections, this is what you need to say to counter their points ...'

A comparison of AASHA's approach with the approach taken by other organizations to get legislation passed, repealed or amended in the past reveals the differences between these approaches. Parallel bills, scattered ownership and civil society reacting to government rather than working with it in a strategic manner marked the formulation and passage of an amendment to the honour killings law in 2004, for instance. Civil society had developed its own draft of the bill but there was a split over issues such as that of terminology, i.e. with some pushing for the term 'murder' to replace 'honour' as the latter, they claimed, came across as a justification of the act. There was also a lack of coordination between civil society and government and a lack of ownership by all the political parties within the government. Thus when the amendment was ultimately passed in 2004, it resulted in the opposition staging a walkout and civil society distancing itself from what it rightly deemed was weak and ineffective legislation. A lack of meaningful coordination and cooperation – in conjunction with exaggerated competition whereby commitment to the issue often took a back seat – between most of the sectors involved ultimately resulted in the bill being flawed in content and disowned by many.

The legislation of the the domestic violence bill has been delayed for similar reasons. It was initially introduced as a private member bill by Sherry Rehman of the Pakistan People's Party. A parallel bill was soon presented by Mahnaz Rafi of the Pakistan Muslim League. The two were eventually amalgamated but other bills, one drafted by a few prominent women's organizations and another drafted by UNIFEM, also began sharing this space. The amalgamated bill that was eventually passed in the NA in 2009 was one that none of the stakeholders was pleased with and much disunity was created between all the players involved. The process was then suspended in the Senate, where it was heavily criticized by the religious parties. Lack of ownership across different parties resulted in few defending it and it eventually lapsed. The fact that the domestic violence bill had been tabled as a private member and not as a government bill also meant that it began its journey from a vulnerable position. Furthermore, it enjoyed no media protection, which meant that space was created for it to be criticized in public.

Implementing the sexual harassment legislation The success of a movement, some social movement theorists point out, must not just refer to the passage of a law but also to its implementation. Although AASHA had met its goal, its members decided that, given that momentum had been built and AASHA had gained significant clout, they would give it two more years and use its platform to facilitate the implementation process. AASHA was not a funded alliance but it chose to bring donors on board at this stage of the process in an attempt to make use of them to further their own implementation vision. AASHA invited them all to a meeting and presented them with a collaborative implementation framework. They explained what their vision for the next two years was, specified what they could do from their platform and suggested that the donors fund whoever they wanted to for the rest of the project. The goal was to have one national strategy and ensure that no one party's work interfered with another's but rather fed into the larger whole.

AASHA's two-year implementation strategy was guided by two goals. The first goal was to set up mechanisms to deal with cases of sexual harassment in the country, and this was their first priority. The second goal was the internalization of the mechanism. These goals were manifest in a multifaceted political strategy that had a number of strands and was developed on the principle of using their two years in the most effective way.

A few examples that highlight their strategy of working through partners for maximum impact include their identifying and approaching key regulatory bodies that had the authority to send out directives (in this case to adopt the Code) to organizations in their domain. Many regulatory bodies have taken this step, such as the State Bank of Pakistan, which has sent directives to all the banks regulated by it, the Ministry of Health, which has sent directives to all its hospitals, medical institutes, attached departments, etc. The same strategy is manifest in AASHA's emphasis on creating resource pools for all sectors (such as the media, the health sector, the police academy, bar associations, etc.) with each resource pool being made up of individuals belonging to a particular sector who are given a comprehensive theoretical understanding of the issue and of the laws. This training becomes one of the means by which the myths surrounding sexual harassment – such as that a woman who faces unwanted sexual attention is being harassed regardless of how she is dressed or the number of relationships she has had in the past – are addressed. AASHA has conducted twenty-five training sessions so far and has prepared almost 500 trainers, who are spreading a discourse about the nature, dynamics and myths of sexual harassment together with legal and procedural information in their respective sectors countrywide.

The desire to facilitate the set-up and implementation of effective structures has also resulted in AASHA using its website to provide information relating to the laws in both English and Urdu. This information includes the original text of the laws, an abridged and easy-to-understand version of the laws and the steps organizations must take to abide by the Code. Similar material, in the form of posters and booklets, is being distributed to a variety of sectors, such as the MoWD and the Chamber of Commerce, for further dissemination. These bodies have been told that they are free to put their own logos on the material and get it reprinted. AASHA has also completed two intense media campaigns for awareness-raising purposes among the general public. They organized twenty television programmes on all the major television channels, published more than three hundred newspaper articles and aired programmes on all the major radio stations in the more recent campaign from November 2010 to January 2011.

Both the laws were passed less than two years ago and only time will tell to what extent they have been effective. Many women have taken the initiative and filed cases, either in their respective organizations or directly with the police. Maliha Husain, the programme director at AASHA, highlights this as a measure of success. She says that 'at this point we are measuring success with the fact that so many cases are being reported all over the country. It is only happening because there is a law and because people are becoming aware of it. They are choosing to report cases in spite of the stigma.'

Interrogating the dichotomies of feminist work

Although many AASHA members had vast experience of engaging in radical political activism as well as working within a development paradigm, they, as a group working on a specific issue with a particular goal in mind, changed their 'discourse and analysis in response to the histories of [their] own engagements with development and with each other and in plural sites and changing times' (Cornwall et al. 2008: 16). It was their familiarity with and experience of working in other paradigms and their analysis of the effectiveness of prior approaches involving the passage or amendment of legislation which resulted in their ability to assess the appropriateness of those paradigms and approaches in the context of achieving their goal. Their strategy was configured on the basis of this understanding. Zia says that 'colloquially, the slogans that Pakistani feminists have used in their political resistance include "men, money, mullahs and the military." This approach has given the movement its structural moorings and clarity with regard to its confrontational and dynamic relationship with the state, the military and capitalist development' (2009: 30).

AASHA's structural moorings were very different. It was inclusive politics – across genders and all sectors of the society – and not confrontation which marked AASHA's multi-pronged strategy. AASHA's systematic engagement with the different segments of society and its ability to instil some level of ownership of the issue among them paid off in concrete ways in the bill's formulation, passage and implementation process. Its willingness to break through the glass wall that has existed between civil society and the state further facilitated the process, as did letting others take the credit for their work.

AASHA's non-confrontational approach and willingness to work with private institutions such as media corporations and with, and often for, the state clearly set it apart from groups such as WAF and other feminists whose politics are based on antagonism or at least some level of scepticism towards such institutions, and most certainly the state. The radical politics that dominated the 1980s and other specific moments since then has been characterized by non-party affiliation, a lack of funding, working through a volunteer base in a largely non-institutionalized setting and an antagonistic relationship with, or at least some level of scepticism towards, the state. These are some of the main characteristics that have long been associated with groups that are termed autonomous and which are thus said to manifest a 'pure' and legitimate feminism (Biswas 2006; Dean 2008; Roy 2011). AASHA's cooperation with the state and private corporatized bodies can potentially open it to criticism and the accusations that are often meted out to women who work in institutionalized structures within the development paradigm – that of not being autonomous and of having 'sold themselves' to demonized structures. Such a criticism is commonly meted out to professional or career feminists, a label given to women who work on women's issues within institutionalized settings that are usually funded by the state or foreign donor agencies, and who may manifest varying levels of cooperation with the state, as has been witnessed in Pakistan since the 1990s (Alvarez 1998; Roy 2011). These feminists are automatically placed in a dichotomous relationship with those who engage in a more radical form of feminist politics.

The problem with categorizing or analysing any feminist approach through analytically simplistic dichotomies is that it can obscure the multiplicity of feminist organizing that defies clear-cut categorization into 'either/or' frameworks, where groups are either radical or institu-tionalized, either autonomous or non-autonomous[7] (Alvarez 1998; Roy 2011). AASHA's approach illustrates 'the plurality, fluidity and unpre-dictability inherent in feminist political action' that is difficult to slot into any neat category (Dean 2008: 290). Thus, while AASHA's strategy of cooperating with institutions such as the state and its dependency on politicians for getting the legislation passed can result in it being labelled non-autonomous, its members' tight control over the larger process and their not letting the representatives of the state dictate terms in any significant manner – for instance, while drafting the bills – are also a marker of their autonomy. The application of any one category to analyse their work therefore becomes insufficient and unsatisfactory and undermines the possibility of understanding the contingencies and flexibility of feminist action (ibid.).

AASHA's strategies also trouble discrete and polarized categories on grounds that are not limited to its relationship with the state or private corporatized bodies. Its members' recognition of the importance of fluidity and the freedom to alter their approach as the need arose, for instance, resulted in their staying away from donor funding before the laws were passed. They felt they could not afford to bind themselves in specific donor requirements. Their decision to accept donor funding in the implementation stage was taken only when the nature of their goal altered[8] and they felt they were in a position to specify the agenda for the donors as opposed to the other way around. Did AASHA become less or non-autonomous when it began receiving funds in a context where its members determined how the funds would be utilized? Furthermore, how do we categorize an alliance (and not an NGO) in which its key members – who are either employed in or run their own NGOs – have hired some staff for AASHA but continue to work as volunteers? Does that make them professional or non-professional feminists? Can we look at the work AASHA members have done over the last ten years and simply state whether it was done in a non-institutionalized or institutionalized setting? Polarizations such as these, which have commonly been used to categorize feminist action, seem to become somewhat irrelevant in such contexts.

AASHA members dissolved their alliance in March 2012 at the end of the two years they gave themselves to give the implementation process a jump start.[9] However, apart from the more practical impact of its work in the country and the lessons those interested in bringing about change can take from studying its approach, AASHA's strategies can continue to serve as a reminder of the limitations of using conventionally understood categories of feminist practices as a point of departure when studying feminist organizing. Looking at feminist work or collective mobilization as a dynamic and multi-pronged process in which those who are involved in facilitating change may alter their strategies to meet specific or changing needs, on the other hand, is a strategy that has the potential to capture the complexity of such work as it happens on the ground (Dean 2008).

Notes

1 Although the term 'radical' has been theoretically expanded to incorporate any action that 'imaginatively construct[s] new ways of seeing the world' in recent work (Dean 2008: 294), I will use it in its more conventional sense in this chapter, i.e. linking it with specific actions and attitudes, such as street protests, anti-statism, etc.

2 Examples of his statements include: all working women should be pensioned off; no one could be punished for rape until an Islamic society was created; and it was better to die than to live in a society that was run by women.

3 My knowledge of AASHA is based on closely following its work since its inception in 2001, and enga-

ging in participant observation and conducting in-depth interviews with its key members from 2007 to 2011.

4 The Code of Conduct can be downloaded in both Urdu and English at aasha.org.pk.

5 This is the date on which the decision in the UNDP sexual harassment case came through.

6 The Commission was established in 2002 to 'examine policies, programmes and other measures taken by the Government for women's development and gender equality; review laws, rules and regulations affecting the status of women', etc. (www.ncsw.gov.pk/).

7 Academics who have studied feminist organizing in different parts of the world have criticized such discrete binary dualisms by drawing upon the idea of 'hybridity', a term that highlights the feminist practice of drawing 'upon both development and movement-oriented modes of mobilization' (Alvarez 1998; Roy 2011: 2). Hybrid politics challenge 'polarized categories of politics' which otherwise 'obscure our ability to understand the specificity of contemporary feminist political mobilization' (Roy 2011: 13, 12). Although AASHA's strategies also challenge polarized categories, the term does not reflect its politics comprehensively. Its strategies are not a product or combination of two differentially conceived categories of action. Some of its strategies – as manifest in its relationship with the state, for instance – have no precedent in any paradigm of action in Pakistan.

8 Dean's study of women's organizations in Britain reminds us that they are not static but can change their goals and strategies over time (2008).

9 AASHA members believe that alliances should not turn into funded NGOs. The purpose of forming alliances, they claim, is to meet a specific goal. Once that goal has been met, the alliance should be dissolved. They are confident that the institutional groundwork they have done and the overseeing bodies they have helped set up will continue to facilitate the implementation of these laws.

References

AASHA (2002) *Situational Analysis on Sexual Harassment at the Workplace*, Islamabad: AASHA.

Ahmad, S. (2001) 'Sexual harassment: a case in Pakistan', *Violence Against Women and Children, Review of Women's Studies*, 11(1/2): 80–101, Centre for Women's Studies, University of the Philippines.

Alvarez, S. (1998) 'Advocating feminism: the Latin American feminist NGO "boom"', www.mtholyoke.edu/acad/spanish/advocating_feminism.html, accessed 1 August 2011.

Biswas, N. (2006) 'On funding and the NGO sector', *Economic and Political Weekly*, XLI(42): 4406–11.

Brohi, N. (1998) *Harassment of Women in the Workplace*, Karachi: Working Women's Support Centre.

Cornwall, A., E. Harrison and A. Whitehead (2008) 'Introduction: feminisms in development: contradictions, contestations and challenges', in A. Cornwall, E. Harrison and A. Whitehead (eds), *Feminisms in Development: Contradictions, contestations and challenges*, New Delhi: Zubaan.

Dean, J. (2008) 'Feminist purism and the question of "radicality" in contemporary political theory',

Contemporary Political Theory, 7: 280–301.

Fisher, W. (1997) 'Doing good? The politics and antipolitics of NGO practices', *Annual Review of Anthropology*, 26: 439–64.

Gangoli, G. (2007) *Indian Feminisms: Law, patriarchies, and violence in India*, Aldershot: Ashgate.

Gardezi, F. (2004) 'Islam, feminism, and the women's movement in Pakistan: 1981–91', in N. S. Khan (ed.), *Up against the State: Military rule and women's resistance*, Lahore: ASR Publications.

Jad, I. (2008) 'The NGO-ization of Arab women's movements', in A. Cornwall, E. Harrison and A. Whitehead (eds), *Feminisms in Development: Contradictions, contestations and challenges*, New Delhi: Zubaan.

Jenson, J. (1996) 'Representations of difference: the varieties of French feminism', in M. Threlfall and S. Rowbotham (eds), *Mapping the Women's Movement*, London: Verso.

Jilani, H. (1994) 'Law as an instrument of social control', in N. S. Khan, R. Saigol and A. Zia, *Locating the Self: Perspectives on Women and Multiple Identities*, Lahore: ASR Publications, pp. 96–105.

Kandiyoti, D. (2008) 'Political fiction meets gender myth: post-conflict reconstruction, "democratization" and women's rights', in A. Cornwall, E. Harrison and A. Whitehead (eds), *Feminisms in Development: Contradictions, contestations and challenges*, New Delhi: Zubaan.

Khan, N. S. (2004a) 'Parliamentary democracy and the women's movement in Pakistan: "still up against the state"', in N. S. Khan (ed.), *Up against the State: Military rule and women's resistance*, Lahore: ASR Publications.

— (2004b) 'Introduction', in N. S. Khan (ed.), *Up against the State: Military rule and women's resistance*, Lahore: ASR Publications.

Khan, N. S. and R. Saigol (2004) 'Women's action forum: debates and contradictions', in N. S. Khan (ed.), *Up against the State: Military rule and women's resistance*, Lahore: ASR Publications.

Malik, L. W. (2009) 'Justice versus honour: social constraints disempowering sexually harassed upper-class Pakistani women', Unpublished senior project, Lahore University of Management Sciences, Lahore.

Menon, N. (2004) *Recovering Subversion: Feminist politics beyond the law*, New Delhi: Permanent Black.

Molyneux, M. (2008) 'The chimera of success: gender *ennui* and the changed international policy environment', in A. Cornwall, E. Harrison and A. Whitehead (eds), *Feminisms in Development: Contradictions, contestations and challenges*, New Delhi: Zubaan.

Mukhopadhyay, M. (2008) 'Mainstreaming gender or "streaming" gender away: feminists marooned in the development business', in A. Cornwall, E. Harrison and A. Whitehead (eds), *Feminisms in Development: Contradictions, contestations and challenges*, New Delhi: Zubaan.

Mumtaz, K. and F. Shaheed (1987) *Women of Pakistan: Two steps forward one step back?*, Lahore: Vanguard Books.

Raja, S. A. (2006) 'Islamization of laws in Pakistan', in I. Alam (ed.), *Religious Revivalism in South Asia*,

South Asian Studies, X: 101–23, Free Media Foundation and South Asian Free Media Association, Pakistan.

Rajan, R. S. (2003) *The Scandal of the State: Women, law, and citizenship in postcolonial India*, Durham, NC: Duke University Press.

Rouse, S. (1988) Women's movement in Pakistan: state, class, gender', *Women Living under Muslim Laws*, Dossier 3, www.wluml.org/fr/node/241, accessed 12 July 2011.

— (2006a) 'Discourses on gender in Pakistan', in S. Rouse (ed.), *Gender, Nation, State in Pakistan: Shifting body politics*, New Delhi: Women Unlimited.

— (2006b) 'Militarisation, nationalism and the spaces of gender', in S. Rouse (ed.), *Gender, Nation, State in Pakistan: Shifting body politics*, New Delhi: Women Unlimited.

Roy, S. (2011) 'Politics, passion and professionalization in contemporary Indian feminism', *Sociology*, 45(4): 587–602.

Saeed, F. (2001) *Taboo! The hidden culture of a red light area*, Karachi: Oxford University Press.

Saigol, R. (2004) 'The shariat bill and its impact on women and education', in N. S. Khan (ed.), *Up against the State: Military rule and women's resistance*, Lahore: ASR Publications.

Tsikata, D. (2008) 'Announcing a new dawn prematurely? Human rights feminists and the rights-based approaches to development', in A. Cornwall, E. Harrison and A. Whitehead (eds), *Feminisms in Development: Contradictions, contestations and challenges*, New Delhi: Zubaan.

Win, E. J. (2008) 'Not very poor, powerless or pregnant: the African woman forgotten by development', in A. Cornwall, E. Harrison and A. Whitehead (eds), *Feminisms in Development: Contradictions, contestations and challenges*, New Delhi: Zubaan.

Woodford-Berger, P. (2008) 'Gender mainstreaming: what is it (about) and should we continue doing it?', in A. Cornwall, E. Harrison and A. Whitehead (eds), *Feminisms in Development: Contradictions, contestations and challenges*, New Delhi: Zubaan.

Zia, A. S. (2009) 'The reinvention of feminism in Pakistan', *Feminist Review*, 91: 29–46.

Zia, S. (2004) 'Women, Islamization and justice', in N. S. Khan (ed.), *Up against the State: Military rule and women's resistance*, Lahore: ASR Publications.

3 | Family law organizations and the mediation of resources and violence in Kolkata

SRIMATI BASU

When Madhumita left her marital home in Kolkata without her one-year-old child one night, frightened by the behaviour of her husband, who allegedly had a 'bipolar mood disorder', there were several paths she could have pursued. She wanted to be back with her child, to have some money to live on, and to be back in the extended family home despite the verbal, financial and emotional turmoil she experienced there and the erratic behaviour and impotence of her husband, if only her family could be persuaded to behave a little better. She could simply have kept things 'in house' – that is, followed the customary path of asking extended kin to intervene, with elders or friends bringing the trouble explicitly to the in-laws' attention, hoping that they could be warned or shamed into modifying some practices. While her natal family had been loath to go down this path, given the greater wealth and connections of her in-laws, they had in fact tried this, with little change effected.

Another informal solution was to involve organizations that functioned as substitute kin, to have someone come to the house and 'mediate' on her behalf: these would include neighbourhood associations, local branches of political organizations (most prominently, the women's wings called *Mahila Samitys*), non-governmental organizations which nonetheless functioned prominently through political networks, and autonomous women's organizations. Madhumita and her natal family had felt hesitant about approaching the political organizations, the most common solution, because her mother-in-law was believed to be a powerful *Mahila Samity* member herself; they had thus come to the deliberately non-affiliated women's organization, which is where I heard her narrative during one evening's collective mediation session. A stronger step would be to engage various facets of the state, with escalating intensity and consequences: to make a GD or 'General Diary' at the local police station as a way of creating a track record of the complaint (this required no investigation or corroboration), to approach a Women's Grievance Cell to make a complaint about domestic violence and/or dowry recovery under statute S498A or S304B (which might well lead to a mediated financial settlement rather than a criminal case), or to file a case at the family court (or the regular civil court, depending on area of residence), where options include mediation, an order for maintenance, and possibly separation or divorce. Each of these options, the mediators suggested, needed to be taken up with a clear recognition of the consequences: thus, bringing in a self-avowed feminist organization to intercede or threatening criminal or civil proceedings might well be perceived by already dissatisfied in-laws as a point of no return. Madhumita ended up following a couple of recommendations: she simply called her mother-in-law and was asked back, and she let the organization know that she would file a GD at the local police station some time when she was over at her parents', in case they needed a paper trail for a later S498A or divorce case (we had no knowledge of whether she did so).

Madhumita's situation helps map the institutional and organizational terrain of marriage mediation, between feminisms, the state and civil society entities. In this chapter, I outline the ways in which organizations working on marital problems inhabit this terrain, including their discursive and political strategies for working on issues of law and gendered violence, and their relationship to women's movements.[1] The three organizations I profile here are: an arbitration cell that places itself within and draws upon the power of the state, an allegedly independent non-governmental organization strongly connected to the ruling political party, and an 'autonomous' women's organization that challenges but also of necessity must work with hegemonic political structures.

My portrait of these organizations as viewed through the lens of mediation cases focuses on political positioning, efficiency, ideology and subjectivity. In line with critiques that feminist scholarship on the state tends to disproportionately emphasize 'policy outcomes' and 'effectiveness', at the cost of attending to the 'discursive and ethnographic examination of how the actors understand and negotiate these new spaces for feminist practice' (Dean 2010: 29), I focus on the lived contradictions between organizational ideology and the practicalities of efficient functioning. How much difference does the closeness or distance from state mechanisms (and their corresponding party structures) make to the strategies an organization may adopt? Given that mediation must necessarily be conducted in constant negotiation with clients and cultural hegemonies and the shadow of the law, are these organizations able to mete out substantially different solutions, despite their ideological differences?

Marked flashpoints of difference exist between organizations – in particular, around issues of marriage, violence, economic autonomy and law. Is marriage a site of subordination, of optimal benevolence, or a strategic site of economic survival? Is violence a non-negotiable act meriting punitive legal action, or a regrettable cultural response correctable through admonition and encouragement? Are women to be encouraged to engage in paid labour to better their bargaining position with respect to marriage, or to accommodate themselves as best they can within marital uncertainties? Should law be avoided, or engaged? I argue here that these organizations differ vastly on these questions, and yet, in operating within a concrete socio-legal space, often strategize in remarkably similar modalities given the practical gender interests that are most urgently at issue. The particularities of the local political field in which they operate means that they have differential access to resources, including institutional access, and hence have different intervention options. However, they are also all governed by broader fields – formal law and informal mechanisms for addressing domestic violence and marital problems, legacies of social movements around gender and class, cultural ideologies of marriage and independence (within, in conversation with or in opposition to feminisms) and, not least, client subjectivities shaped by these dynamics – which in effect delineate a more limited compass of action.

Women's organizations, social movements and the state

'Women's movements are neither homogeneous nor pure products of modernization and development, but rather are embedded in particular histories and geographies,' Ray contends (1999: 159). The Indian 'women's movement', aptly described as 'one of the many burgeoning efforts at reassertion of citizens' claims to participate as equals in the political and development process' (Agnihotri and Mazumdar 2005: 50), is perhaps characterized above all by its heterogeneity (Kumar 1993; Chaudhuri 2004; Khullar 2005): from anti-nationalist struggles through challenges to caste and religious and language hierarchies, against development trends and land policies and price rises, foregrounding sexuality and delineating sexual violence, part of mainstream political parties and regional parties and radical and subversive political groups. Contrary to spectres of Westernized infection as the origin of women's rights, and despite the overwhelming public visibility of elite urban women in the movement, a broad swath of 'mass struggles' from 'spontaneous or non-party platforms' has involved marginalized and subaltern groups with women in prominent roles, many of which (like minority groups in other nation-states) tend not to foreground gender difference as the basis of rights claims (Sen 2005: 84, 91–2). All these movements have drawn from, and in turn have influenced, global movements (including the UN Decade for Women and its legacies, but also movements around labour and sexuality and anti-fundamentalism), while being focused on developing specific national lexicons of protest and resistance (Roces 2010).

Indian women's organizations, though presenting challenges to family and community, have heavily focused on the state as the site for a broad range of complaints and claims, as a partner and collaborator, as the source of economic entitlements and the protector of human rights. Input from those representing 'women's rights' has been formally integrated into the post-colonial state in documents such as *Towards Equality* (CSWI 1974) and *Shramshakti* (Agnihotri and Mazumdar 2005: 71*)*, or through the national and state Women's Commissions and academic departments, to name but a few prominent avenues. 'Progressive legalism, developmentalism and empowerment' (Madhok 2010: 224) have been critical foci in seeking legislative and policy change, even when institutionalization falls short of feminist visions (Rajan 2003; Menon 2004). As critiques of feminist institutional reform have demonstrated (Merry 1999; Sack 2004; Santos 2004; Hautzinger 2007; Lazarus-Black 2007), mainstreaming often means that substantive questions of gender equity are lost in translation to practice. Often, the problem lies in the gap between 'practical' and 'strategic' gender interests, to follow Molyneux's useful distinction (1985), such as in imperatives to find quotidian material solutions, whether or not larger political questions are solved. Nonetheless, the impact of the women's movement is prominent in India, as witnessed in a number of areas depicted in this chapter: institutions such as the family court, laws such as IPC 498A (against domestic violence), trends such as mediation (in opposition to litigation), and the dense network of organizations attending to women's issues from a variety of approaches.

The 'state' itself is heterogeneously constituted, incorporating ideologies of gender equity while keeping other hierarchies in place. Similarly, organizations are constituted through global, national and local dynamics, specific histories and modes of action, 'simultaneously inside and outside the dominant discourse and institutions' in both working with the state and trying to transform it (Kelly 2005: 474). Indeed, the very difference between the two becomes increasingly blurred as we can no longer take 'the boundaries of the state as self-evident or view … it as a preconstituted and coherent actor', nor ignore the ways in which NGOs with 'feminist goals' become 'implicated' in the 'illiberal underside of neoliberal governmentality' (Sharma 2006: 62, 78–9). Sharma's example of hybrid GONGO (government/NGO) organizations (to which a couple of the organizations profiled here are kin) perfectly exemplifies this point: she argues that the presence of GONGOS 'constructs a reified image of the State as an authoritative yet leaner entity', 'degovernmentalizes the State and proliferates nodes of governance outside of its formal structures', 'increasing entanglement' while appearing to be more separate (ibid.: 78). As development funds and global feminisms shape the viability of particular issues, NGOs are also caught in contradictory relationships between donors, the state and their clients, often in competition for funds and favours (Chowdhury 2005).

The complex affiliations through which such organizations function may be thought of as a 'political field' which 'includes actors such as the state, political parties and social movement organizations, who are connected to each other in both friendly and antagonistic ways, some of whose elements are more powerful than others, and all of whom are tied together by a particular culture'; an organization jostles for 'stakes in the political field [that] are both symbolic and material' (Ray 1999: 8). Ray argues that because 'the precise set of interests that dominate at a particular moment ... are formed out of struggle and negotiation within a political field, [t]hus at any given point, a women's organization pushing for change must be aware of the power of the state vis-à-vis the other political players in the field's distribution of power' (ibid.: 14). Importantly, 'their identities are shaped by the fields within which they are acting collectively' (ibid.: 159) – that is, both organizations and the actors who inhabit them are constituted through these negotiations.

The three organizations profiled in the following sections, arising out of this diverse history, represent different legacies of the women's movement. The first, a product of mainstreaming feminism, promoting alternative dispute resolution through governmental initiatives, is spatially and administratively tied to the state but imagined as a modern form of community settlement; here, troubled marriages are managed with an eye to reconciliation for women's alleged protection, but the agents have no obvious social movement connections. The second, a non-governmental organization with deep connections to state/left politics, illustrates more recent neoliberal trends of empowerment and self-governance; it is related to the women's wing of the ruling party but, critically, located and governed as independent of the state and party, thus publicly committed to social justice through class empowerment, with gender as a secondary concern. The third, an organization with a long history in the autonomous women's movement, customarily positions itself in opposition to the state, and thus bears links to long traditions of feminist oppositional mobilization. The first two may be regarded as variant forms of the GONGO (Sharma 2006), but all three work in partial collaboration as part of a legal and culturally plural system of claim-making, while also in conflict over favours, resources and politics.

The political context is critical to the nature of the interventions. These organizations are in West Bengal, governed for thirty-five years by the Communist Party of India (Marxist) (CPI[M]) and its Left Front allies, within but frequently in opposition to the larger central government of India. Ray diagnoses the city of Kolkata, site of her (and my) fieldwork, as a 'hegemonic field that is powerful and concentrated' around the ruling left party, the CPI(M). Scholars studying the long-term governance of West Bengal by the left have emphasized, however, that stereotypical understandings of 'communist states' do not apply fully in this context, because while some Marxist rhetoric is strategically deployed in political frameworks, the ruling parties also work through complex rural and urban constituencies, local and national political coalitions, development trends and legal processes (Roy 2003; Majumder 2010; Chakrabarty 2011). Alliances go deep, such that not only are the daily functioning and form of the institutions profiled here shaped by the state, but also, importantly, are subjectivities and forms of desire and comportment, whether in affinity with or opposition to the ruling government.

Women are prominently present in left movements in India, even if the predominant attitude of such movements has been to 'relegate' 'the resolution of women's issues' to the ever-deferred 'post revolutionary period', to be 'distrustful of any open analysis of patriarchal dominance' as a distraction from class struggles (Sen 2005: 81). Armed agrarian struggles such as the Naxalbari movement were unable to integrate women into the structures or incorporate their perspectives, and particularly struggled around questions of sexuality, sexual violence and motherhood (ibid.: 85; Roy 2008). However, Sen points out that participation in such movements could be positively transformative for women: being part of 'day to day practical democratic processes' and much greater freedom than they had in work, family or other realms could enhance women's 'political and personal achievement' (Sen 2005: 95).[2]

Women's organizations connected to the party perfectly exemplify these contradictions in gendered power. They benefit from political networks and capital, and attribute personal and societal empowerment to the party and government's alleged progressivism and success; as Ray says of *Mahila Samitys*, they find themselves 'protecting and defending the state and even offering protection and patronage to others' (Ray 1999: 93). But they are constrained in the gender transformations they can facilitate, debilitated by 'loyalty' and 'deference', often 'self-censoring their critiques' (ibid.: 92–4). Autonomous women's organizations, on the other hand, often follow a more radical gender politics but have to work in an environment where both issues and funds are determined by the parameters of the ruling party, limiting their scope and effectiveness and making for ambivalent choices (ibid.: 95). Ray's study of Mumbai's diffuse political culture and strong autonomous women's movement in the 1990s, with no single party having dominated the political process that deeply, serves as a telling contrast: women's movement organizations mobilize around a variety of issues, and the small women's wing of the CPI(M) – JMS – has to negotiate for visibility and resources in competition with others (ibid.: 114–15, 119).

The realm of marriage mediation, correspondingly, reflects a variety of approaches to marriage and economic entitlement. For those who regard gender as a primary axis of subordination, and violence an enabling tool of this control, economic impoverishment associated with marriage is a systematic and not coincidental outcome of gender roles in the modern nation-state. If economic inequalities, on the other hand, are seen as the fundamental problem, then the corresponding focus is on women's economic self-reliance, whatever the state of their marriages. In yet other discourses, pragmatic social reform goals rather than radical measures are emphasized: helping destitute women, urging men to be better husbands, preventing divorce in families, ensuring a better state and nation through enhancing well-being, are seen to be the optimal good. More practically yet, some groups concentrate specifically on dimensions of governmentality, such as improving efficiency through mediation and avoiding legal bottlenecks by relying on customary dispute resolution. These very different motivations are all enacted within the same field of marriage mediation, with varying ranges of commitment to feminism and hegemonic registers of femininity, both between and within organizations.

'Family assistance': of and in the state

There were very high hopes for community mediation, called *shalishi* in Bangla, during my 2004/05 fieldwork. Encouraged by the proliferation of alternative dispute resolution methods in courts and among non-governmental organizations, and invoking customary village-level arbitration fora, the state government and the ruling party at that time had envisaged a network of *shalishi* fora at various local levels to supplement *and* complement formal legal settings, including structured venues for semi-formal mediation, as in this section.[3] At the *Paribarik Paramarsho O Shahayata Kendra* ('Family Advice and Assistance Centre' would be a rough translation) in a medium-sized town about an hour from Kolkata, arbitration sessions lasting about three to four hours were held every Friday. The unit was physically located inside one of the police posts in the town, advertising the *Mahila Pulish Tadanta Kendra* (literally, 'Police Investigative Centre for Women'; syntactically, it could also be read as 'Women Police Investigative Centre', appropriate given the prominence of female police officers here). There was a different police station in town which functioned as a Women's Grievance Cell investigating criminal complaints. The unit I observed was meant to be focused on *shalish* or arbitration, and sent people off to the other police unit or formal courts as necessary.

On one of my first visits, when I was being shown around by one of the constables, a motorcycle pulled up with two women and a man. Approaching the constable, one of the women introduced herself as being with a non-governmental organization in town, and said of the other woman, 'She is having some trouble at home and wants to report it.' The constable responded, '*Ekhaney, jara shongshar korben tader jonyo*' (my translation, 'this place is only for those who want to pursue marriage' does little to capture the sense of *shongshar/sansar* as embodying notions of family, domesticity and worldliness). She recommended that the group go to the other police station to register a complaint or seek maintenance. To approach this unit, thus, is to foreground reconciliation as a putative outcome. This approach is in line with some family court venues I studied in the context of my larger project, where the primary focus of 'counselling' is on reconciliation and maintaining the integrity of the family unit, as well as increasing processual efficiency (Basu 2012). As in the courts, where the official counsellors were often senior women from the women's wing of the ruling party, here too those who undertook such 'counselling' characterized themselves as helping women economically, even as they worked within hegemonic notions of domestic control and family integrity. Domestic violence was a significant issue in every case I observed here, and unlike in other venues, there was no attempt to deny or deflect it; rather, in line with strategies of reintegration, it was reviled and a corrective strategy suggested, with no attempt to see it as an insurmountable problem in the marriage.

The 'counselling' (their term) board consisted of a local female magistrate from the lower courts, a male doctor, a female lawyer, the male supervisor of the centre and the female Officer-in-Charge [OC] of the Cell. The 'board' had been given the authority to summon witnesses and draw up arbitration agreements but had no civil or criminal enforcement authority beyond that. However, because the OC and a magistrate served on it, they seamlessly invoked these other formal roles during proceedings: in several cases, they would make a move as if to begin to jail a man accused of domestic violence, as a starting point to get him and his family to begin negotiating. The spatial arrangements also spoke to configurations of power and the involvement of family and community. The board members sat on a row of chairs behind a wooden screen, across the table from a bench for the couple. But every other available seat was occupied by other family members and even neighbours, and a continuous row of heads peered in over the top of the screen; they were all allowed, indeed encouraged, to attend.[4]

Asghar Ali and Firoza Begum, who had two daughters (one a year and a half and one seven months old), had come to the forum accompanied by a female NGO worker from nearby Madhyamgram, and numerous relatives and neighbours from either side. Asghar Ali had not shown up for two previously scheduled sessions; this was his first appearance. He testified that he used to drive a van for a salary, but at the time of the meeting worked on commission setting up wireless towers for much less money. Asghar's father was a carpenter. Firoza, who had been at her parents' for eight months by that point, alleged that Asghar beat her regularly with his father's tools, didn't provide her with money for food and clothing, and that she had to make do with a very meagre income from sewing. She claimed he took an axe to many of her things, and that he habitually stole rice. Asghar defended himself by saying, 'It's wrong to beat up someone, but when I come home from driving the van there's no food ready, and she curses if I say anything.' Asghar's father provided a long testimonial about Asghar's drug problem, during which his very poor in-laws had financially helped with his rehab, but confessed that Asghar had relapsed and feared that this case might be his in-laws' revenge.

The board members observed out loud that Firoza seemed to have a quarrelsome nature, and contradictorily that she seemed very young, not yet mature. The chair asked both Firoza and Asghar what they wanted, to which neither replied. Her parents argued against sending her back given the violence with carpentry tools. Firoza too said at this point, 'How can I stay there?' (*Ki korey thakbo?*). The doctor on the board reminded her in rejoinder, 'We don't call you here unless you want a healthy marriage' (*Shusthobhabey shongshar kortey chai na bolley amra daki na*) – in other words, that this was a venue where only subsisting marriages, deemed 'healthy' by definition, could be considered. He told them that the board would not force her to return, and that they would have to decide whether she should go back. Firoza's mother continued to defer to him for a decision: 'Whatever you [collectively] think is best' (*Apnara ja bhalo bolben*). Dr B, without answering directly, passionately expounded out loud: 'It's inhuman if only a morsel of this is true. I feel like beating them up; the father and son would both be in jail if it wasn't for this arbitration.'

Finally, Firoza said: 'I'll go if you take the responsibility' (*Apnara jodi dayitto nen, jabo*). The board worked out a deal for the family whereby they were all to come back in a week, and at that time the question of whether Asghar's behaviour was likely to improve could be settled with some offer of proof from his family, following which Firoza could go back with them and questions of money would be settled then. But Firoza was also given a series of admonitions: 'Make sure you cook – you're married, what do you mean you won't cook?' (*Ranna korbey – biye hoyechchey, ranna korbey na!!*). She was scolded for characterizing the rice that Asghar got from his mother as 'stolen', reminded her that they were the same family and that she should ignore his mother's snide remarks. She was reprimanded for having brought her old and sick father-in-law to tears through her allegations about his son.

This board worked by evoking formal legal provisions even as it circumvented them, incorporating community sanctions and governmental surveillance to extend its reach. Outrage was expressed at violence, and the punitive power of the board was deployed to curb both physical violence and economic neglect, apparently to secure optimal protection for women. But the vector of '*shustho shongshar kora*', of 'healthy conjugality', was the driving force, with 'health' seeming to consist of a perfect balance of familial roles without conflict. There was no attempt to destabilize structures of power in the extended family within which violence is arguably embedded and rendered permissible, nor to empower Firoza in any way other than by issuing the threat of continued monitoring by the board. It is impossible to tell whether the family's economic marginality and her youth and lack of education (she was illiterate beyond being able to sign her name; he could not even do that) figured in their failure to encourage her to improve her economic situation or to alter the living situation, in contrast to the later solutions focused on women's economic self-reliance. The promotion of marriage ideologies and the authoritarian discipline of the board, among other modes of operation, make it the sort of organization trenchantly critiqued by feminist groups focused on violence; yet ironically, its very existence as an informal venue for mediating questions of violence and money in marriage is a legacy of the impact of the women's movement.

Approaching NGOs: political connections

Suraha (literally 'solution', known also as the Socio-Cultural Research Institute), an organization located in a primarily residential street in south Kolkata, is technically an NGO, but was started by Shyamali Gupta, one of the most prominent female Left Front leaders, at one time president of the women's wing of the dominant party. 'Counsellors', mostly but not exclusively women, including several lawyers, counsellors from the family court and others with strong party connections, sat at clustered tables for open office hours three evenings a week, and were almost continually busy. Marital mediation was not the only reason people came to the sessions: problems included physical and financial harassment by families towards couples, defrauding attempts, or intimidation from neighbourhood goons. Quite often, people came with explicit referrals from local political representatives, and in looking for solutions, counsellors sought the active assistance of *Mahila Samitys*, in a seamless connection between NGO and party. Raka Ray argues that in the political nexus of the state, being an NGO associated with a prominent political figure means that the organization is able to benefit from non-governmental status by having access to some categories of funds, while also drawing upon its political networks and its deep connections with the governmental sector to get its goals accomplished (Ray 1999: 92–4). *Suraha* is formally an NGO, thus different from the *Mahila Samitys* or party women's wings that Ray focused on, but with essentially similar instrumental and pragmatic advantages.

Leaders in left-affiliated women's movement organizations, however, tend to prioritize class over gender, as the rich contradictions in Ray's interview with Shyamali Gupta (then the president of *Paschimbanga Ganatantrik Mahila Samity* [PBGM] but also subsequently the founder of *Suraha*) exemplifies:

> Feminist or womanist groups believe in gender oppression. We do not. We believe in class oppression. Like us, there are men who are oppressed. But it is true that social oppression is a little higher in the case of women because as a section of society, not as a class, women are backward. It is true that family and society are male dominated. I prefer to call it not oppression but domination. (Ibid.: 77)

The statement perfectly reflects the relegation of gender to a 'post-revolution' priority in favour of the primacy of class (Sen 2005), ironic in the predominantly middle-class milieu of the centre (in terms of the class background of the counsellors, though not necessarily of the clients). Gender oppression is acknowledged as an add-on – indeed, as a different order of problem ('not oppression but domination') – though the work of this organization is manifestly centred around intra-familial discord and violence, rather than the remediation of any class-based inequities.

At Suraha, there were no obvious attempts to repair marriages at all costs, or to tolerate violence for the sake of economic stability. The organization was of course not under any legal directives to favour reconciliation, unlike the family courts or the 'Family Assistance' centre, though the issue gets murkier when one considers that some of the family court counsellors, who were driven by reconciliation ideologies in those jobs, worked as mediators here as well. Sessions generally focused on concrete legal strategies, and ways to set up the issues most advantageously for the client, including making available personal, political and professional networks. Very often, consideration of women's economic resources was an explicit part of developing a working strategy. As a senior member said in an interview, what most bothered her was women clinging to marriage rather than facing the problem: she would like to ask of clients, 'Why are you just waiting for the maintenance award? If you were illiterate and you had no means of supporting yourself that would be one thing; cut off all relations and stand on your own legs.' A recently (and swiftly) widowed client whose in-laws were trying to seize the marital house and bank assets, for example, was the subject of a long discussion of ways in which she needed to begin to make a living, including suggestions such as having a paying guest in the home or finding a job with daily wages (in addition to other legal moves concerning the assets).

In a complicated legal case in which counsellors were strategizing about initiating criminal investigations on grounds of torture against the husband and in-laws, the young woman, about to leave looking depressed and discouraged, was told by a counsellor: 'Remember, this case is only one thing, it is not your life. Whatever happens with the case, you need to take care of yourself.'

A more extended example better illustrates the constraints of agency and legal possibility within which such advice may be offered. The client, Padmini, a twenty-three-year-old woman who had begun a diploma in computer administration after her BA, came in with allegations of severe emotional abuse and control of mobility and privacy by the husband and in-laws. She emphasized her Marwari ethnicity, describing Marwaris as a small and conservative community; members of her marital household played to this fear by telling her repeatedly that, for the community, divorce meant 'a big ugly mark on the forehead', that she would not be able to remarry. In answer to the critical question 'Do you still love him and want to stay?', Padmini said vehemently, 'No, I feel hatred.' Various counsellors chimed in with recommendations: she needed to ask her mother to draw up a full list of expenses for the wedding, and gather all receipts for jewellery and other items preparatory to filing a case on the grounds of violence and dowry recovery. She was reminded that her jewellery, including the four gold sets her in-laws had given her, was her property. Padmini sought to reclaim the wedding expenses of Rs4–500,000 back, to use towards a business or further education, but a lawyer clarified that the proportion spent on entertainment or hospitality, a very large proportion could not be legally recovered, though they could try for the rest. She was to report back after her family had taken these steps, for further guidance. One of the counsellors said, by way of parting, 'There is no such thing as a stamp on the forehead from divorce.' 'If there is, lots of Marwari boys have that stamp too,' another added.

While the primary focus of these sessions was on legal strategy and economic self-sufficiency, these practicalities were framed by implicit assumptions that marriage was not necessarily the optimal solution, that deference to in-laws or violence from them need not be a norm, and that positive alternatives for women existed. It was Padmini's choice of severance rather than return which launched these suggestions, but in contrast to what may have happened in other venues, she was never pressed to consider marriage as the inevitably better option. The contrast with solutions offered to Firoza is stark: it is, of course, impossible to determine how far Padmini's different class and educational status affected her economic options, her ability to pursue legal recourse energetically, and hence her reliance on marriage (and violence within it), but the organization's focus on living beyond marriage was conspicuously different to that of the venue considered earlier.

Within the political field of women's organizations in Kolkata, this organization carries optimal authority in mediating non-governmental and state realms, and deploys these connections skilfully. The proffered suggestions above are in line with Ray's finding that while leaders in left parties are apt to minimize the salience of gendered power in public pronouncements, grassroots, 'front-line' women workers are often sympathetic to the problems posed by domestic violence. They work towards negotiating settlements, often by using political connections, even though party leadership does not wish to assign visibility to domestic violence, sexual assault or the gendered division of labour, and prefers to quietly deal with such problems internally (Ray 1999: 89). Their subjectivities are thus reshaped through their clients' situations and the resultant encounters with the political field: while the founder publicly endorses the primacy of class oppression, her organization routinely tackles the materialities of gendered violence, confronts the intersectionalities of gender and class, and promotes women's autonomy. It sketches out strategies that foreground economic self-reliance, even if they are directed towards individual empowerment rather than towards transforming class relations or furthering state governance. It thus works in rhetorical rivalry but practical alliance with autonomous women's organizations and feminisms.

Choosing violence: an 'autonomous' women's group

Nari Nirjaton Pratirodh Mancha ('Forum Against Oppression of Women', most often called *Mancha* or 'Platform/Stage') is a long-standing autonomous women's organization with the reputation of being stridently radical and vocal, speaking to gendered violence, sexism and classism within the legal system, and institutionalized corruption. Present members recount in interview that, according to organizational history, it came together in protests over a case in the early 1980s when a woman ran in flames from her in-laws' home, from precursors such as women's study circles and an emergent national movement, foregrounding anti-violence work as central to their identity. Ray describes it as originally being an umbrella entity of 'new, non CPI(M) affiliated women's organizations' against the dominance of the CPI(M) party, having lost allies along the way because of its political critique, but having earned 'grudging admiration' for its resolute opposition (ibid.: 95, 101). Maitreyi Chatterji has long served as its charismatic leader, but the core members are a mix of age groups and classes, including professors, journalists, office workers, informal sector workers and career left political activists, who often engage in energetic debates about policy and feminisms.

Mancha works both through public awareness campaigns, and support and counselling for individual cases. Despite differences in background, counselling sessions look remarkably similar to those of the previous venue. Sheets are laid out on the floor of a residential apartment on Friday evenings for members to sit on, and they gather to hear clients as a group. Occasionally, a person may be sent off to an adjacent room with an individual to work on something specific, or if there are too many waiting clients. There is an explicit commitment to having women narrate their own accounts, rather than the customary form of having a family member who can tell a tighter story (*guchchiye bola*) speak. Emphasizing women's control over their lives, however, also means ceding to the limited options women may consider best, and working within unsatisfying cultural accommodations.

One evening, Molly brought her eight-year-old daughter, her brother and a married neighbour couple to the session, so that they could 'explain things in case she can't say it all properly'. Her brother knew one of the senior members of the group, and had been invited to bring his sister. The men were artfully dispatched to the next room with the little girl, allegedly to keep her away from this conversation; when they had left, a member explained to Molly that at the Forum they believe it best to let a woman tell her own story. Molly then narrated a happy marriage of ten years ('the normal happy conjugal life', '*khub shukher dampatya jibon, jerokom hoi*') until her husband's elder sister moved back into town, to which she dated a recent sharp deterioration in marital relations. Her husband came home every night now via his sister's house, acutely unhappy with Molly. Later, however, she recounted that while her in-laws had been keen on the match and specified they wanted no dowry, after the wedding, which included donation of appropriate goods ('properly, the usual way', '*thikbhabey, jemon hoi*'), the in-laws now harangued her constantly about poor-quality and scant dowry goods. Molly complained that her father-in-law and sisters-in-law drank all day, and that once her father-in-law had misbehaved so badly towards her that she left; his family later arranged for them to live in a separate flat. Much of the focus of her husband's present ire seemed to be violent jealousy over Molly's brother's friend, who had helped them to negotiate the mortgage. He refused her household money, locked her inside the house when he went out, and regularly asked her to leave him; she had finally moved to her parents'. His sexual dissatisfaction had become a constant complaint: she said with some difficulty, 'He is not happy with conjugal life, not satisfied with sex' ('*o bibahito jiboney shukh pachchey na*', 'sex-*e satisfied noy*'). He had lately begun saying he wanted to marry someone else and thus needed a divorce. Molly had begun working for a direct marketing company, but stopped once her husband started coming to the office to throw loud fits; the boss said they liked her work but she should put her marriage first for now, possibly meaning she was creating too much disruption but that she could go back later.

Sujata, an experienced member in her forties, a professor by occupation, succinctly laid out three trajectories of advice for Molly on behalf of *Mancha*, which Molly was to consider further when she got home, and later discuss with her family. First, she assured Molly that the question of maintenance was not closed to her simply because her husband always told her she would not get a paisa of his money: because he had a government job, they could help her file a '125CrPc' order to allocate part of his salary according to the judge's determination. Maintenance, Sujata emphasized, was not tantamount to asking for divorce, but an entitlement during the subsistence of the marriage too. Secondly, she argued, if her husband was not going to pay her expenses then he could not also object to her working. 'How long is he going to keep you locked up?' she queried. 'Just go out when he goes to work. He'll eventually get tired of harassing you at work if you keep going.' She contended that Molly might be surprised to learn that many people in that company were likely to be in similar positions, and so *Mancha* advocated that she keep her boss apprised of the potential trouble and hope it would eventually end. Thirdly, and interestingly last, she asked Molly what outcome she herself wanted; Molly repeated her earlier statement that she wanted the marriage to continue. Sujata proffered as *Mancha*'s recommendation that, in that case, they believed her position would be much stronger if she went back to the marital home. There would be violence, but she would need to learn to deal with it and stand up to it. She suggested provocatively, 'You smack him a bit too next time' ('*Apnio duto merey deben porerbar*'), speculating that he would be really startled by that, and might hit her harder that time in retaliation, but would think twice the following time.

The usual weighing of legal options by the group followed: Molly had already been to the police station to file a couple of GDs (General

Diaries), but they considered whether it might not be time to register an FIR, a First Information Report of a crime. The group regarded the *Mahila Samity* in that area with some wariness, but decided nonetheless that Molly would benefit from them being apprised of the situation, given the organization's reach and surveillance; a *Mancha* member would take care of this. Molly was also told that the best thing her family could do would be to drop in on her regularly every evening, as a reminder to her husband that someone was watching out for her. Amid the chaos of numerous suggestions, Sujata returned in closing to her original advice to Molly: 'You might be wondering what sort of women's organization you have come to, with these suggestions of running out and beating husbands up. But what we want to say to you very clearly is: you need to be strong [*shokto*] here. Unless you confront him strongly yourself there won't be a good resolution for you.'

Several moments of this session (and Madhumita's case, which opens this chapter) indicate the feminist politics of this group: their insistence on women telling their stories, on women actively managing their futures, their insistence on honouring agency and women's decisions, even those they consider physically or ideologically unwise. Contrary to popular perceptions of advice given by feminist groups, they do not lead with advice about a drastic break or the benefits of divorce. They offer practical advice about legal manoeuvres and workplace etiquette, even showing a willingness to approach the left women's unit they are wary of for Molly's sake, thus working strategically both through state solutions and the necessary political allies of the state to access effective forms of power. There are no comfortable solutions to offer, however, and the message is fundamentally one of tough love, building (economic and social) independence, living with her chosen decision as best she can. In effect, they send her back to the violence (of her own free will), with full knowledge of its inevitability – indeed, with the remarkable idea of retaliating in kind so as to rise above fear and intimidation, even if bodily injured, to make livable room for herself in her violent world. They recommend not an imagined outcome of domestic bliss and family integrity, as with Firoza, but alternative forms of support, including her natal family, and economic resources, both maintenance and wages. The organizational imperatives of protesting about violence against women, and radical feminist critiques of patriarchy, may not be obviously satisfied in these solutions, but they advance their visions on other fronts: foregrounding the client's subjectivity as a feminist imperative, working to maximize legal potentialities of maintenance and criminal law (established substantially through women's mobilization), and pushing the boundaries of gendered expectations of work, mobility and violence.

Conclusion

'What would you like to do with respect to your marriage?' The question inevitably (if sometimes only rhetorically) posed to women as part of public mediations of troubled marriages assumes a modern subject of the nation-state who can access legal provisions and economic remedies, negotiating the array of organizational choices available for her help to find the perfect option. The responses, however, lead to a set of invariably difficult choices, governed by legal limitations, cultural preferences for staying within marriage and avoiding legal or other external intervention, problems with livelihood and residence, further exacerbated for poor or non-literate subjects. Organizations that help navigate this terrain may be chosen for their familiarity or their reach, their anonymity or their notoriety, with some recognition of the connections they might enable and sometimes an unrealistic sense of their capabilities, but not necessarily of their ideologies of gender or their attitudes to violence.

These three examples of marriage mediation organizations are spaces of intervention that all emerge from the women's movement's engagement with the state on questions of family and violence (as also from other social factors, like the rise of alternative dispute resolution [ADR] and neoliberal ideologies of empowerment). They work with very different goals, from social reform based on 'healthy marriage' to the transformation of class relations to a primary focus on anti-violence work. In practice, however, neither the particularities of their client bases nor the usual trajectories of action (nor the furtherance of their stated goals) line up neatly, as '[a]ctivists within these movements consciously work to understand and assess the possibilities offered by the field within which their organizations are embedded, negotiating optimal results given existing conditions' (Ray 1999: 159). Nor is the difference merely at the level of individual negotiation: despite ideological differences, organizations operate within local political fields of left hegemony and autonomous feminist marginalization, and larger contexts of the visibility and institutional influence of the Indian women's movement, and global feminist movements. The landscape of legal possibilities, from courts to mediation to claiming maintenance to police reports, as well as rhetorical parameters about gender, violence and empowerment, is determined by the legacy and imbrication of those layers. Thus across the board, strategies engage mainstreamed feminist ideas of domestic violence as abhorrent and women's access to economic resources as essential, even as they differ conspicuously on cultural discourses of family harmony and the components of a healthy marriage. They all acknowledge the practical material benefits of sustaining a marriage even as they evoke alternative futures outside it (some more hesitantly than others). They invariably work with a canny sense of the possibilities of plural institutional options, legal and political, but also familial and community-based. This is not to overlook the specific histories that give each organization a particular configuration and force in the political field, but a reminder of the cultural, political and legal constraints governing activist engagements with law, marriage and violence.

Notes

1 This data is drawn from an extended ethnographic project on Family Law and Family Violence in Kolkata, India, for which I have conducted research since 2001, in two extended periods of fieldwork in 2001 and 2004/05 with ongoing annual investigations since then. I have observed a variety of family law, domestic violence and marriage-mediation-related settings in Kolkata, including participant observation of the family courts, the Women's Grievance Cell and a variety of organizations that undertook marriage mediation, field visits to litigants' homes with counsellors, and interviews with judges, counsellors and feminist activists. My total observational and interview archive in Kolkata consisted of 234 cases. Mediations were primarily conducted in Bangla (Bengali), interspersed with occasional English and Hindi. Names of mediators and litigants are pseudonyms.

2 Stree Shakti Sangathana's life history narrative of 'Pramila Tai' provides a vivid example of Sen's point on greater freedom and community (2008).

3 The move was ultimately turned down by the legislature. Among various protests about the scope and nature of authority of these units, there was a prominent concern among those not affiliated with the ruling party that the units might be overly influenced by the political connections and interests of litigants. Talwar and Samity (2002: 8) affirm the profound influence of political alliances in *shalishi* cases.

4 In other counselling settings, while an occasional family member was called to mediation sessions, the focus was on talking to couples individually and then jointly.

References

Agnihotri, I. and V. Mazumdar (2005) 'Changing terms of political discourse: women's movement in India, 1970s–1990's', in M. Khullar (ed.), *Writing the Women's Movement: A Reader*, New Delhi: Zubaan, pp. 48–79.

Basu, S. (2012) 'Judges of normality: mediating marriage in the Family Courts of Kolkata, India', *Signs*, 37(2): 469–92.

Chakrabarty, B. (2011) 'The Left

Front's 2009 poll debacle in West Bengal, India', *Asian Survey*, 51(2): 290–310.

Chaudhuri, M. (2004) *Feminism in India*, New Delhi: Women Unlimited.

Chowdhury, E. H. (2005) 'Feminist negotiations: contesting narratives of the campaign against acid violence in Bangladesh', *Meridians: Feminism, Race, Transnationalism*, 6(1): 163–92.

CSWI (1974) *Towards Equality: Report of Committee on the Status of Women in India*, New Delhi.

Dean, J. (2010) *Rethinking Contemporary Feminist Politics*, Basingstoke: Palgrave.

Hautzinger, S. (2007) *Violence in the City of Women: Police and Batterers in Bahia, Brazil*, Berkeley: University of California Press.

Kelly, L. (2005) 'Inside outsiders: mainstreaming violence against women into human rights discourse and practice', *International Feminist Journal of Politics*, 7(4): 471–95.

Khullar, M. (ed.) (2005) *Writing the Women's Movement: A Reader*, New Delhi: Zubaan.

Kumar, R. (1993) *A History of Doing*, New Delhi: Kali for Women.

Lazarus-Black, M. (2007) *Everyday Harm: Domestic Violence, Court Rites, and Cultures of Reconciliation*, Urbana-Champaign: University of Illinois Press.

Madhok, S. (2010) 'Rights talk and the feminist movement in India', in M. Roces and L. Edwards (eds), *Women's Movements in Asia: Feminisms and Transnational Activism*, London: Routledge, pp. 224–36.

Majumder, S. (2010) 'The Nano controversy: peasant identities, the land question and neoliberal industrialization in Marxist West Bengal, India', *Journal of Emerging Knowledge on Emerging Markets*, 2(1): 41–66.

Menon, N. (2004) *Recovering Subversion: Sexual Politics beyond the Law*, New Delhi: Permanent Black.

Merry, S. E. (1999) *Colonizing Hawai'i: The Cultural Power of Law*, Princeton, NJ: Princeton University Press.

Molyneux, M. (1985) 'Mobilization without emancipation? Women's interests, the state and revolution in Nicaragua', *Feminist Studies*, 11(2): 227–54.

Rajan, R. S. (2003) *The Scandal of the State: Women, Law and Citizenship in Postcolonial India*, Durham, NC: Duke University Press.

Ray, R. (1999) *Fields of Protest: Women's Movements in India*, Minneapolis: University of Minnesota Press.

Roces, M. (2010) 'Asian feminisms: women's movements from the Asian perspective', in M. Roces and L. Edwards (eds), *Women's Movements in Asia: Feminisms and International Activism*, London: Routledge, pp. 1–20.

Roy, A. (2003) *City Requiem, Calcutta: Gender and the Politics of Poverty*, Minneapolis: University of Minnesota Press.

Roy, S. (2008) 'The Grey Zone: the "ordinary" violence of extraordinary times', *Journal of the Royal Anthropological Institute (n.s.)*, 14: 316–33.

Sack, E. J. (2004) 'Battered women and the state: the struggle for the future of domestic violence policy', *Wisconsin Law Review*, pp. 1657–740.

Sangathana, S. S. (2008) 'Pramila Tai', in M. E. John (ed.), *Women's Studies in India: A Reader*, New Delhi: Penguin, pp. 157–64.

Santos, C. M. (2004) 'En-gendering the police: women's police stations and feminism in Sao Paulo', *Latin American Research Review*, 39(3): 29–55.

Sen, I. (2005) 'A space within the struggle', in M. Khullar (ed.), *Writing the Women's Movement: A Reader*, New Delhi: Zubaan, pp. 80–101.

Sharma, A. (2006) 'Crossbreeding institutions, breeding struggle: women's empowerment, neoliberal governmentality and state (re)formation in India', *Cultural Anthropology*, 21(1): 60–95.

Talwar, A. and S. M. Samity (2002) 'The Shalishi in West Bengal: a community response to domestic violence', *Women Initiated Community Level Responses to Domestic Violence: Summary Report of Three Studies. Series: Domestic Violence in India: Exploring Strategies, Promoting Dialogue #5*, Washington, DC: International Center for Research on Women, pp. 14–30.

4 | Contemporary feminist politics in Bangladesh: taking the bull by the horns

SOHELA NAZNEEN AND MAHEEN SULTAN

Introduction

This chapter will take on a few of the major challenges in contemporary feminist politics in Bangladesh, i.e. take the 'bull by the horns'. We do this by focusing on two salient challenges faced by the feminists in Bangladesh: 'NGO-ization' and the generational shift in the feminist movement. We explore the following questions. First, how have women's and feminist organizations[1] dealt with the NGO-ization process and how are they adapting in the post NGO-ized phase? Secondly, what is the nature and impact of generational shifts on feminist activism in Bangladesh?

Concerns over and anxieties about the NGO-ization of the feminist movement, which unfolded in historic and context-specific ways, are not new. The NGO-ization of the feminist movement has been critiqued extensively (Lang 1997; Alveraz 1998). Recently, feminists have re-evaluated their critique of NGO-ization (Hemment 2007; Alveraz 2009), which has led to a more nuanced analysis of the impact of NGO-ization. This chapter aims to contribute to this growing body of literature.

The NGO-ization of the feminist movement refers to the process by which issues of women's collective concerns are transformed into isolated development projects without taking the social, political and economic context into consideration (Jad 2004). It is closely connected with the promotion of modes of organizational forms and practices based on neoliberal values (Alveraz 2009). Bangladesh makes an interesting case study because of the large NGO sector and the fact that 'NGO-ization' of the women's movement started much earlier than in the rest of South Asia.

Our analysis begins by focusing on the organizational level, which is largely underexplored in the Bangladeshi and other contexts. We argue that the impact of NGO-ization on organizational autonomy, agenda and accountability is varied. A difference can be noted between small local women's organizations and some national women's organizations.

The latter group was able to mitigate and minimize the impact of NGO-ization. NGO-ization has also had some positive impacts on the feminist movement since it helped to link women's organizations to different societal actors, granted access to policy spaces and better organizational capacity, and increased outreach. We also argue that in the post-NGO-ized phase, feminist organizations have tried to raise resources from alternative sources and focus on mobilization to counter funding constraints and excessive policy focus vis-à-vis movement-building; and have been somewhat successful in negotiating these spheres.

Like NGO-ization, generational shifts within the feminist movement and their impact on feminist activism and whether an intergenerational movement can be created are much debated issues (AWID 2008). We aim to contribute to this debate by focusing on the generational shift in the feminist movement in Bangladesh, which is strongly linked to NGO-ization; but remains under-researched. We find that there is a generational divide between those feminists who constituted the vanguard of the autonomous women's movement in the 1970s and those who are today part of a 'professionalized' academic and/or NGO culture and how, where and on what issues they mobilize. Given that the younger women grew up in a context where Women in Development/Gender and Development were mainstreamed and during the NGO-ization of the movement, their expectations are different and they have a 'professionalized'/monetary approach to undertaking women's empowerment and movement-related work. Although a clear divide exists, our data shows that the lines are blurring, given that the priorities and ways of working within even established feminist organizations are changing. We argue that a key challenge for feminists is to ensure that women in their twenties are engaged. Our analysis shows that the possibilities for engaging this group and creating an intergenerational movement in Bangladesh depend on the class structure of the movement and how different generations deal with the threat to women's rights from conservative religious political groups.[2] The latter has created a scope for solidarity-based action between generations. How far this scope is realized depends on how class and gerontocracy within the movement are addressed by women's rights organizations.

Most of the data used in this chapter was collected as part of two larger researches conducted for the Pathways of Women's Empowerment Research Programme Consortium. The first study explored how feminist organizations build constituencies for demanding gender justice. This research was undertaken in 2008/09 and focused on three pioneer national-level women's organizations:[3] Bangladesh Mohila Parishad

(BMP), a mass-level women's organization; Naripokkho (For Women), a feminist activist organization; and Women for Women (WFW), a feminist research and policy advocacy organization. The second study, conducted in 2009/10, investigated how changes in donor funding structures and strategies affected the way women's rights organizations mobilize. It focused on five organizations, selected to capture the diversity of women's organizations in Bangladesh:[4] Doorbar network, an autonomous feminist network of small women's organizations;[5] Banchte Shekha (Learn to Live), a feminist NGO; Bangladesh National Women's Lawyers' Association (BNWLA), a professional women's association; Bangladesh Mohila Ovibashi Sramik Association (BOMSA), a migrant women workers' association; and Kormojibi Nari (Working Women), an activist organization. The key data collection methods were open-ended interviews, group discussions and organizational document analysis. For the second study, participatory workshops and interviews with donor agency staff were also conducted. We also consulted Web materials, blogs and secondary sources and conducted interviews with university students and young professionals engaged in promoting women's rights to gauge the views held by these groups.

The women's movement, the NGO sector and the state in Bangladesh

How feminist organizations choose to promote women's rights issues and interact with other societal actors is influenced by the following: a) the role of the international gender and development discourse which created scope for funding various gender projects and programmes; b) the expansion of the NGO sector; c) the wider social and political context in Bangladesh.

Bangladesh became independent through a war with Pakistan in 1971. The state is hierarchical by class and gender. Patron/client relations form the basis of social/political relations between groups (Goetz 2001). The state role in promoting women's rights has been contradictory, and in the early years influenced by the availability of donor funding. It has at times enacted progressive laws and policies and undertaken various development initiatives for promoting women's rights and at other times acted to sustain male privilege (Jahan 1995).

On the other hand, Bangladesh has a vibrant women's movement whose history can be traced to the anti-colonial movements, first against the British and then the Pakistanis (ibid.). Over the years, women's/the feminist movement has focused on a wide variety of issues, including women's economic empowerment, political participation, violence against women, legal reforms, gender mainstreaming in public policies, etc. (ibid.). There is a diversity of women's and feminist groups which range from small, local-level *samity*s to larger membership-based associations to mass-level national organizations. Despite the presence of strong women's groups and a track record of electing female prime ministers since 1991, gender equity issues do not have currency in formal politics. The espousal of Islam by the military dictators during the late 1970s and 1980s and the tacit and overt alliances formed by the two main centrist parties (the Awami League and the Bangladesh Nationalist Party) with the Islamist parties to form governments from 1991 onwards have made it difficult for feminists to raise with political actors issues that deal with religion. In the 1980s and early 1990s, the role played by Islamist parties in opposing the gender and development agenda and actors who work on these issues helped create issue-based coalitions and solidarity movements among women's organizations and development NGOs.

The NGO sector in Bangladesh expanded as donor funding increased in the 1980s.[6] It is not a monolithic sector; it ranges from organizations with a purely service delivery focus to social-movement-building ones (Kabeer 2002). Given that during the military dictatorship development NGOs were penalized for political affiliation, most chose to pursue an apolitical agenda, focusing on service delivery and awareness-raising and consultation rather than structural change (Hossain 2005). The focus on service delivery was also fuelled by the availability of donor funding and the rise of good governance agendas which advocated NGOs as an alternative and later as a complementary channel for delivering services (Sanyal 1991; Rahman 2006). This apolitical development agenda continued to be pursued in the post-authoritarian phase,[7] largely because of the polarized civil society space where pursuing a particular rights-based agenda is interpreted as aligning with either the Awami League or the Bangladesh Nationalist Party, thus leading to losing one's credibility and standing and, at times, political repercussions (Nazneen and Sultan 2009). NGOs have over the years actively promoted women's rights and gender equity, with many of them focusing on establishing women as clients of services and creating access to microcredit for income/employment generation. They have also employed significant numbers of women.

Besides women's/feminist organizations and NGOs, donors are a strong actor in promoting the women's empowerment agenda. The availability of donor funding led to the proliferation of gender development projects and to the creation of a particular discourse on women's empowerment. However, the proliferation of these projects has also placed women's organizations in a difficult position, where their activities have been characterized as 'Western imports' by the wider public (Nazneen et al. 2011a). The expansion of the NGO sector, which is taken as shorthand for civil society in Bangladesh, and the dominance of the development discourse have led women's and feminist organizations to distinguish themselves from NGOs.

NGO-ization and women's organizations

In this section we discuss how women's organizations and feminist activism negotiated or dealt with the NGO-ization process and how they are adapting to the post-'NGO-ized' phase. We show how the dominance of development policies and programmes has affected women's organizations and how they are having to adjust to the realities of a post-developmental-aid and NGO-ized phase caused by the increasing scarcity of direct funding. We also explore how the NGO-ization process affects the agenda, autonomy, agency and accountability of different types of women's/feminist organizations. Molyneux (2001) points out that the ability to act autonomously in setting a feminist agenda is a key aspect in the construction of the feminist movement. Autonomy means that organizations remain accountable for promoting feminist interests to their constituencies.

The changes in the international and national aid architecture in the post-NGO-ized phase have forced many women's/feminist organizations to reposition themselves in relation to development aid and resources. These adjustments include changes in ways of mobilizing and coping with reduced financial resources while competing for such resources. Faced with the challenge of mobilizing with shrinking financial resources, organizations that used mass mobilization strategies or had outreach services are re-evaluating their strategies and reassessing what is possible in a changed political and historical context.

In Bangladesh there is a variety of women's organizations, which differ in their nature, leadership, values and resources, and the ways in which they have negotiated their position within the development paradigm and developmental funding regimes. Some of these organizations are membership based, seeking to address the interests of women as a whole, while others seek to serve disadvantaged women. Their formal structures vary: the terms used are *samity* (association), *shangathan* (organization, which may or may not be a legal body) and *sangstha* (institution) to denote the different degrees of formalization of these organizations.

The less formalized organizations, operating at the village level, are the *Mahila Samitys* or women's associations. They were set up to provide training and relief to poor women and engage in various cultural and social activities. Some of these small associations were also encouraged by the cooperative movement. Their main goal was to ensure that women received services, loans, training or even relief in the form of wheat or rice. We found that many of these smaller local associations and regional women's organizations[8] have 'worked with' the NGO-ization process and have benefited from it, but with a price to pay. With the growth of the formal NGO sector and an increase in donor funding, smaller organizations were exposed to the developmental NGO model of funded projects, professional staff, management by a few persons, or even one individual, and a more formal board. A number of the smaller women's organizations took advantage of the increased interest in and funding for 'women's development' and developed the skills and capacities to compete in the world of project funding or even take on subcontracts in larger projects managed by larger NGOs. Other enabling factors were the availability of funding for women's development as well as donors' willingness to work with women-headed NGOs. This led to a greater recognition of smaller local women's NGOs and an increase in resources for organizations to restructure themselves. Although their interests lay in women's development, in order to work towards this goal they had to take whatever means and resources were available. This resulted in small, scattered projects and often ad hoc interventions for the women they were seeking to serve, with their objectives and activities being adjusted to the available funding. However, in the interaction with other NGOs, feminist networks and other civil society groups promoting human rights, some of these organizations are now more able to participate in and contribute to debates around women's rights and gender equality. A case in point is Banchte Shekha, which illustrates how a small organization with village women as members grew into a woman-headed NGO which is principally serving women in a larger area and playing an active role in policy-making.

However, Banchte Shekha's change came at a significant cost. A unique feature of Banchte Shekha before it received external funding was the direct role that village women played in implementing and managing the programme, and the supportive role of local people and government officials in providing resources and training for women. A fundamental change after receiving donor funds was that its accountability is no longer to members or the people the organization works for. A more NGO-type General Body and Executive Committee was introduced with social workers and elite as members. Accountability is now vertical, to the board and to the donors, with the board taking a back seat to the executive and to the funders.

In fact, most of these smaller and regional organizations were not in a position to determine the terms of their engagement with larger or funding NGOs. To survive, they had to learn the rules of the game of development NGOs. Some have been able to retain their original spirit of challenging gender inequalities and discrimination, and they believe that they are still contributing to the movement towards equality and development, even while they have accepted NGO-ization.

There is another group of organizations for whom NGO-ization was more problematic and who tried to strategically engage with the process. Some women's organizations covered by our research illustrate this trend. All the eight case study organizations started out on a purely voluntary basis and six of them started as membership organiza- tions. Their *raison d'être* was to respond to women's rights issues that their founder members had identified as burning issues. They did have other means of raising funds, such as carrying out training and consultancies on gender and development or women's rights issues (in the case of Naripokkho, WFW, BNWLA) and through donations (BMP and Naripokkho). The impetus for seeking external financial support and adoption of the project model arose out of appreciation of the limitations of voluntary activism in expanding outreach and sustaining activities. For example, Naripokkho wanted to ensure that financial resources were available to its own members so that some of them could become involved on a full-time basis on the priority advocacy and research work. Similarly, for BMP, external support was needed to recruit several full-time staff and arrange for funds for its publications, training, workshops and meetings. BMP and BNWLA felt the pressure to respond on a larger scale and extend their activities to more women. In the case of BOMSA, which was founded by women migrant workers, it was not possible for them to sustain their activities without financial support as they did not have the economic means to volunteer their time.

In spite of the felt need for increased resources, a few organizations were hesitant about taking donor funding and wary of the implications it would have for their nature and identity. In fact, even after years of taking project funding and adopting many elements of the NGO identity, these organizations are still sensitive about the NGO label. To many of them, to be so labelled is seen as an insult to the activism and their social movement character. For example, Kormojibi Nari took great pains to clarify that they are not an NGO. They claimed: 'We are an organization of women workers. Women workers are at the centre of our work' (Sultan 2011: 4). All of the organizations studied (other than Banchte Shekha) argued that they were not NGOs, though they are registered with the NGO Affairs Bureau,[9] and stressed their identity as membership and social-movement-based organizations.

Given their self-perception as being different from development NGOs, how, then, do they deal with development aid and projects? Among the organizations researched, a few benefited from available resources without compromising their principles. For both BMP and Naripokkho, the decision to accept donor funding was a major one. It led to many debates about organizational autonomy and accountability to core constituents. In order to protect their autonomy, the organizations made sure that there was a consistency between their organizational goals and objectives as articulated in their constitutions and the specific donor's mandate and objectives. Secondly, to retain control over their agenda and maintain their autonomy, the organizations decided not to allow their core activities or the overall organization to be dependent on external funding. For example, Naripokkho consciously decided not to accept core funding for the organization, choosing to keep external funding limited to projects, so that there would be no risk of external interference with core organizational activities. BMP's project was formulated in such a way that it enabled them to do what they had been doing before but in a better-resourced way, which resulted in better record keeping and documentation and support to voluntary members by having full-time staff to carry out support activities. Finally, strategic choices about programmes and priorities were set by the membership in all four of the national organizations (BMP, BNWLA, Naripokkho and WFW). The organizations established formal rules so that the project staff are not in decision-making positions and members steer the projects. In each case, there was a feeling that the funding they receive is more than balanced by the voluntary contributions of members in terms of time, professional inputs and other resources. Most organizations are confident that if external funding were to stop overnight, activities might have to be reduced but the organization would not be fundamentally affected.

While autonomy, accountability to members and adherence to founding principles and values are maintained in certain national women's rights organizations, nonetheless external funding has influenced them in various other ways. All of them have gone through processes of institutionalization, having to register with relevant government authorities. Organizational structures and procedures have become more formalized and the standardization of accounts, monitoring and reporting are positively valued. Various concepts and definitions, such as outcomes, results, outputs and objectives, have become part of their daily vocabulary. Projects limit the organizations' ability to project time frames, which is often resented, as illustrated by the quote from a BNWLA member below:

> BNWLA felt that some approaches and processes that donors insist on are not appropriate for the issues being addressed. This leads to conflict over how things could be implemented. For example, court cases and legal processes are lengthy and time-consuming, and project time-frames can be too small to showcase successes. (Nazneen et al. 2011a: 26)

Projectization and NGO-ization have also affected organizations in which voluntarism was valued. Members' time has been monetized, creating a division between paid staff and volunteer members. While senior members continue to devote a substantial amount of voluntary time in organizations such as BMP, BNWLA, Karmojibi Nari and the Doorbar network, these organizations are finding it harder to mobilize new volunteers (see below). Projectization has monetized activities that were formerly carried out by volunteers, which may act as a disincentive to future voluntary work. Voluntary members are often in a governance or supervisory role with regard to paid staff, which creates hierarchies among membership and staff. Finally, the organizations have evolved from groups of activist women with social and affective bonds of friendship and common backgrounds to formal organizations bringing together women and men from different backgrounds.

The wider international development and women's rights discourse, changes in funding trends and the epistemic power of the donors have also influenced the agenda and mobilization strategies of women's organizations. Advocacy styles, for example, have become more media and event focused, as these can easily be quantified as a measure of influence for the external funders. While working on issues closely linked to founding principles or those that seemed important in the context of changes at the national or international levels, these organizations are also sensitive to international and national trends. Although the organizations we studied chose their own agenda and were not greatly influenced by donor funding, it should be noted that certain issues, which had gained priority in the international gender and development discourse, were picked up by all these organizations. This points to the epistemic powers and influence that donor discourses have over international development agendas, which in turn impact on the national level.

The case study organizations also emphasized advocacy for policy and legal reform in recent years and focused more on lobbying the state. A certain style of advocacy has developed in the process. For example, Kormojibi Nari worked on the labour code based on the ILO conventions and BNWLA on various legal provisions based on CEDAW. A focus on the state is not new but a concentration on this form of activism indicates a qualitative change, whereby constituency-building for structural change takes a back seat.

The issue of NGO-ization needs to be put in perspective, and therefore we need to be aware that, for these organizations, there is life besides and beyond funding. All of the case study organizations researched were not entirely project based in their activities, even while receiving significant donor funding. They had activities and identities beyond funded projects. When asked to list and prioritize resources, these organizations felt that while financial resources were important, they were not the most important factor in achieving their goals or making an impact. The leadership of the founders of the organization and membership strength, time and commitment were identified as more crucial to their work than financial resources.

The reputation or the goodwill of the organization was also considered to be an important resource, although in some cases this depended on the extent and visibility of their activities (supported by funded projects). This reputation gave these organizations access to various fora and enabled them to become members of various national and government committees, thus increasing their influencing role. They have become actors to be consulted, who contribute to public opinion and policy-making, extending their roles beyond project activities. Relationships and partnerships with the government and women's organizations have been built, whereby women act as experts or advisers, or even implement contracts and provide services in government programmes, both nationally and regionally. While closeness to the government can be a disadvantage (e.g. you cannot criticize them as freely) the advantages are felt to be worth it.

The partnerships and networks the organizations entered into were important resources and a means of getting their messages across. This fosters constituency-building for, and helps to bring about, change. While project resources can sometimes support participation in networks and coalitions, this is considered an important arena of influence for mobilization as a whole, and organizations see it as work that is not limited to projects. Another strategy for constituency-building was to strengthen the membership base that the organization claims to represent. For instance, Kormojibi Nari and BOMSA constantly face the challenge of devising ways by which the membership can contribute to the sustainability of the organization without being a financial drain on it.[10]

These non-financial resources mentioned above have gained new significance in the post-NGO-ized phase when funding for women's rights and for small and medium-sized organizations is shrinking. The case study organizations are exploring alternative funding sources and ways to raise financial resources. Banchte Shekha had explored private sector contributions, bank loans and asset-building as other ways of raising money. A few are actively considering mobilizing resources from the private sector, while being conscious that private firms and individuals might have their own agenda, which may not necessarily match theirs. Participating in tenders and bids for various donor and government calls for proposals was also an option that BNWLA and BOMSA took up.

The alternative understanding of resources, different strategies to access other types of financial resources and non-project-based strategies for gaining influence and voice through constituency-building, networking and building relations with the government, international agencies and other social movements are some of the ways of working that will increasingly play a larger role in the post-NGO-ized period. Recent reflections among the organizations have emphasized that they need to think ahead strategically and shape the social, economic and political forces at play instead of being shaped by them.

Generational divide

Younger feminists (in their twenties and thirties) use the term 'feminist impasse' to describe the generational divide between the vanguard feminist groups of the 1970s and themselves (Siddiqui 2011). This impasse pertains to the divergence in views and attitudes of these different generations and the way they choose to engage with the feminist movement. We focus on the following categories of young people (mostly women but also some men), although these categories are not always mutually exclusive: a) urban, middle-class students/professionals who are members of a woman's rights/feminist organization; b) urban, middle-class students/professionals who are not members of women's rights/feminist organizations (but may be a part of other movements or groups); c) middle-class professionals or students who are members of women's organizations and are based in small towns or semi-urban areas; d) members of associations that represent the interests of working-class women.

The more established feminist organizations are facing a crisis in terms of recruiting and retaining young members. One of the leaders of a pioneer feminist activist organization, Naripokkho, lamented the absence of younger members in their fold and pointed to 'apathy, consumerism, and the appeal of conservative forces'[11] as the reasons why fewer younger women join women's/feminist organizations. While these factors do contribute towards younger generations' disengagement with these organizations, there are other issues in play.

While NGO-ization of the movement had some positive impacts in terms of increasing the outreach of feminist organizations through allies and 'sidestreaming' (Alveraz 2009) feminist analysis and discourse into other arenas, it has also led to the development of a particular approach to conceptualization and mobilizing for women's rights. A case in point is BNWLA, founded in 1979 as a professional women lawyers' association. Senior leaders of BNWLA, all veterans of the movement, pointed out that NGO-ization and donor funding had a profound influence on how the younger generation of female lawyers engaged with the organization's activities. They argue that the younger members take a more professionalized (i.e. gender- and development-oriented and -projectized) approach to women's rights, where provision of legal aid to a large number of women clients and drafting changes for legal reforms are prioritized. In contrast the older members felt that they espoused a more movement-oriented focus which stresses consciousness-raising and street agitation. Though the older members themselves have engaged in providing legal aid and drafting legal reform, this emphasis on different strategies, along with anxieties around NGO-ization, has contributed towards an idealized notion of feminist activism that was espoused by the autonomous feminist groups in the 1970s and 1980s. The younger members argue (and the older members agree) that a professionalized approach does not imply that they are less committed to feminism, but both admit that it does show that the younger members came to experience and view gender issues in a context where the 'NGO' model of 'doing gender' projects is ubiquitous. It also points to how gender issues are integrated in academia and development training programmes, emphasizing a gender and development approach. Paradoxically, it is the very success of feminist researchers and activists of the 1970s and 1980s in incorporating gender into academic programmes and development organizations' training which has led to the promotion of the gender and development approach in these programmes.

NGO-ization and donor funding also had an impact on monetizing the labour used for organizational activities. Most of the organizations under study had to hire project and office staff as they expanded and took on various projects. This created a clear division between the staff and the members, with those belonging to the younger generation particularly at times feeling undervalued for voluntarily doing the same type of work as the staff. The younger (and new) members feel that they should be compensated for their time. Both BNWLA and the Doorbar network reported that this has created tensions between the staff and younger members, and also between the younger and older generations of the membership within these organizations (Nazneen et al. 2011a; George and Nazneen 2010).

A clear impact of NGO-ization and donor funding can be felt in the way different generations perceive voluntarism. It should be noted that members of these selected case study organizations interviewed place a high value on voluntarism and members' time is counted as a key resource. All of the case study organizations started off with volunteers, with senior members regularly volunteering their time (Nazneen et al. 2011a). The smaller women's organizations that are members of the Doorbar network also reported high levels of voluntarism among the founder members (George and Nazneen 2010). However, there has been a decrease in voluntarism among the younger members. This decrease perhaps reflects both attitudinal and socio-economic realities. The attitudinal issue, a professional approach towards investing their time, was discussed above.

Also, younger women members have less family support and greater financial pressures which require financial compensation and reduce their ability to contribute voluntary time. In addition, there is a socio-economic class dimension to voluntarism. Some of the members of the Doorbar network, which largely consists of small local organizations, and organizations such as BOMSA, whose members are from a lower- to lower-middle-income group, found it financially difficult to volunteer their time (Nazneen et al. 2011a). In fact, the members of these groups argued that donor funding and projects have enabled them to participate in promoting women's rights. They also felt that upholding voluntarism as the normative ideal of feminist politics placed them at a disadvantage. Given that most of the feminist organizations were composed of and led by middle-class professional women, these women could afford to provide unpaid labour, which working-class women were unable to do. In fact, the socio-economic class dimension of voluntarism calls into question the normative ideal of voluntarism in feminist politics, which relies on unpaid female labour.

What stops the urban-based educated young feminists belonging to the middle and upper-middle income groups from joining the more established women's/feminist organizations? The lack of space and democracy within these organizations is cited as a key reason. Siddiqui's (2011) article points out that many of these organizations are led by charismatic leaders, who have led their organizations effectively. However, very few of these organizations nurture rank-and-file leadership and provide space for younger members (discussed later in this section). This is not a unique feature of the feminist movement, but is common to other social movements in Bangladesh. Some of the younger feminists working in various gender and development projects said they were afraid of the '*Khalamma* brigade' (aunty brigade) in these organizations and stayed away from formally engaging in their activities. They preferred alternative ways of engaging with and contributing to the movement. However, they also admitted that during crisis periods (for example, the backlash against the National Women's Development Policy from conservative quarters), it is the *Khalamma* brigade which leads and actively resists oppositional forces. This group also admits that they themselves have shied away from street activism during these periods.

Another constraint that younger women experience is the issue of time. Some of the interviewees pointed to time as the most crucial factor. Membership requirements are too rigorous, making it difficult for them to join these organizations. One of our interviewees, a young professional working in a project on gender justice, said,

> Oh, I wanted to join X [an established feminist organization], I admire them a lot. But they require you to be present at so many trainings and meetings. I realise this is for broadening our views and concepts around women's rights etc. But I work full-time and have other household chores and child care duties to carry out. I don't get any help from the extended family members. They are busy and we are not living with them. So, I prefer something that would be more fluid and flexible, hence my engagement in cyber activism. I also do my bit through the project I work on. (Interview, YF 1, August 2009)

Besides these issues, some of the young urban middle-class feminists pointed out that the vanguards of the movement have failed to engage with the emerging debates and issues that matter to younger people. Siddiqui (2011) pointedly asks whether some of the established feminist organizations have lost relevance for the younger crowd. This question is troubling given that young women (and men) have been active in other movements, such as the anti-corruption campaign and environmental movements. The organizations leading these movements and campaigns have garnered mass support and a following among the younger group. In addition, both men and women (particularly students) have actively participated in various issue-based campaigns for women's rights, such as the anti-sexual-harassment movements based in public universities since the late 1990s. These movements evolved spontaneously and were organized and led by students, and though the movements are counted as part of the women's movement in Bangladesh, they were not led by mainstream women's organizations. This indicates that there is interest among the urban middle-class youth in engaging with particular issues pertaining to women's rights. Though the established feminist organizations have expressed support for these groups, they have yet to create effective links with these flatter and fluid movements.

One of the reasons behind their inability to establish effective links may be that feminists belonging to the established organizations have failed to capitalize on the new modes and forms of mobilizing. Environmental organizations, such as Bangladesh Paribesh Andolon (BAPA), or the anti-corruption campaigns coordinated by Transparency International, Bangladesh, have created interest among the youth through using innovative means to package their message and involve the youth. They use photo exhibitions, film shows, cartoon competitions focusing on corruption, boat rallies on the river to protest against encroachment on the river, and established 'friends' networks among young members. Older members have toured the country and talked to school and college students. All of these activities prompted younger members to join the movement. Links with the influential senior leaders through tours and discussions have also ensured that younger members have had informal channels for expressing their opinions and accessing the leadership.

The Internet, particularly media such as Facebook, and the mobile phone have become key ways of transmitting messages and organizing young people, and was effectively used during the recent anti-sexual-harassment movement by students at one of the public universities.[12] There are sites and blogs where various gender rights issues are debated.[13] Established feminist organizations may have some Web-savvy members, but the organizations themselves (at least the selected case study organizations) have poorly constructed and managed websites and are absent from this vibrant new public (cyber)space. Some of the young feminists we interviewed, who are professionals in development agencies, also argued that the 'old guard' were no longer in touch with emerging issues. These include gender issues in the corporate, energy, transport and ICT sectors and the cultural sphere (i.e. sexualities, 'girl power', etc.). These organizations have also been critiqued both internally and externally for failing to adequately focus on and take into account the newer issues pertinent to rural poor women, such as the rights of female migrant workers and female agricultural labourers, or gender issues within the trade unions (Nazneen et al. 2011b; Azim 2011). Admittedly, the established organizations have focused on 'conventional' issues, such as violence against women, women's political representation or economic empowerment, because equity has not been achieved in any of these areas. How the established women's organizations create cooperative relationships with leaders of organizations that represent specific group/class interests, such as the migrant women's associations (e.g. BOMSA) and women in trade union groups, such as the Awaj Foundation, may be a critical factor in building an intergenerational movement.

The disengagement felt by the urban middle-class young women towards the feminist movement does not mean that the rank and file of established feminist organization is thinning out. In fact, among the selected case study organizations, feminist professional networks, such as BNWLA or the women workers' cells of Kormojibi Nari, reported that their membership among young women in small district towns has increased. The Doorbar network also reported an increase in the number of organizations based in small towns wanting to be network members. The reasons behind this increase are the following. First, young professional women in district towns and small local-level women's organizations expect to be able to access donor funding and information by joining the network. Secondly, they expect to use the social capital gained through establishing links with national-level organizations in their negotiations with local authorities. Thirdly, individual members and smaller organizations gain visibility and strength by being members of national associations/networks. Besides these instrumental reasons, these new members have a genuine desire to be part of a wider community that works on women's rights with a strong commitment to advancing gender equality.

Whether these new members play a significant role depends on: a) how much space is provided to these smaller, locally based groups within these larger networks; and b) whether the new issues that are identified and promoted by these groups will be taken up by the established feminist groups. What the research on Bangladesh Mohila Parishad, Naripokkho and Women for Women shows is that within the larger feminist coalitions, very few groups based outside the capital, Dhaka (whether led by and composed of younger women or not), have the scope for exercising leadership. This does not mean various negotiations do not take place within these feminist coalitions. However, the voices of the smaller groups are usually marginalized in many of these larger networks. The Dhaka-based national organizations are able to assume leadership in these coalitions because they have the financial and other resources (Nazneen and Sultan 2010). Women's organizations have been largely composed of and led by elite and professional middle-class women in Bangladesh. Undeniably, the inclusion of these new (and younger) members based in small towns within organizational ranks and feminist coalitions has changed the socio-economic class composition of the movement. The impact of this shift is not visible yet.

The established feminist organizations are aware of these shifts and have tried to reach out to younger women. Bangladesh Mahila Parishad, Naripokkho and BNWLA have specific programmes, such as discussion sessions, workshops, training sessions and consultations, through which they engage with adolescents and young women. They know that these engagements are important and are aware that in order to survive they need to create a second tier of leadership. Many of the established leaders in these organizations – for example, Naripokkho's leaders – say that they are 'tired' and 'need fresh blood' (George and Nazneen 2010). Some organizations, such as BNWLA, point out that without a second generation of leaders the organization cannot be sustained. The main problem seems to be that of retention and sustained interest. As a Bangladesh Mahila Parishad interviewee put it, 'It's not that the young people do not come and work with us. They come when they are students, they volunteer with us throughout their student days. But as they enter professional life, they discontinue. The pressures are tremendous and they drop out' (interview, BMP respondent, 3 July 2008).

What becomes evident is that there is a divergence within the feminist movement in Bangladesh along generational lines. This divergence is strongly influenced by geographical location and class identity. Although there have been episodes in which effective collaboration between generations has taken place, the future of creating an intergenerational feminist movement is still unclear.

Conclusions

The above discussion on the two key challenges faced by the feminists in Bangladesh – NGO-ization of and the generational divide within the movement – shows the following.

Feminist/women's organizations have been affected differently by NGO-ization, depending on their size, resources, leadership and location (whether local or national). The agenda, autonomy and accountability of smaller, local-level women's organizations were more affected by the NGO-ization process compared to those of the national-level organizations, which managed the process in a more strategic manner. Adoption of the NGO model and acceptance of external funding increased organizational capacity, leading to the development of more formal financial and administrative procedures and processes within the case study organizations. NGO-ization also increased outreach and access to alternative spaces. On the other hand, NGO-ization has affected and in many cases constrained the way the women's rights agenda is framed and enters the wider social movement arena. In the post-NGO-ized phase, with scarce external funding, women's/feminist organizations have been forced to re-examine their mobilization and funding strategies.

NGO-ization has further aggravated the generational divide within the movement through 'professionalizing' feminist activism for urban professional middle-class women. The established women's organizations face difficulties in recruiting and retaining young members as volunteers. Urban youth and young professionals also feel disconnected from the movement because of time pressure, and failure of the established feminist organizations to identify what these groups consider priority issues and effective use of new modes and spaces for mobilization. However, the socio-economic class composition of the movement is changing with young women professionals in the semi-urban areas and small towns joining feminist networks. New types of organization created by working-class women have also emerged and play an active role.

These trends and changes discussed above challenge the dichotomies that pervade the discussion on feminist politics, such as privileging voluntarism over 'professionalized' activism or labelling feminist organizations as movement oriented or as NGO-ized (Roy 2011). They show that the women's organizations have a more hybrid way of functioning. They also bring sharply into focus how leadership and engagement of elite and middle-class women in feminist movement-building have led to a model of feminist activism that privileges unpaid female labour.

Can Bangladeshi feminists create a strong intergenerational movement using alternative modes, strategies and ways of mobilizing? It depends on the following. First, the emergence of working-class feminist/women's organizations and active participation by women in semi-urban areas represent possibilities for the expansion and strengthening of the movement. Whether this potential is realized will depend partly on how the established women's organizations respond to these groups. Secondly, given that established women's/feminist organizations are having to explore alternative resources (partnerships, constituency-building, etc.) and means for mobilizing, they could benefit from accessing and using the new modes and spaces that the younger generation uses and inhabits. Whether the younger generation is interested in collaborating with or joining feminist groups will be a key determinant. Finally, the generations have collaborated with each other when right-wing groups have threatened women's rights or on specific women's rights issues such as the anti-sexual-harassment movement in public universities. Whether these episodic collaborations turn into long-term cooperation remains to be seen.

Notes

1 Not all women's organizations are feminist in nature since they may not aim to change power relations through structural change (Molyneux 2001). The organizations researched for the Pathways study discussed in this chapter characterize themselves as feminist organizations though their origins may have not have had an explicit feminist character.

2 In 2008 and 2010, the Islamist political groups mobilized against the National Women's Development Policy, arguing that the policy's stand on women's control over property might be used to change the sharia law on women's inheritance. The government watered down the policy despite protests by women's groups.

3 These organizations were chosen because of their pioneering role in strengthening the women's movement in Bangladesh. They also capture the diversity of national-level feminist organizations in Bangladesh.

4 The organizations were selected based on the following criteria: a) women-headed organization; b) established before 2000; c) works on women's rights (not only service delivery or welfare issues). The criteria were set to ensure that comparator organizations were selected in Ghana since this was a inter-country study to trace the

impact of the Paris Declaration (2005) and the Accra Agenda for Action (2005).

5 This network includes 540 small women-headed organizations functioning at the local level.

6 About 80 per cent of villages have NGOs (Nazneen and Sultan 2009).

7 Bangladesh embarked on a new democratic period after the fall of General Ershad in 1990.

8 These trends are exhibited among a number of the smaller, local-level members of the Doorbar network and also of the NCBP (National Committee for Beijing Plus 5) set up by WFW.

9 A requirement for receiving foreign funding.

10 BOMSA membership of 7,000 women migrant workers; BMP membership of 120,000 women activists; Doorbar network membership of 540 local-level women's organizations; BNWLA membership of 1,200 women lawyers and KN with up to 450,000 women workers organized in cells – all of them trying to find ways of making the membership active in local resource mobilization or contributing financially to the organization.

11 Comments made by Shireen Huq at the Pathways of Women's Empowerment, South Asia, closing conference in July 2011.

12 Facebook was effectively used by one of the victims of sexual harassment to update the status of her hearing and also by students and colleagues who supported her cause. It became a key tool to protest the university's decision to take action against the perpetrator, but also to chastise the victim by urging her to 'behave properly'.

13 See the recent debates on Facebook regarding Rumana Manzur, an assistant professor at Dhaka University, who was blinded by her husband. Also see *Forum* magazine (July 2011), where Dristipat's (an Internet group) female members wrote extensively on this. Most of the members of this writers' collective are young professionals.

References

Alveraz, S. E. (1998) 'The Latin American feminist NGO boom', www.mtholoyoke.edu/acad/latam/schomburgenmoreno/alveraz.html, accessed 10 March 2003.

— (2009) 'Beyond NGO-ization? Reflection from Latin America', *Development*, 52(2): 175–84.

AWID (2008) www.awid.org.

Azim, F. (2011) 'Woman of the New Millennium in Bangladesh', Paper presented at the Pathways of Women's Empowerment South Asia hub closing conference, 26–28 July 2011.

George, S. and S. Nazneen (2010) *A Review and Reflection on Networking as a Strategy for Movement Building*, Unpublished report for Naripokkho on the Doorbar network, Dhaka.

Goetz, A. M. (2001) *Women Development Workers*, Dhaka: UPL.

Hemment, J. (2007) *Empowering Women in Russia: Activism, Aid and NGOs*, Bloomington: Indiana University Press.

Hossain, N. (2005) *Elite Perceptions of Poverty in Bangladesh*, Dhaka: UPL.

Jad, I. (2004) 'The NGO-ization of Arab women's movement', *IDS Bulletin*, 35(4): 34–42.

Jahan, R. (1995) 'Men in seclusion and women in public: Rokeya's dreams and women's struggles in Bangladesh', in A. Basu (ed.),

The Challenges of Local Feminisms: Women's Movement in Global Perspectives, Boulder, CO: Westview Press.

Kabeer, N. (2002) 'Citizenship and the boundaries of acknowledged community, identity and affiliation and exclusion', IDS working paper 171, IDS, Brighton.

Lang, S. (1997) 'The NGO-ization of feminism', in J. Scott, C. Kaplan and D. Keates (eds), *Transitions, Environment, Translations: Feminisms in International Perspectives*, London: Routledge.

Molyneux, M. (2001) *Women's Movement in International Perspective: Latin America and Beyond*, London: Palgrave.

Nazneen, S. and M. Sultan (2009) 'Struggling for survival and autonomy: impact of NGO-ization on women's organizations in Bangladesh', *Development*, 52(2): 193–9.

— (2010) 'Reciprocity, distancing and opportunistic overtures: women's organisations negotiating legitimacy and space', *IDS Bulletin*, 41(2): 70–8.

Nazneen, S., M. Sultan and M. Mukhopadhyay (2011a) *Mobilising Resources for Women's Rights: The Role of Resources, Synthesis Report: Bangladesh*, Dhaka: BDI and Pathways of Women's Empowerment Research Programme Consortium.

Nazneen, S., N. Hossain and M. Sultan (2011b) 'National discourses on women's empowerment: continuity and change', IDS Working Paper 368, IDS, Brighton.

Rahman, S. (2006) 'Development, democracy, and the NGO sector: theory and evidence from Bangladesh', *Journal of Developing Societies*, 22(4): 451–73.

Roy, S. (2011) 'Politics, passion and professionalization in contemporary Indian feminism', *Sociology*, 45(4): 587–602.

Sanyal, B. (1991) 'Antagonistic co-operation: a case study of nongovernmental organizations, governments and donors' relationship in income generating projects in Bangladesh', *World Development*, 19(10): 1367–79.

Siddiqui, S. (2011) 'Sultana's nightmare', *Forum: The Daily Star Monthly Magazine*, 8 March.

Sultan, M. (2011) *Mobilising for Women's Rights and the Role of Resources, Karmojibi Nari: A Case Study*, Dhaka: BDI and Pathways of Women's Empowerment Research Programme Consortium.

5 | Offline issues, online lives? The emerging cyberlife of feminist politics in urban India

TRISHIMA MITRA-KAHN

In millennial debates about the articulation of and participation in the political, the transnational lament regarding the 'mysterious disengagement' (Putnam 1995: 68) of people from civic and political life is routinely juxtaposed with affirmative assertions citing the proliferation of a certain kind of politics that eschews conventional organizational forms and participation patterns. The latter declaration is founded mainly upon early, large-scale, exemplary examples of cyber activism (McCaughey and Ayers 2003) and is being revised in light of Web 2.0,[1] which seems to aid the proliferation of quotidian political praxes by people from the global middle class. These political praxes, driven by the credo of 'everyday life' (Bang 2004, 2009; Shah 2010), are moving away from traditionally organized representational politics and are emphasizing the 'emic' or the insider point of view (Hymes 1970) while agentically creating and investing in a deliberative and discursive politics of articulation. In post-liberalized India the lives of middle-class[2] urban women, some of whom come from a generation that has grown up digital (Shah 2010), are being negotiated within the fundamental paradox of expanding education and employment as avenues to reimagine gender relations and rising neoliberal and Hindu right-wing discourse on womanhood, seeking to curtail any such reimagining. In this respect the spaces afforded by Web 2.0 appear to be critical for the emergence of middle-class women's contentious political action; spaces that might otherwise be mired in ambivalence or silence within the mainstream cultural geography of Indian feminism. The Internet has proved to be instrumental for some women's examination, critique, transgression and subversion of the interoperable gendered socio-political and cultural scripts that their lives are increasingly subject to and subjectivized by.

Rather than offer an overview of the 'everyday change making' (Bang 2009) within online feminist politics in urban India, this chapter emerges from the minutiae of the ethnographic field to focus on the articulations of the political within, and subjectivities produced in, a selection of non-mainstream[3] online women-led campaigns. It does so in order to explore, if somewhat descriptively, how young middle-class women are engaged in 'a micropolitics of becoming' (Connolly, quoted in Bang 2004: 14), developing 'small' tactics for 'making a difference' (Bang 2009: 22) to their social worlds. To accomplish this, I explore three campaigns: the Blank Noise Project, India's first and largest youth-led, voluntary, online public arts-based campaign against public sexual harassment, Please Mend the Gap, and 'A Valentine for India': Stand up to Moral Policing. The research sample is limited to campaigns led by a fairly cohesive socio-economic cohort of young, urban, middle-class, English-speaking, educated/employed women, most of whom are in their late twenties or early thirties. The analysis herein is constrained by the newness of the campaigns researched, some barely a few months old, and by the sheer speed with which these and many others seem to be continuously evolving. A glaring omission is the lack of focus on individual women's blogs, or on Ultra Violet India's first avowedly feminist blog, where seemingly individualized textual productions signal a move towards a broader collective understanding of issues that affect middle-class women's lives. A significant analytical oversight is the overlooking of the sheer number of young middle-class men who form an integral part of online campaigns, though this is generated by my incipient data collection. Therefore the research herein is in no way exhaustive and should be considered introductory.

This chapter is organized as follows. I begin by placing the development of the cyberlife of feminist politics in urban India within the context of contemporary post-colonial Indian feminism and within the trajectories of certain dictates of ideal womanhood averred, albeit distinctly, in neoliberal and Hindu right-wing discourses. I then focus on the emerging politics and activism against public sexual harassment, or what has hitherto been termed 'eve-teasing' in India, by examining the Blank Noise Project. I find that newer campaigns on public sexual harassment, such as Please Mend the Gap, are enabled by Blank Noise's pioneering efforts to break the silence on public sexual harassment and prise open various dialogic spaces. Therefore a large part of this chapter focuses on Blank Noise's political praxes. I then discuss a street protest, 'A Valentine for India', against 'moral policing' or the regulation and surveillance of women in urban public space. In 2009, moral policing manifested itself in a series of violent physical attacks on middle-class women in southern Indian cities and in its wake different forms of protest politics sprang up in many urban metropolises; my focus is on one such protest.

The underlying leitmotif of this chapter is that an affirmative, hopeful, playful politics which seems to saturate these new articulations of feminism contests the multiple hegemonies that regulate the corporeality of middle-class women's gendered lives. Analysing these offers the possibility to 'break new ground and increase [our] understanding of feminism, organizations, and social movements' (Martin 1990: 202) and indicates the emergence of a cyberlife of feminist politics in urban India.

Contextualizing the emergence of the cyberlife of feminist politics in post-liberalized urban India

To account for the rise of young, middle-class, urban women's everyday politics, it would be inadequate to simply focus on the 'opening up' of the IT industry in 1995, which changed the Internet in India 'from its largely academic origins in the late 1980s' to 'the dynamic environment of today' (Wolcott and Goodman 2003: 566). Instead, a focus on the sociocultural geography of what Mary E. John (1998) calls the 'watershed decade' of the 1990s, in conjunction with the ideological feminism that the post-colonial Indian women's movement (IWM)[4] has historically privileged, offers greater analytical merit in contextualizing the emergence of online feminist politics.

It is by now common knowledge that the IWM has had to strive to *do* feminism in an environment hostile to feminist politics as Western and elite, and sometimes from within its own ranks. Many women's groups that today form the urban IWM emerged out of the dissatisfaction with the lack of discursive spaces for feminist politics within left-wing political parties (Menon and Nigam 2007), and 'the cutting edge' of the early post-colonial IWM was its 'socialist feminist stream' (Mehta 2008). Further, in the face of the 'reneged promises' of newly independent India on material livelihood issues for the 'vast majority of the nation's women' (John 1996: 126), early feminists could not speak from the vantage point of a select few and refer to their realities. The urban IWM's feminism as a politics of representation was thus envisioned quite similarly to an anthropological endeavour to push against its middle-class leadership and composition. This phenomenon has been termed by Mary E. John as Indian feminism's 'split subject' (ibid.: 128), with the activist/theorist middle-class feminist self and the socio-economically underprivileged *other* women as the objects of activism and enquiry. The split subjectivity of feminist politics was 'precisely the way' by which the IWM could 'proclaim its *Indianness*' (ibid., emphasis in the original), thereby claiming its legitimacy for

Indian women and simultaneously negotiating the 'anxieties' around its privileged composition (Roy 2009: 349). Elsewhere, Naisargi Dave (2011: 10) makes a similar point, arguing that early Indian feminism, fairly consistently, exercised 'cultural caution' in addressing certain issues which could potentially 'imperil' it with a 'bourgeois taint'.

John notes that the ability to produce selves and others has never been a straightforward process, but to conceive of feminism 'autobiographically' was 'unthinkable' in the early post-colonial moment (John 1996). Yet the more-than-autobiographical nature of Indian feminism did not prevent a focus on forms of violence against women such as dowry and rape, *the* focus of the early urban IWM, which cut across caste, class, region and religion; a point John makes. However, some other forms of cross-cutting violence such as 'eve-teasing' or the sexual harassment of women in public space, while theorized by feminists (Baxi 2001; Phadke 2003), saw sustained activism and the institutionalization of ameliorative mechanisms, other than the legal, such as *Jagori*'s Safe Delhi campaign and *Pukar*'s research-based advocacy on gender and public space emerge less than a decade ago. In light of the fact that it was the lobbying by some groups from within the IWM which led to the promulgation of India's first and only specifically addressed law on 'eve-teasing' – the Delhi Prohibition of Eve Teasing Act 1988 – the reasons for a broader ambivalence on the issue are varied and complex and cannot be fully developed within the context of this chapter. Yet a few arguments can provide the requisite analytical insight. Some authors have suggested that a silence on public sexual harassment develops from within the broader movement's conceptualization of the issue as one of class, and not necessarily feminist, politics (Phadke 2003). Popular culture in India, manifest in films and advertisements, has routinely presented the issue as a matter of class in its frequent caricaturing of incidents where a modern or Westernized upper-class woman is pitted against a lower-caste/class man, even though data from surveys and safety audits suggest that 'regardless of class, profession, or identity', urban women 'are vulnerable to sexual harassment' (Women in Cities International 2010: 70) and perpetrators from a range of socio-economic classes. Others have cited the episodic, spontaneous or 'one-off' nature of public sexual harassment hindering the development of issue-specific conceptual frameworks (Chakravarti et al. 2008) and the overshadowing of the issue by the exclusive focus of women's groups in the 1980s on sexual harassment in the workplace. Thus public sexual harassment remained unaddressed in its specificity, with early activism on the issue confined to ad hoc groups of feminists, academics and university students primarily in Delhi who strove to bring it within the ambit of the wider anti-sexual-harassment agenda but confining it to harassment at metropolitan universities. Groups demanded that universities be constituted as workplaces but advocated broadening the legal definition of the term (for a discussion, see ibid.) and highlighted the issue from the perspective of a duty of care that universities had towards their students and employees. Therefore it is unsurprising that the bulk of young urban middle-class women's non-mainstream political organizing is focused on public sexual harassment, an area of ambivalent silence for the broader urban IWM.

The 'watershed decade' of the 1990s, with the increased institutional visibility of feminist goals and politics beside rising right-wing Hindu religious fundamentalism, caste-based political assertions and the state's abrogated welfare responsibilities in its turn towards a free market economy, proved to be a locus of many feminist anxieties and dilemmas. Relevant to this chapter are the constructions of an essential womanhood and normative femininity that emerged in the period, both from within the fundamentalist and neoliberal projects, as the model for an 'ideal gendered citizenship' in post-liberalized India (Sunder-Rajan 1993: 130; see also Oza 2001). The neoliberal construction was nowhere more visible than in the newly privatized media's consumerist rhetoric heralding the arrival of a 'new Indian woman' (Sunder-Rajan 1993); the 'Modern and Indian woman' (Munshi 2004). This discourse centred on promoting the image of Indian women as educated and employed but within the seamless and seemingly unproblematic imaginaries of wives, sisters and mothers (Sunder-Rajan 1993). The right-wing discourses on womanhood developed within a politics that was more generally beset with misgivings regarding the gendered modernity that economic liberalization and cultural globalization were purportedly generating. Propelled by the idea of gender chaos, dystopic visions on what would happen to Indian culture and Indian women as India 'opened up' to the West promoted a further normative discourse on womanhood. Appropriating the IWM's lingua franca of agency and autonomy, right-wing discourses invoked the power of various Hindu goddesses as well as called upon Indian women to embody the Hindu ideal of the chaste, devoted, perfect wife (i.e. *pativrata*) to resist Westernized modernity. All of these discourses were in frequent public-sphere circulation, made possible by the privatization and expanding range of the print and visual media. In millennial India, young women are now being encouraged to submit to another idyll – a 'modern urban sexy middle class progressive but respectable woman' (Phadke 2005: 74). The women researched herein are the first generation under the panoptic gaze of women's magazines, films, advertisements and indeed the state (Oza 2001), which vigorously promote this virtuous sexual desirability. They are being told, for example, in advertisements, that women 'who attracts stare[s] from a male crowd on a street, bus, or in any other public place – a harrowing experience of everyday sexist harassment' (Sunder-Rajan 2004: 189) should consider this harassment as emblematic of their sexual desirability (Sunder-Rajan 1993: 132).

Feminist theorists have been at the forefront of pointing out the broad contours of the potential impact of these schizophrenic discourses on the lives of women. They have also pointed to the flattening of subjectivity that occurs in the frequent recourse to Indian woman in both neoliberal and right-wing discourses. They have consequently concerned themselves with the hyper-sexualization of women; either being promoted in various guises by neoliberal discourses or to be resisted as a Western scourge in right-wing imaginings. It has also mattered strongly to the left-leaning IWM that the middle class, from the 1990s, 'sets the terms of reference of Indian society' as a whole (Jaffrelot and van der Veer 2008: 19) and therefore feminist concerns have centred on the stabilization of a poly-vocal female subjectivity that both discourses aim to achieve through their alignment of womanhood with a peculiarly middle-class incantation. This normalization of womanhood is what activists in India have historically drawn their battles lines against. While some have indicated the unsuitability of the object/subject divide in light of these and other temporal developments (John 1998), and have called for a politics to be addressed to the discursive regulation of womanhood or 'cultural policing', the broader IWM's 'response is remarkable only in its absence' (Phadke 2003: 4569).

But the ambivalence of conceptual spaces cannot fully capture why many middle-class women have come out on to the streets and into cyberspace to protest against sexual violence, with their lives being subject to the surveillance regimes of normative gender ideals. Almost all the women researched herein seem to want to negotiate this terrain themselves. Some refuse to see their political praxes within the metonymy of either feminism or the IWM and are instead investing in a do-it-yourself grammar which lays claim to equality as entitlement and seems not to use the vocabulary of women's rights. Yet the grammar of equality and citizenship, which many young women frequently resort to, is enabled by early Indian feminism, whose 'original socialist vision' (Mehta 2008) did not preclude the usage of 'liberal' vocabularies suscribing to 'rights' and 'equality' (John 1996: 127). It is perhaps the messy intersections between the frameworks that the IWM has opened up for young middle-class women to organically critique hegemonic discourses, the relative lack of specifically addressed activist politics on certain forms of representational and sexual violence, the hyper-circulation of ideas on an ideal womanhood, an overwhelming desire to agentically chart their own avenues for dissent and redress, critically underscored by Web 2.0, that contextualize the emerging cyberlife of feminist politics in urban India.

Returning the gaze

Street sexual harassment In 2003, twenty-four-year-old Jasmeen Patheja decided to write her Master's thesis on 'eve-teasing' at the Srishti School of Art, Bangalore, a city touted as India's IT capital. While recruiting research participants, Patheja was struck by women's recalcitrance towards eve-teasing. Confronting views such as 'it happens every day, it's normal', or 'complete denial' (Blank Noise 2005), Patheja wondered whether asking women about public space would lead to greater insight. Not only did the number of women willing to speak to her rise from nine to sixty but 'groping, fear, vulnerable, weak, staring, and feeling sick' emerged as a large part of the affective narratives. The 'denial towards eve-teasing as an issue' led Patheja to propose collective action to resist such street-based harassment (ibid.). The availability of Internet spaces was crucial here. Without access to a communicative and low-cost/free space where Patheja could 'take the issue to the streets, while including a wider base of participants' (ibid.), collective action would remain Patheja's soliloquy. Thus began the Blank Noise Project, which is today a critical node within broader youth-led online activism in India. Newer campaigns focused on similar issues are appropriating Blank Noise's political praxes, manifest in online information exchange, testimonial writing and direct street-based action. Newer campaigns have taken on board Blank Noise's refusal to treat eve-teasing as trivial and women as 'eves' who titillate men with their presence in public space (for a discussion, see Baxi 2001). As Patheja notes:

> I want to build collective ownership of the issue of street sexual harassment. Where Blank Noise is concerned I think it is ... attempting to think about collective responsibility. We are driving the point that no one is outside the issue – you are responsible as a spectator, as 'perpetrator' and even as a survivor – we collectively need to address the issue instead of ignoring it or believing that it is someone else's job to fix it.

Today Blank Noise Project is composed of its four blogs (the original website, the 'action hero' blog, the 'spectator special' blog, and *Blank Noise Guy*), Facebook, YouTube and Twitter presence, and city-based Google groups. It spans seventeen cities in India and has a membership of more than one thousand unpaid, middle-class, English-speaking volunteers. The writing team on the blogs functions as the de facto leadership and team members refer to themselves as coordinators or super-action heroes. As with early IWM groups, people join Blank Noise 'not through the structure of formal association but through informal networking' (Sen 2000: 58) such as word of mouth, through friends who are already members, and through blogosphere and media coverage of its activities. There is a small core membership (Annie Zaidi, Blank Noise's Bombay coordinator, places the number at between twenty and fifty) that meets mainly through Web 2.0 to discuss, debate and organize campaigns. Even though membership is steadily expanding and is not conceived of in classical social movement terms, most members never meet face to face. For Blank Noise, its online presence is the organization and helps to moor its activities in the absence of physical space (Angelina 2011).

Former coordinator Hemangini Gupta provides an overview of Blank Noise Project's politics:

> We are looking at power relations, or trying to at least ... The basis of what it [Blank Noise] is and where it is coming from seems to be a queering of spaces to challenge a sort of male supremacy and violence that seems inbuilt in the public space. Basically it's a challenge to the assumption that a certain kind of power equation is 'alright' and we have been defiant about confronting this.

Blank Noise is remarkably different from its 2003 avatar, where the original blog was the online documentation of Patheja's public art interventions. In the early stages, with 'one foot in the art world and the other in the world of political activism' (Felshin 1995: 9), Patheja's focus remained on 'interrogating victimhood' (Blank Noise 2005). An early exhibition she undertook was an installation of clothes women wore at the time of being harassed with posters delineating the specific sections of the Indian Penal Code that deal with eve-teasing alongside. Playing on how middle-class women moderate their demeanour and appearance on city streets – through attire, for instance – in an attempt to resist the male gaze, the installation tested the limits of provocation and satirized law that frames eve-teasing as an offence that outrages a woman's modesty. This early exhibit is now an online campaign called *Did you ask for it*, where women email scanned images or send clothes worn at the time of harassment. As one of Blank Noise's first campaigns, *Did you ask for it* interrogates attire's semiotic function and implicitly plays on how middle-class women internalize or negotiate the demands of sexual purity in conjunction with self-expression. In August 2011, when Delhi witnessed its own iteration of the global Slutwalk march called the *Besharmi Morcha* (Protest of the Shameless) and the public sphere was rife with debates on its cultural suitability, it is important to highlight that *Did you ask for it* has been testing the limits of provocation, through a Dionysian laughter at modesty, since 2005.

Between 2005 and 2007 Blank Noise moved away from victimhood and engaged with 'public confrontation' (ibid.). The original blog's utility was expanded to post information on how to join and participate in 'street interventions', on existent laws on sexual harassment, and how to file a report with the police. Hyperlinks to global projects such as *Hollaback* and *Bitch* magazine as well as links to the websites of IWM groups such as *Jagori* and *Pukar* were put in place. Methods to donate electronically, to cover website upkeep and basic campaign-related costs, were initiated as 'most of the money came from personal finances, Jasmeen's art project money, and a few private donations' (Annie Zaidi, personal communication).

Today Blank Noise runs a series of online campaigns and 'street interventions', though the two cannot be neatly separated into the virtual and the physical. Nonetheless, online or textual campaigns include the Action Hero Testimonials (where women submit personal narratives of street sexual harassment as stories of resistance), Museum of Street Weapons (an online pictorial archive of the everyday items women carry with them to protect against potential harassers), and the Step by Step Guide to Unapologetic Walking (a toolkit compiling actions women can take while traversing public spaces without fear of harassment). These form the larger part of Blank Noise's activities, but street interventions such as 'Y R U looking at me?', 'take back the night', 'Dear Stranger' and 'I never ask for it' are undertaken in cities with greater membership.

Most street interventions, which are collaboratively planned through emails and online discussions, evince a carnival-like quality and a certain political theatricality, and borrow techniques from global feminist movements and protests. For example, in 'Y R U looking at me?' Blank Noise members stand in silence at traffic intersections with red reflective tape on their bodies that spells out the phrase. Once the traffic lights turn green, members disperse into the crowd, handing out leaflets on street sexual harassment. The intervention is 'gay triumphant, and at the same time, mocking and deriding' (Bakhtin 1984: 11–12) of the gendered status quo of the street, and Blank Noise hopes to disrupt the idea of 'woman as image' and 'man as bearer of the look' (Mulvey 1992: 27). The logic that prevails in the different street interventions is similar: urging women to deliberately draw attention to their bodies, engage the male gaze and register their right to public space. If eve-teasing functions as power to 'threaten one with trouble ... to keep one out of trouble', the performativity of the female body as 'unanticipated agency' 'reverses the gaze, and contests the place and authority of the masculine position' (Butler 1990: viii). While performing on the streets, women seem to remain unaffected by critics who view such performative posturing as celebrating women's victimization instead of their strength (Roiphe 1993).

As a performative critique of street sexual harassment, Blank Noise views the issue within the continuum of gendered exclusions middle-class women face in urban public spaces. For Blank Noise, eve-teasing is resolutely about the violent manifestations of the male gaze on the street, and thus the group believes that harassment can be mitigated by returning the gaze and reclaiming streets. Yet Blank Noise is also quick to understand why women do not do so, apprehending fear and specifically 'the fear of being violated' as the operating logic. Fear is thus

> often camouflaged or concealed by 'appropriate behaviour.' Mothers warn their daughters about what to wear – it must be 'respectable;' women cover themselves with shawls and stoles; middle class women do not take public transport if they can help it; young girls need male escorts at night. Fear is mitigated or mediated by denying the city: covering up the body, choosing to walk on the side of the road with no men; the ladies' special bus; the 'safe' mall over the bustling street market. (Patheja and Gupta 2007)

And so, to 'mitigate' fear, Blank Noise asks women to embody their action hero spirit. Since 2006, Blank Noise has collected over two hundred action hero testimonials, narratives written by women documenting how they did 'not surrender to the power on the street'.[5] Blank Noise's approach to breaking the silence on street sexual harassment and its attempt to formulate redress are deeply rooted in the heteroglossic 'action hero' identity; at the bare minimum, testimonials and street interventions are not written and performed by victims but by action heroes who are encouraged to document stories and tactics of resistance as well as share reasons for not responding/reacting to harassment. If street sexual harassment 'accomplishes an informal ghettoization of women' (Bowman 1993: 520) by restricting their access to work and/or educational spaces or to 'privatized spaces masquerading as public space' (Phadke 2007: 1514), Blank Noise advocates that a woman become an 'action hero', a *flâneuse* who 'engages the risk' (Phadke et al. 2009) that lurks in public space.

The ideological and techno-social space that Blank Noise has opened up has greatly benefited newer campaigns which seem to borrow from its philosophy of collective action and collective responsibility and are focused on a politics that John would call the 'autobiographical'. These include Fight-Back (2011), a Bombay-based Internet campaign against gender-based violence, Be the Change (2011), a group of students from Delhi University working on institutionalizing a 'zero tolerance approach' to sexual harassment, and Let's Talk About It (2011), a campaign led by young men in Delhi against sexism and gender-based violence. Be the Change regularly organizes protest demonstrations predicated on the idea of *Bol ke ab bus aur nahin* (Say enough, no more) and urges its Facebook followers to 'Break the Silence! Act Now!' Philosophical synchronicity apart, it is important to highlight the considerable overlap in membership, loosely defined, between Blank Noise and these newer emergent online campaigns. Similarly, in Delhi, Please Mend the Gap (PMG) has recently emerged to fight sexual harassment in urban public space. In March 2011, a young middle-class woman was molested and verbally abused on the metro in New Delhi. Her friend, Rosalyn D'mello, and D'mello's flatmate, Malini Kochupillai, were appalled at the woman's narration of the incident. Not only did most commuters turn away while the woman was screaming for help (some even asked her to quieten down), but police personnel seemed hesitant to lodge a formal complaint. Incensed, D'mello wrote a letter which went 'viral'[6] hours after being published on Facebook. The viral note also received publicity on Blank Noise's Facebook page and within the Indian blogosphere. Instead of minding the gap, a group of women and men decided to mend it, and PMG began soon after. PMG's methods include online petitioning and street-based protest performances such as flash mobs that are similar to Blank Noise's street interventions. Yet unlike Blank Noise with its creatively indeterminate politics, PMG explicitly sees itself as an advocacy group and has concrete goals; at present the group is in the process of putting forth its demands via the submission of an online petition to the Indian prime minister, the chief minister of Delhi and the head of Delhi Transport. Like Blank Noise, PMG queries protectionist vocabularies. If Blank Noise refuses to submit to the idea of modesty interpellating sexual harassment, so too does PMG, which questions the efficacy of a 'woman's only' metro compartment: 'We did not ask for a "women's only" compartment ... We're not asking for reservation. We're asking for respect.'[7] However, there are significant, if not fundamental, political divergences between both groups' approaches towards conceptualizing strategies to combat harassment. While PMG focuses on the criminality of harassment, highlighting the availability of legal redress and demanding better information relating to the legal assistance available to victims, Blank Noise remains unconvinced about the recourse to law as necessarily positive or an effective solution. Former coordinator Hemangini Gupta argues: 'Should we be allowing the state to legislate an issue where there is so much grey even with how it is understood and defined – from "looking" to physical violence?' (Angelina 2011: 67), and Blank Noise has highlighted the fact that 'natural processes of justice' are often handicapped in dealing with 'actions that violate personal and physical space', which 'are often fleeting or done on-the-run and sometimes hard/impossible to prove'.[8]

Nonetheless, these different approaches coalesce on, and reaffirm, the idea of consciousness-raising as shaping the content of online articulations and street interventions. If in the 1970s consciousness-raising was 'the feminist method' (Alarcon 1997: 289) in the Anglo-American context, through which women 'understood the world in a different way' (ibid.: 293), so too in these new formations that evince the usage of a similar political strategy. Consider PMG co-founder Malini Kochupillai's views:

> For me, the most important goal for Mend the Gap is to raise awareness among men and women across socio-economic class boundaries about what sexual harassment is, and how they can confront it, and also to educate men that this kind of behaviour is unacceptable. Women need to stop brushing harassment in public spaces off as 'men will be men' ... We have been using Facebook and Twitter and flash mobs to do this.

Consciousness-raising, then, is the larger part of what these women have set out to do, and this seems to be deeply underscored by the political-as-personal. In performative critiques of sexual harassment, women hope to subvert the male-centred gendering of urban public space. Their political praxes emanate not from any primordial form but through communication and the everyday exchange of information on blogs and in online discussion fora. The everydayness of such communicative exchange aspires to break the silence on what has hitherto been understood as a seemingly trivial phenomenon, and it does so by asking women to participate in a discursive 'collective witnessing' (Oliver 2001) of public sexual harassment. The process of witnessing, be it through writing action hero testimonials or participating in street protests, alleviates the trauma of being given 'othered subjectivity' (ibid.: 7). When women take part in such a politics of witnessing, via consciousness-raising tactics, the harm done to one's subjectivity by forms of violence can be assuaged by assuming the position of an acting subject. This potentially opens the door to another subjectivity: the action hero.

Surveillance and regulation While public sexual harassment seems to be the overwhelming focus of non-mainstream online Indian feminist politics, activism against discourses that censure women's lives in public space is also emerging, with the catalyst being an attack on a group of women and men in a pub in Mangalore, a city 200 miles from Bangalore on 24 January 2009. On the day, activists from the Shri Ram Sene, a Hindu right-wing fringe group loosely affiliated to the established right-wing parties such as the Bajrang Dal and the Vishwa Hindu Parishad, physically assaulted a group of women and men. The group declared that women were 'cocktail drinking floozies' (Susan 2009) who were desecrating Indian culture, and women wearing Western clothes were later physically assaulted in Bangalore. Pramod Muthalik, the Sene's leader, pledged to disrupt celebrations of Valentine's Day in the state, and vowed to wed unmarried couples found together on the day. The Mangalore pub assault reflects an increasing trend of 'moral policing' by state and non-state actors in urban India, manifest in the shutting down of 'dance bars', right-wing protests against obscenity and the immoral depiction of women in film and art,[9] and more generally in public-sphere discourses where culture and modernity (used interchangeably with Westernization) are discursively constructed in stark opposition.

In the wake of the Mangalore pub assault, numerous spontaneous protest politics emerged in urban India, most famous of which was the Pink Chaddi campaign that asked women to 'pub *bharo*' (fill the pub) and send *chaddis* (panties) to the Sene as a way to say 'pants to Indian bigots' (ibid.). Lawyer Namrata Kotwani, who was twenty-five at the time, notes that 'seeing the constitution die by a thousand cuts every day' in the Sene leader's media interviews swung her into action in New Delhi. At this moment of 'social crisis', Kotwani turned to the 'layer of support through the web and internet' she had at her disposal (Harcourt 2002: 154). On 3 February 2009, she sent an email to Blank Noise Project, the Caferati LISTSERV which is an online network of young Indian writers whose editor is Annie Zaidi from Blank Noise, and an Indian members-only political discussion group called SATIN, seeking participants for a protest demonstration she planned. Kotwani was convinced that India sorely needed a valentine, and on 14 February 2009 the 'A Valentine for India': Stand Up to Moral Policing campaign, made possible by an email chain, descended upon New Delhi's Jantar Mantar, a space synonymous with political protest in the city. Banner-wielding women and men chanted '*Dharam Rakshak bahut hain, samvidhan ki rakhsha kon karega?*' (There are many protectors of morality, who is going to protect the constitution?) and demanded the right to 'associate freely, as they please, when or where they like' (Kotwani, personal communication). Kotwani clarifies that the demonstration was motivated by the sense of outrage she felt at the Mangalore pub assault but impelled by the 'abridging of people's rights', not only those abridged in the pub assault. She notes:

I am concerned about law and order, freedom of expression and association, autonomy in private life, and religious choice. Muthalik was targeting inter-religious relationships in a very obvious way and our sympathies lay only with fairly affluent girls who were beaten up at the club. But what about the harassment of Muslim boys by party activists? That of course got no media attention beyond perfunctory reporting. My thought was why not organise a protest as a means of getting attention for the idea that politically we have certain rights guaranteed to us by the constitution and no one can bully a citizen one fine day merely because their sensibilities have been affected.

Though the demonstration is placed within the broader context of protecting constitutional rights and seen 'as an act of citizenship', Kotwani seems also to be driven by the need to challenge the ontology of normative moral codes and a lack of women's agency apparent in the 'patrifocal gender relations'[10] (Gupta and Sharma 2003) that the Sene's politics promoted:

I am not a champion for Valentine's Day – I'll be the first one to admit that it is an excuse for greeting card companies to sell their trashy chocolates and lame greeting cards ... But why are young middle-class women being treated like cattle and rounded up before dark every evening?

For Kotwani, unexamined moral codes are dangerously constraining for middle-class women, and this view is shared by the protesters who joined her. Many had never met each other or Kotwani and had simply responded to an online call for action. Via her protest, Kotwani interrogated and momentarily displaced the moral and gendered codes of propriety that middle-class women are supposed to uphold in service of the nation, and highlighted how the everyday life of seemingly empowered women is circumscribed by forms of violence and newer renditions of the patrifocal gaze. Paradoxically, such violence appears to increase with women's rising presence in public space. Undeterred, Kotwani and her fellow protesters, rather than submitting to the Sene, challenged what the Sene symbolically signifies. They displayed a critical consciousness and straightforwardly demanded autonomy, though not via the vocabularies of women's rights, in an environment where the threat of retribution was high.

There are indeed many parallels to be drawn between Kotwani's protest and the IWM's early street protests, not the least of which is the understanding that some protest moments may or may not change into sustained advocacy/activism. Some middle-class women seem to be drawn to these forms of protest politics and some seem to be drawn to, as substantiated by the number of women who attended it, the foreign import, the *Besharmi Morcha*. This seems to be Kotwani's greatest success – not the theatricality of the one-off protest, but the dialogues and debates she and other post-pub campaigns have enabled on middle-class women's lives with the aid of laptop, drink and underwear.

Afterword

The articulations of the political within the cyberlife of feminism in urban India are singularly premised on critiquing and challenging 'women's fundamental out-of-placeness' in public space (Phadke et al. 2009: 190). Middle-class women seem to be continuously testing the limits of what 'counts as activism, what counts as community, collective identity, democratic space, and political strategy' (McCaughey and Ayers 2003: 1–2) and are challenging the hermetic sealing of categories such as local/global, sexual/political, self/other. The rising forms and levels of violence against women in urban metropolises in conjunction with the contradictory messages of provocation, purity and desirability have ensured an epistemic 'lived messiness' of middle-class women's lives (Heywood and Drake 1997: 8). Organizing against harassment and moral policing, but contesting broader socio-political relations therein and beyond, the women researched in this chapter are aware that the locus of oppression is within their social hinterlands. It would be erroneous to read these new politics as little more than heteroglossic solipsism; these evolving forms of consciousness-raising-based organizing are at heart a collective witnessing of different, but not discrete, forms of violence. If we abjure the idea that the emerging political must have clearly articulated aims at the outset we can validate the process in action; the gradual transformation of the victimized or censured subjectivity into a collective 'action hero' identity. This is the hermeneutics of what most campaigns hope to achieve, be it Blank Noise's sustained performative advocacy, PMG's emerging initiatives, or Kotwani's demonstration. Very little of this would be possible without the Internet, which has been indispensable for the political desire of these women's anger to be put to the service of collective contentious action.

The political praxes of these women suggest synchronicity with the urban IWM's early activism. While the potential for subversion might ultimately be contained by the carnivalesque quality of these new politics, which seem to disrupt but not dislodge the status quo, consider the evolution of IWM's anti-rape and dowry campaigns. As one of the first nationwide feminist campaigns in the 1980s, these relied heavily on the 'shock value' (Gangoli 1996: 334) of street theatre. How epistemologically different is 'Y R U looking at me?' from the street play *Mulgi Zali ho* which was first staged in 1982 by activists in Bombay? Kotwani's demonstration resembles the *Holi* protests that were carried out in the 1980s by students from Delhi University against the molestation of female students. Blank Noise's utilization of culture-jamming techniques is quite similar to the irony deployed in the 'Unholy Greetings' campaign by the group Gender Study Forum against sexist language used in cards manufactured by an Indian greeting card company (Chakravarty et al. 2008).[11] Further, testimonial writing is quite similar to the 'open letter' tradition inaugurated in the wake of the Mathura rape case and subsequently reworked into letter-writing networks by LGBT organizations in India (Dave 2011). Eschewing newness as it does, there is a distinct youthfulness to middle-class women's politico-ideological repertoire, and this needs to be charted further to account for how such discursive similarity has been achieved without dialogic engagement with the broader IWM. We cannot deny, however, the borrowing of grammars from the putative

West. Unlike the early IWM, which was cautious about appropriating Western vocabularies, a new generation of middle-class women does not seem to be a priori dismissive of Western grammars solely on the grounds of their lineage. Blank Noise is not culturally defensive about its early activities, borrowing from the global Hollaback movement's repertoire; *Did you ask for it* derives some of its ontology from the North American Clothesline Project. Similarly, Kotwani remains inspired by the works of Lily Ledbetter, and in my interviews with Blank Noise members, names such as Betty Friedan and Kate Millett routinely appear. Future research must be open to a focus on what happens to feminist vocabularies when they travel.

For now, the women researched herein do not profess to speak to, or of, 'citizens without a city' (Appadurai 2001: 27) in their articulations on violence against women. They are critically reflective of how their multiple markers of privilege shape their understanding of violence, the solutions they propose, the politics they espouse, and the manner in which they do so. Not content with self-reflexivity, Blank Noise and PMG have started to think beyond the cyber and are either translating their campaigns into vernacular Indian languages, initiating bilingual campaigns or working with various civil society groups. We do need to ask, however, whether the middle-class action hero is reinforcing regimes of control over lower-caste/class men in urban areas, given the impunity with which police from the state of Uttar Pradesh targeted lower-caste/class men while carrying out 'Operation Majnu'[12] against eve-teasing in 2005. There seem to be no easy answers, but PMG and Blank Noise state that victims and perpetrators cut across age, class, caste and religion. Blank Noise has shown a remarkable ability to critique its praxes as it evolves. For example, one of its early campaigns, 'photographing the perpetrator', was stopped after heated debates ensued on its blog and internal critiques emerged within the organization as the pictures of 'perpetrators' clearly involved lower-caste/class men. Keen not to create a 'normativized framework of perpetrators' (Hemangini Gupta, personal communication) and aware of the ethical issues involved in photographing men, sometimes without their consent, Blank Noise eventually disbanded the campaign. Issues of class are thus not unacknowledged by the group and yet this perhaps explains why Blank Noise keeps ascribing to its aesthetic (i.e. public art) status which it has clearly moved on from but which provides it with the necessary 'licence' (ibid.) to do politics. While the concept of class contextualizes how Blank Noise and PMG organize and perform their politics, their activities are unsuitable to be read through the lens of millennial Indian middle-class activism (Fernandes 2004) that sociologists have contextualized as 'sociocultural anxiety' (ibid.: 2427) in relation to very specific class and not necessarily democratic interests. It is a fair assessment that many new Internet campaigns seem to be in a symbiotic relationship with visual and Internet media coverage of (middle-class) incidents in forming their political consciousness. Yet Fight-Back has today metamorphosed into a broader platform on gender-based violence after the initial politics was addressed to a specific incident of a middle-class woman's molestation covered by the visual media. Blank Noise's demands for the reclaiming of public space and Kotwani's frequent recourse to autonomy do not seem to be reproducing class interests in the name of gender, for class-based privileges such as education and employment provide women with 'greater access to public space' (Phadke 2007: 1513), but 'privilege ... does not bestow on even a limited number of women, an unlimited access' to public space (ibid.: 1514). Therefore there remains the need to formulate research trajectories that account for and locate class but are not constrained by the limits simplistic class-based analyses pose.[13]

Critiques based on the digital divide are not superfluous; notwithstanding the access the women researched herein have to the Internet, in a country of over a billion people only 12 million women use the Internet and most not within their homes.[14] (Though the online presence and cyber activities of the Dalit north Indian women's *Gulabi Gang* [pink vigilantes] must also be noted.) We do need to ask whether the reliance on Internet spaces to do politics is producing 'regulated, subordinated, and disciplined state subjects' (Brown 1995: 173) who are being afforded a sufficient degree of political agency so as not to engage with structural causality. The creative consumption of forms of global capital such as the Internet seems to produce, in the Indian case, a subject whose adoption of the 'master's tools' (Lorde 1995) is nothing new in the wider context of activists who have historically done so. Many IWM groups have contested forms of hegemony from within the systems of governmentality they seek to oppose, such as the state and NGO partnerships that arose in the *Mahila Samakhya* programmes of the 1980s.[15]

The possibility of keeping alive these new practices seems shaky; what appeared to be an open public sphere is today evolving into a corporatized private sphere within the purview of global intellectual property (IP) laws, national Internet surveillance and cyber clampdown policies. The appropriation of moral rights by the commercial platforms these women use calls into question not only the epistemic status of information ownership but ownership in itself (Mitra-Kahn n.d.). Ironically, and in part as a measure to engage with these issues, Blank Noise is open to the idea of a trusteeship or an NGO. PMG is working with *Jagori* to produce a bilingual booklet on sexual harassment, though it is keen to stress that it 'doesn't want to become an NGO or have the agenda co-opted by one' and is 'selective' about choosing organizations to work alongside (Malini Kochupillai, personal communication). While the broader IWM is debating the efficacy of the NGO model on grounds of depoliticization and the careerization of feminism (see Roy 2009), Blank Noise and PMG seem to be initiating dialogues within precisely those spaces, 'born out of the search for resources and sustainability … to support movement-building work' (Batliwala 2008: 18), which are today indicted of engendering political apathy. Never has a time for intergenerational dialogue seemed more apropos.

I hope that the deliberately provocative title of this chapter has sufficiently displaced the 'clicktivist' (White 2010) appraisals that have been recently been offered by some Indian feminists in their dismissals of online activism as being a 'click away' (Mehta 2008). Nothing seems to be more obvious than the fact that rarely do Indian middle-class women content themselves with being 'bad grrls' on the Internet (Wilding 1997). Their everyday political almost always blurs the duality between online and offline worlds; though online discourses and debates are a mode of activist praxis in themselves. Middle-class women for whom the Internet is an appendage to their everyday lives are displaying an ingenious use of Web 2.0 in service of the political and are adding to the *casus belli* of Indian feminism. By turning the feminist gaze on themselves, making the object the subject of feminist enquiry, not effortless or easy in the least, some middle-class women appear to be creating and reinventing political praxes while furthering Indian feminism's historical project to denaturalize 'woman', 'feminist' and the 'political'.

Notes

1 Web 2.0 refers to 'the proliferation of user-created content and websites specifically built as frameworks for the sharing of information and for social networking, and platforms for self-expression such as the weblog, or using video and audio sharing' (Hands 2011: 79).

2 The unwieldy category of the middle class seems to have become a catch-all term homogenizing diverse groups of people with various levels of capital and its myriad forms. For the purposes of this chapter, I find it useful to recognize Fernandes and Heller's (2006) three-pronged categorization. Therefore, when I use the term middle class, I point to women from the 'Dominant Faction' (ibid.: 500) of a group of

people 'whose economic opportunities are not derived primarily from property ... but rather from other power-conferring resources', such as access to forms of cultural and social capital.

3 Demarcating between mainstream and non-mainstream cyber feminist politics in India is essentially a political exercise. The demarcation is even more tenuous given that many new campaigns are led by a combination of veteran Indian women's movement activists and young women who are entering the feminist public sphere for the first time. In this chapter, I have chosen not to include some cyber campaigns such as *Jagori*'s SafeDelhi campaign, *Pukar*'s online research centre, which pursues online activism explicitly as a mode of activism, or *Bell Bajao*, the global NGO Breakthrough's online initiative to end sexual violence focused on educating men. Instead my focus is on campaigns that represent women's first engagement with politics in the physical and virtual public spheres. I inflect this further to focus on those campaigns which have no recourse to (or choose not to have) institutional support or funding.

4 In referring to the Indian women's movement, which 'is not a monolithic construct', I note the 'various initiatives' that 'feed into a network of women's groups and contribute to the growth of the process of feminist thought' (Phadke 2003: 4575). I further inflect this to focus on urban middle-class-led women's groups and feminist scholarship, though this 'cannot be thought of and does not claim to represent all Indian women' (Roy 2009: 353).

5 actionheroes.blanknoise.org/.

6 Going viral is the speedy spread and circulation, around the Internet, of an email, blog post, online video, online marketing campaign, etc.

7 delhibytes.wordpress.com/2011/04/18/please-mend-the-gap/.

8 blog.blanknoise.org/2001_09_01_archive.html.

9 It is important to note that protests against obscenity have also received support from feminists in India, but this support must be differentiated from how right-wing groups framed the issue. For a discussion, see Oza (2001).

10 Gupta and Sharma (2003: 280) borrow from anthropological theory to posit patrifocal gender relations as 'kinship and family structures' which give 'precedence to men over women', subordinate the 'individual to family', with 'patrilineal inheritance' and lineage based on 'patrilocal descent'. Women's roles in patrifocal relations are underscored by 'chastity and subservience'.

11 I thank Dr Pratiksha Baxi for making this point and drawing the *Holi* protests to my attention.

12 Operation Majnu is an initiative against 'eve-teasing' led by various police departments in northern Indian states. It was started in 1998 in Uttar Pradesh and in 2005 received widespread condemnation for its targeting of lower-caste/class men and physical assaults on unwed couples in urban public spaces.

13 It is important to also highlight that not all online feminist campaigns are about middle-class women. For example, the online campaign to free Soni Sori, a young primary school teacher from Chhattisgarh who was brutally tortured, sexually assaulted by police personnel and has remained incarcerated since October 2011 based

on unproven allegations that she is a Maoist, continues to be run by a team of middle-class journalists, activists, bloggers and film-makers. For more, see sonisori.wordpress.com/.

14 www.iamai.in/PCov_Detail.aspx?nid=972&NMonth=2&NYear=2006.

15 For a comprehensive discussion of the *Mahila Samakhya* programmes, see Sharma (2008).

References

Alarcon, N. (1997) 'The theoretical subject(s) of this bridge called my back and Anglo-American feminism', in L. Nicholson (ed.), *The Second Wave. A Reader in Feminist Theory*, London: Routledge, pp. 288–99.

Angelina, M. (2011) 'Digital natives' alternative approach to social change', in N. Shah and F. Jansen (eds), *Digital Alternatives with a Cause: Book Two, To Think*, Bangalore: Centre for Internet and Society, pp. 64–76.

Appadurai, A. (2001) 'Deep democracy: urban governmentality and the horizon of politics', *Environment & Urbanization*, 13(2): 23–44.

Bakhtin, M. (1984) *Rabelais and His World*, Bloomington: Indiana University Press.

Bang, H. (2004) *Everyday Makers and Expert Citizens: Building Political not Social Capital*, digitalcollections.anu.edu.au/bitstream/1885/42117/2/Henrik.pdf.

— (2009) *'Yes We Can': Identity politics and project politics for a late-modern world*, www.uvm.edu/~dguber/POLS293/articles/bang.pdf.

Batliwala, S. (2008) *Changing Their World: Concepts and Practices of Women's Movements*, Toronto: Association for Women's Rights in Development (AWID), www.awid.org/eng/Issues-and-Analysis/Library/Changing-Their-World.

Baxi, P. (2001) 'Sexual harassment', *Seminar*, 505, www.india-seminar.com/2001/505/505%20pratiksha%20baxi.htm.

Be the Change (2011) www.facebook.com/groups/234311546587591/.

Blank Noise (2005) Frequently asked questions, blog.blanknoise.org/.

Bowman, C. G. (1993) 'Street harassment and the informal ghettoization of women', *Harvard Law Review*, 106(3): 517–80.

Brown, W. (1995) *States of Injury: Power and Freedom in Late Modernity*, Princeton, NJ: Princeton University Press.

Butler, J. (1990) *Gender Trouble: Feminism and the subversion of identity*, New York: Routledge.

Chakravarti, U., P. Baxi, S. Bisht and J. Abraham (2008) 'Reclaiming spaces: gender politics on a university campus', in R. Coomaraswamy and N. Perera-Rajasingham (eds), *Constellations of Violence: Feminist interventions in South Asia*, New Delhi: Women Unlimited, pp. 218–58.

Dave, N. (2011) 'Activism as ethical practice: queer politics in contemporary India', *Cultural Dynamics*, 23(1): 3–20.

Felshin, N. (1995) *But is It Art? The spirit of art as activism*, Seattle, WA: Bay Press.

Fernandes, L. (2004) 'The politics of forgetting: class politics, state power, and the restructuring of urban space in India', *Urban Studies*, 41(12): 2415–43.

Fernandes, L. and P. Heller (2006) 'Hegemonic aspirations: new middle class politics and India's democracy in comparative perspective', *Critical Asian Studies*, 38(4): 495–522.

Fight-Back (2011) www.fight-back. net/.

Gangoli, G. (1996) 'The right to protection from sexual assault: the Indian anti-rape campaign', *Development in Practice*, 6(4): 334–40.

Gupta, N. and A. K. Sharma (2003) 'Patrifocal concerns in the lives of women in academic science: continuity of tradition and emerging challenges', *Indian Journal of Gender Studies*, 10(2): 279–306.

Hands, J. (2011) @ *is for Activism: Dissent, Resistance and Rebellion in a Digital Culture*, London: Pluto.

Harcourt, W. (2002) 'Women's activism on the Net', *Gender, Technology and Development*, 6(1): 153–7.

Heywood, L. and J. Drake (1997) *Third Wave Agenda: Being Feminist, Doing Feminism*, Minneapolis: University of Minnesota Press.

Hymes, D. (1970) 'Linguistic method in ethnography: its development in the United States', in P. L. Garvin (ed.), *Method and Theory in Linguistics*, The Hague: Mouton, pp. 249–325.

Jaffrelot, C. and P. van der Veer (2008) 'Introduction', in C. Jaffrelot and P. van der Veer (eds), *Patterns of Middle Class Consumption in India and China*, New Delhi: Sage, pp. 11–34.

John, M. E. (1996) *Discrepant Dislocations: Feminism, Theory, and Postcolonial Histories*, Berkeley: University of California Press.

— (1998) 'Feminisms and internationalisms: a response from India', *Gender and History*, 10(3): 539–48.

Lorde, A. (1995) 'Age, race, class, and sex: women redefining difference', in B. Guy-Sheftall (ed.), *Words of Fire: An Anthology of African-American Feminist Thought*, New York: New Press, pp. 284–92.

Martin, P. Y. (1990) 'Rethinking feminist organizations', *Gender & Society*, 4: 182–206.

McCaughey, M. and M. Ayers (2003) *Cyberactivism: Online activism in theory and practice*, New York: Routledge.

Mehta, K. (2008) 'Women's movements in India', *Seminar*, 583, www.india-seminar. com/2008/583/583_kalpana_ mehta.htm.

Menon, N. and A. Nigam (2007) *Power and Contestation: India since 1989*, London: Zed Books.

Mitra-Kahn, T. (n.d.) *Hollaback, Grrl: (Cyber)feminist praxis and emergent cultures of online feminist organizing in urban India*.

Mulvey, L. (1992) 'Visual pleasure and narrative cinema', in M. Merck (ed.), *The Sexual Subject: A Screen Reader in Sexuality*, London: Routledge, pp. 22–34.

Munshi, S. (2004) 'A perfect 10 – "modern and Indian": representations of the body in beauty pageants and the visual media in contemporary India', in J. H. Mills and S. Sen (eds), *Confronting the Body*, London: Anthem, pp. 162–81.

Oliver, K. (2001) *Witnessing: Beyond Recognition*, Minneapolis: University of Minnesota Press.

Oza, R. (2001) 'Showcasing India: gender, geography, and globalization', *Signs*, 26(4): 1067–95.

Patheja, J. and H. Gupta (2007) 'Fear as experienced by women in their cities', Paper presented at 'Dealing with fear: what holds societies together', Akademie

Schloss Solitude, 18–20 October, www.dealing-with-fear.de/Symp1/patheja_gupta.html.

Phadke, S. (2003) 'Thirty years on: women's studies reflects on the women's movement', *Economic and Political Weekly*, 38(43): 4567–76.

— (2005) 'Some notes towards understanding the construction of middle-class urban women's sexuality in India', in R. Misra and R. Chandiramani (eds), *Sexuality, Gender and Rights: Exploring Theory and Practices in South and Southeast Asia*, New Delhi: Sage, pp. 67–81.

— (2007) 'Dangerous liaisons: women and men: risk and reputation in Mumbai', *Economic and Political Weekly*, 42(17): 1510–18.

Phadke, S., S. Ranade and S. Khan (2009) 'Why loiter? Radical possibilities for gendered dissent', in M. Butcher and S. Velayutham (eds), *Dissent and Cultural Resistance in Asia's Cities*, Oxford: Routledge, pp. 185–203.

Putnam, R. (1995) 'Bowling alone: America's declining social capital', *Journal of Democracy*, 6(1): 65–78.

Roiphe, K. (1993) *The Morning After: Sex, Fear and Feminism*, Boston, MA: Little, Brown.

Roy, S. (2009) 'Melancholic politics and the politics of melancholia: the Indian women's movement', *Feminist Theory*, 10(3): 341–57.

Sen, S. (2000) 'Toward a feminist politics? The Indian women's movement in historical perspective', World Bank Working Paper Series no. 9, www.onlinewomeninpolitics.org/india/indian.pdf.

Shah, N. (2010) 'Knowing a name: methodologies and challenges', in *Digital Natives with a cause? Thinkathon*, Position papers, Museum of Communication, The Hague, pp. 13–33.

Sharma, A. (2008) *Logics of Empowerment: Development, Gender, and Governance in Neoliberal India*, Minneapolis: University of Minnesota Press.

Sunder-Rajan, R. (1993) *Real and Imagined Women: Gender, Culture and Post-Colonialism*, London: Routledge.

— (2004) 'Real and imagined women: politics and/or representation', in L. Racow and L. A. Wackwitz (eds), *Feminist Communication Theory: Selections in Context*, Thousand Oaks, CA: Sage, pp. 187–202.

Susan, N. (2009) 'Why we said pants to India's bigots', *Observer*, 15 February, www.guardian.co.uk/commentisfree/2009/feb/15/india-gender.

White, M. (2010) 'Clicktivism is ruining leftist activism', *Guardian*, 12 August, www.guardian.co.uk/commentisfree/2010/aug/12/clicktivism-ruining-leftist-activism.

Wilding, F. (1997) 'Where is feminism in cyberfeminism?', www.obn.org/cfundef/faith_def.html.

Wolcott, P. and S. Goodman (2003) 'Global diffusion of the Internet I: India: is the elephant learning to dance?', *Communications of the Association for Information Systems*, 11: 560–646.

Women in Cities International (2010) *Learning from Women to Create Gender Inclusive Cities: Baseline Findings from the Gender Inclusive Cities Programme*, www.womenincities.org/pdf-general/gicp_baseline.pdf.

6 | Illusive justice: the gendered labour politics of subnationalism in Darjeeling tea plantations

DEBARATI SEN[1]

Amid the colourful, happy faces of Nepali tea pluckers on Indian television and the occasional newspaper article about the abuse of trafficked Nepali women in Delhi, there is a striking paucity of information and research about the political involvements of average Nepali women (plantation workers) in their community's quest for political autonomy within India. In this chapter, I inscribe the centrality of women in contemporary Nepali politics and locate the gendered historical consciousness that women have developed amid important political transformations in Darjeeling. I use Nancy Fraser's conceptual distinctions between 'politics of recognition'[2] and 'politics of equality' (Fraser 1997, 2000) to frame the specificity of political transformations in Darjeeling, but move beyond the recognition–redistribution dilemma to locate Nepali women plantation workers' complex positionalities within Nepali struggles for political and cultural autonomy. I contend that an intersectional feminist approach is essential to address the limitations of the recognition–redistribution dilemma in aiding a well-rounded understanding of women's strategic positionalities within Nepali subnationalism.[3] This approach helps us understand the gendered ramifications of subnationalism in India's north-east as well as locate the specificity of Nepali women's subjectivities within discussions of contemporary South Asian feminisms.

It is too easy to characterize women plantation workers' political actions either as a struggle for subnational and ethnic recognition, whereby Nepali males set the political agenda, sidelining women labourers' wage bargaining issues, or as simply a struggle for more labour rights, wherein women encounter male domination in all spheres of their lives, such as household, community, workplace. The multiple marginalities of Nepali women plantation workers (i.e. their marginalization in their workplaces, in the households and as Nepalis, since they are part of a minority community in India) make them complex subaltern agents for whom cultural 'politics of recognition' has material and affective consequences in their communities and workplaces. The latter articulates a politics of equality which has symbolic and gendered implications.

The gendered marginalization of women in Darjeeling remains embedded in a political field (Ray 1999) with mutually overlapping social, political and ethnic terrains that deny women plantation workers both respect and higher wages. Hence it is crucial to apply a feminist intersectional lens and account for ethnicity and gender within a single framework to understand women's cultural struggles in Darjeeling, to extend and reformulate Fraser's 'recognition–redistribution' dichotomy, and emphasize their intertwining to take note of women's complex positionalities within Nepali subnationalism. I argue that women's agency within Nepali subnationalism has to be understood in terms of place-based meaning-making that attends to their everyday work and household practices of negotiating patriarchy. Meaning-making is as much economic as it is a cultural redefining of oneself in the midst of multiple marginalities. I contend that meaning-making occurs through an appropriation of the language of subnationalism, i.e. the politics of recognition, to reinterpret workplace and household situations in bolstering claims for higher wages and other kinds of redistribution of power and resources within the plantation hierarchy. The concept of meaning-making helps us discern how women plantation workers code their equality claims in the language of ethnic exceptionalism and recognition (as hill women). It may seem that Nepali women plantation workers are giving in to dominant male hegemonic plans about Darjeeling's future. However, I see such place-based meaning-making practices as interruptions to the suppression and silencing of women's voices within subnationalist politics, as revealed to interlocutors like me during ethnographic encounters. Women's narratives point to the evolution of a particular form of gendered historical consciousness through which Nepali women plantation workers find a way to express how political shifts in Nepali labour and ethnic politics have engendered 'interstitial politics' (Fraser 1997; see also Sen 2009, 2011). The post-communism cultural politics of subnationalism helped women address issues of structural violence, by having the freedom to express themselves as proud *pāhāḍi*[4] workers, but such modalities did not question other forms of structural limitations facing the Nepali workforce. Nepali women plantation workers, irrespective of their present political affiliations, feel that the Gorkhaland movement has empowered them in some aspects of their lives as much as it has disempowered them in other arenas. To elucidate my point further, I offer an ethnographic vignette.

One crisp winter morning Lachmi, a tea plucker, and I set out to meet the other twelve women plantation workers in her tea-plucking group whom Lachmi oversaw. Lachmi was in a particularly bad mood that day, lamenting her inability to negotiate a job for her youngest son in the plantation bungalow as a guard. As we walked away from her home into the plantation she pointed out to me a Nepali male *chaprāsi* (field supervisor) and said to me, 'Do you see him, sister; they are the bane of our existence, those *chamchās*.[5] Here I am, always encouraging the girls in my group to work hard so that our company makes more money, and here they are, roaming around all day and misreporting to the manager and owner to prove their efficiency.' In response to this comment, I asked Lachmi why there were no women field supervisors – *chaprāsis*. She replied:

> There is no reason why we women cannot become *chaprāsis*, but who will fight that battle? Are the unions of any use? They are only interested in Gorkhaland and *partybazi*.[6] Our *sāhib*[7] always listens to the wrong kind of people, the insincere Nepali men, who tell him that women are untrustworthy and drink too much – worthless. We might not know how to run the country like Indira Gandhi, but we know how this plantation works and we are *pāhāDis*; we work harder than people in the plains.

Encapsulated in Lachmi's words are deep frustrations with the plantation manager and his male henchmen's close surveillance of women workers. Also notable is anger over the local labour union's preoccupation with *partybazi* without engagement on any questions of women workers' empowerment. Her sarcastic comment about India's first female prime minister has to be contextualized as disgust for the negative sexualized representations of the 'Darjeeling Girl' (Leichty 2002) through which Nepali women have become the 'other' of mainstream Indian femininity. Her negotiation of these existing frustrations is articulated through pride in a *pāhāDi* identity, which many plantation workers used as a motivational reference for their toil. In doing so they defended the essentialized image of a hill worker that the male leaders of the Gorkha National Liberation Front (hereafter GNLF) carefully constructed, and it was a key cultural trope through which the broader Nepali community maintained its distinction in the local economy of difference; distinguishing them as people of substance, different from the Adivasis in the plains and mainstream Indian identity. Ethnic pride and loathing for sexist labour practices perpetuated within Nepali politics mark the complexity of women's political engagements in Darjeeling.

Thus a feminist understanding of women's agency in Darjeeling's tea plantations must acknowledge that women are not only marginalized as labourers within tea plantations; they are also stereotyped and sexualized as untrustworthy subjects within the middle-class Indian discourse of femininity and the patriarchal Nepali community. Additionally, women are also part of the Nepali community, which is itself culturally marginalized with the Indian nation. Therefore women are marginalized in complex ways resulting from 'multiple patriarchies' (Chatterjee 2001) and their ethnic, economic and political manifestations. In response to such multiple marginalizations, women use cultural tropes of an essentialized *pāhāDi* identity. These symbolic tropes hinder the possibility of raising important work-based issues in the plantation, such as the need for new shoes in the monsoon or a small loan for their child's education. Yet a job for the male members of the household, claims for which are couched in languages of ethnicity and subnationalism, also has material consequences for these women. Thus, Dorothy Hodgson rightly points out that production and reproduction of minority identity, whether ethnicized or subnationalist, in response to larger political economic forces, is a gendered process (Hodgson 2001).

These gendered everyday material and discursive manifestations of the 'politics of recognition' are absent from the existing literature on subnationalism in India (Kohli 1997; Dasgupta 1997). The paucity of information about the creativity of poor women in Darjeeling is perpetuated by the increased media focus on and scholarly interest in the struggles of the broader Nepali community within India. The latter focuses on diagnostic moments of ethnic anxiety, decentralized territorial arrangements and forms of violence (Samanta 1996; Lama 1996), in which men are disproportionately represented, barring a few instances in which women become martyrs. But a detailed ethnography of everyday realities (Roy 2007) helps us move beyond seeing Nepali women as victims, silent bystanders or heroes. Instead, it upholds women's complex subjectivities, and how through their labour and influence women uphold the symbolic economies of struggle, the critical cultural work they do to make the movement meaningful for average people, despite dictatorial and corrupt leaders, and setbacks in the movement.

South Asian feminists have engaged with the question of women's agency within existing production systems (Banerjee 1991; Fernandes 1997), calling attention to the multiple overlapping forms of oppression women suffer because of 'multiple patriarchies' (Chatterjee 2001;

Lynch 2007). Existing works on women's marginalization within labour unions focus on informalization of the production process, formation of masculine entrepreneurialism among labourers who exploit other labourers (Chari 2004), and domination of trade unions by regional and national-level political parties (Fernandes 1997). What requires closer examination are relations between a community's desire for subnational autonomy and the work-based subjectivities of women, who are part of a feminized labour force and bear the brunt of multiple marginalizations and patriarchies.

Relating subnational desire and workplace dynamics is essential for complicating the relationship between ethnic identity formation and working-class politics in India. Ethnicity, within discussions of working-class identity formation and mobilization, either has been seen as a force fragmenting the working class, or is overlooked by trade unions in creating greater solidarities. These are important starting points for comprehending the relationship between ethnicization and labour union politics, but I provide a different angle to these approaches by looking at ethnicization of working-class identity in the context of 'multiple patriarchies' (Chatterjee 2001) within the working class: patriarchy in the households, male domination in the labour unions, and plantations run by upper-class Nepali men and non-Nepali groups. Women plantation workers' desires have to be understood against the backdrop of a struggle to be as respectable as the male members of their society and in conjunction with their struggle to be included as equal cultural citizens in India.

Following Deborah Elliston, I suggest we need a 'more dynamic and processual theorization of labor as a social practice by situating it within a much larger field of social practices and meaning'. I emphasize, through the findings in this chapter, that the microprocesses of labour, or place-based meaning-making of labour, provide an opportunity to acknowledge the complexity of subnational politics, related desires and their workplace manifestations. These everyday realities of labour in Darjeeling's plantations reveal that 'political subjectivities and positioning are themselves produced and enacted and in ways that are in deep dialogue with social projects of (re)producing difference and hierarchy' (Elliston 2004: 625).

In the rest of the chapter, based on seven years of intensive ethnographic research, which includes detailed interviews with 146 plantation workers from four plantations in Darjeeling and adjoining areas, I begin with a discussion of contemporary Nepali working-class politics in Darjeeling and existing work-related stereotypes about Nepalis in

India. This is followed by a discussion of the emergence of Nepali pride and its workplace ramifications and another section on the conflicts between workplace justice and the desire for cultural recognition. The last section, based on workers' narratives, locates the effects of subnational desire on worker identity.

The rise of Nepali ethnic pride and gendered reinterpretation of plantation work

Popular interpretations of the Gorkhaland movement locate it primarily as a subnational movement for greater recognition of the marginality of Nepalis and for promoting greater inclusiveness and more rights for Indians of Nepali descent by creating a separate state – Gorkhaland. The modalities of this ethnic struggle had important gendered implications for plantation labour processes, as stated by Lachmi in the opening section. Women plantation workers' public support for their 'home-grown' movement, necessitated by the search for greater respect for Nepalis as Indian citizens, also created a silence around labour issues in general and women's labour issues in particular, which were not seen as this movement's priorities or were regarded as a distraction.

The first thing that strikes anyone on a tea plantation is the monotony of the labour process. Workers begin plucking tea leaves very early in the morning, with a short break for lunch. They work in bands of ten to sixteen, usually supervised by a Nepali male *chaprāsi* and occasionally managers who walk around checking the quality of plucking, but also to see whether anyone is slacking.

The strictures of this low-paying routinized work affected women's perception of themselves as labourers, compounded by the absence of any union support for their needs and intense envy within households generated by their economic opportunities. They frequently used the word '*lati*' (stupid, ignorant) to describe themselves. In their statements to me, there was emphasis on gradually becoming more stupid, almost implying that plantation work produces this negative effect on workers. Another phrase that recurred in their conversation was '*hami bolnu birsechu*', 'we have forgotten how to speak'. The latter expressed their fear of arguing with the managers and senior male members of their community.

These negative reflections were aggravated by the poverty of their daily lives. They blamed the plantation for all their misery and complained incessantly about the lack of proper pay and effective unions. Phulrani, now fifty-two years old, told me: 'Of course our condition is a bit better than when I started. Then we were threatened that we would be stripped naked if we did not pluck and clean well. The managers and *chaprāsis* were abusive. Even now they are very harsh, but at least we get our salaries.' She then said, 'The last good thing that the union did for us was in 1984 [pre-GNLF], when they fought for making most workers permanent, and soon after, the retirement benefits started. That was twenty years ago. Our wages are little compared to what the times demand, but we have been doing the same work for ages.'

Phulrani, in her comments, was referencing the mid-1980s, when the Marxist parties – such as the CPI(M), Communist Party of India (Marxist) – still dominated labour unions and modalities of plantation labour politics were different. Her comments also allude to the absence of any discussion over plantation workers' wages and living conditions in the new turn towards an identity-based local movement brought about by the GNLF.

The references to being 'stupid' and 'losing the power to speak' were always connected with the growing lack of options in women plantation workers' conversations. There was also a notion of being tied to the dictates of the *thikā*/wage, which recurred in my interviews about work and plantation life in Darjeeling. The phrase implied the discipline imposed by the insufficient wage that limited workers' economic options, and the lack of any demand for a wage increase on the part of unions. The small wage limited the scope for better education for their children. It made workers dependent on informal money-saving ventures. I also interpreted the use of the phrase 'being tied to the wage' as a way for plantation workers to express how other systems of patriarchal control worked through the wage. Women workers could never ask for more wages because the management was tied by the state permitted minimum wage, which was uniform through the Darjeeling area. However, the dictates of the *thikā* were made ever more binding by the male union leaders devoting their attention to the needs of the local political party, the GNLF. *Thikā* was used to denote the strict disciplining of their work life, and the verbal abuse from the male managers and male supervisors, which governed how women lived and worked in the plantation premises.

To cope with these strictures women workers often displayed ethnic pride in everyday conversations about work to describe their sincerity and skill. This was also a way for them to counter the existing gendered stereotypes about Nepali workers within India, which the plantation managers and Nepali supervisors used against them to discipline them more. Male plantation managers and NGO workers repeatedly cautioned me about the three Ws in Darjeeling that any respectable person has to reckon with: Women, Weather and Wine. Apparently the three things were untrustworthy and could not be relied upon and lead to the many obstacles of everyday life in Darjeeling, plagued as it is by chronic male unemployment and socio-economic underdevelopment. These images, popularized by colonial and post-colonial institutions and the dominant Indian middle class, mask important questions of injustice that face women from Darjeeling, ironically at times perpetuated despite their own communities' mobilization efforts. These images dominate how women plantation workers find meaning in their everyday work lives.

The use of *pāhāDi*-ness[8] was therapeutic, as this provided plantation workers with a chance to reinterpret their work life in meaningful ways. The investment in seeing oneself as hard working, sincere and skilled was psychologically gratifying in a climate of intense disciplining within plantations and male domination at home. Women desired to present themselves honourably, to outsiders like me, and also to themselves, since they wanted to live up to middle-class norms of respectability against which their popular images were formed. This is where the subnational desire and systems of identification were instrumental; the home-grown union run by GNLF provided women with a new language to understand and cope with their marginality. Nepali workers could now freely express their pride in being Nepali, which was not possible within CPI(M)-dominated unions. The management also strategically engaged in meeting the ethnic needs of their workers by building Nepali Buddhist temples, holding Hindu ceremonies and involving workers, or sending out text messages in order for a Nepali boy to win the *Indian Idol* contest.

Most plantation workers I came across expressed their marginality by referring to themselves as *pāhāDi*, seeing themselves as different from people in the plains. It is not a simple class-, race- or caste-based difference, but implies personality type, with characterizations such as 'simple', 'hard working', 'loyal' and 'honest'. It implies a particular kind of personhood. Among Nepalis in India, the invocation of *pāhāDi*-ness was pronounced because Nepalis found in this usage an effective way of maintaining their distinctiveness from plains people, whom they perceive as oppressors, as cunning, smart and privileged. *PāhāDi*-ness simultaneously expresses marginality and pride/difference. Nepali plantation workers took pride in their *pāhāDi* identity. Many Nepali women would say, '*hami pāhāDi majale kām garchu*', 'we *pāhāDis* work with great zest', or '*India lai bachaunu ko lagi pāhāDi lāi chahincha*', 'to save India you need a pāhāDi' (alluding to the presence of Nepalis in the Indian army and as guards in Indian homes). Political parties in the hills also used *pāhāDi*-ness strategically to build local party loyalties. These careful self-interpretations were also critical for the development of a gendered historical consciousness among women plantation workers. In their referencing of the pre-GNLF period (in Phulrani's comment and Chhaya's later) one can discern how women developed a deep understanding of the structural inequalities facing them, even within their own party and GNLF unions.

Cultivation of *pāhāDi*-ness meant being good workers who were not interested in disrupting work. This was a way for Nepali workers to maintain their distinctiveness from the plains plantation workers, which continues even today, as reflected in Lachmi's comments. In the post-Gorkhaland movement period from 1989 to 2007, the local state and labour unions in Darjeeling were dominated by the GNLF. During 2005–07 (before the second Gorkhaland movement),[9] the focus of the GNLF was on getting the Nepali people in Darjeeling recognized as 'tribal' so that they could get special benefits from the federal government. This involved the 'reinvention' of Nepali 'tribal' tradition, although the majority of the Nepali people adhered to the Hindu caste system, and observed various religious and cultural practices depending on caste affiliations. However, preoccupation with this new cultural turn defined the focus of the party and the local state in the late 1990s and early 2000s.

Since its inception, the GNLF positioned itself as different from the plains people's parties, especially the Marxist parties, such as the CPI(M). The left-wing unions had no room for specific Nepali concerns and no place for Nepali pride. Making Nepali people conscious of the stigma of the 'red' party and its principles was a deliberate move to engender a new politics of difference to break away from corrupt hegemonic communist unions. Adherence to any of the principles of the 'red' party was considered incongruous with the political demands of the emerging Nepali state within India. Therefore, the worker-centric policy of the communist unions did not receive priority on the GNLF agenda.

One of the offshoots of this differentiation was that the GNLF encouraged plantation workers to work hard and not engage in militant trade unionism, which was a marked feature of unions in the plains. Many women workers told me that they understood the value of work because this was the only way they could survive. Workers in Darjeeling distinguished themselves from non-Nepali workers in the plains, who, according to my informants, were communists and did not want factories to survive. As proof of this claim they cited the numerous plantation closures in the plains. It seemed from their narratives that the unions in the plains tea plantations were uselessly conducting a movement to stop work, just because of their party affiliation. In my interviews, workers like Lachmi expressed their opinions about unionization, along with Nepali pride. Expressing pride was a positive motivation for average Nepalis, who had to suffer the consequences of negative stereotypes about them.

In regular conversation workers always related their hard work to the quality of the tea produced, as if their labour were of a different kind, like their ethnicity, climate and environment. These frequent statements implied that the distinct flavour of Darjeeling tea was a direct result of the value of the Nepali labourers. Workers creatively used their knowledge about the distinctions between aromatic/ expensive teas within India to project their ethnic identity in strategic ways. Workers knew about the high price of Darjeeling tea since they were all but forbidden to consume this green gold. Factory supervisors checked whether women from the sorting department were stealing tea. Nepali pride in work was always laced with complaints about the lack of water supply within plantations, lack of restrooms at work, the undemocratic plantation practices, and union-busting. However, the hegemonic ideology of GNLF's current vision became meaningful for average workers because of pre-existing desires for self-recognition. These self-proclamations about being hard-working *pāhāDi* workers, on the other hand, became beneficial for the GNLF in putting labour issues on the back burner.

Male GNLF members were constantly engaged in making the 'Nepali community' more conscious about its ethnicity. Being equal citizens of India and gaining respect became the priority, not improving the existing conditions of labourers within Darjeeling. A survey of documents (Samanta 1996) at the time of the formation of the Darjeeling Gorkha Hill Council reveals that the demand for Gorkhaland was accompanied by a request to increase the quota for Nepali men in the army, the abrogation of the Indo-Nepal Treaty of Peace and Friendship, and more direct funds from the central government in Delhi for general development of Darjeeling. The central government, which also regulates the wages of plantation workers through the Tea Board of India, was never requested to increase the wages for plantation workers. Gorkhaland became a panacea for all the evils that existed within Darjeeling. The consequences of hegemonic subnational politics are evident from everyday conversations. The celebration of and adherence to this *pāhāDi*-ness has produced certain kinds of silences in the workplace, as I discuss in the next section.

Desire for workplace justice versus desire for ethnic recognition

Like Lachmi, most women complained that honest women workers were never adequately rewarded because of the lack of a 'system', implying rampant nepotism in the plantation and the absence of a systematized collective bargaining mechanism to voice these demands. The constant reference to the 'system' alluded to the gendered structural inequalities in the plantations, which prevailed despite the plantation owner's new interest in meeting his workers' ethnic needs. Women workers often made a distinction between the patterns of union activities. Older women workers (who were adults during the Gorkhaland agitation or had worked for many years) claimed that when communists dominated the unions, the union leaders were always looking for reasons to embarrass and challenge the management. The primary focus was to improve the quality of workers' lives within the plantation. So leaders took notice of women workers' issues. Even if leaders did not tell the management about the need to promote women tea pluckers to the position of clerks or *chaprāsis*, they would push for raising the compensation for each extra kilo of tea leaves plucked, and since women plucked more, they made more money.[10] Eventually, with the popularity of ethnic issues during the Gorkhaland movement of the 1980s, the concerns of union leaders shifted to the building of a hegemonic Gorkha identity. For decades there have been no specific demands for a wage increase.[11] I was told by women in Sonakheti, the union's energy was devoted elsewhere, to motivating the unemployed Nepali male youth to work for their party and fight the battle for a Nepali homeland. Men acceded because of rising unemployment and the hope that party work would eventually secure employment in the Darjeeling Gorkha Hill Council, a decentralized administrative body formed after the first Gorkhaland movement in 1989.

The GNLF did not have a pronounced and active women's wing, although it enjoyed public support from most women plantation workers, and in many instances coerced families to send one woman representative to *dharnas* (meetings). One of the older plantation workers once told me, 'The male members of our families do not care about us, they are jealous and they talk about us badly, although we do everything to keep them happy.' Women were only too happy to see the male youth get involved with the union–party nexus; the latter offered potential for making important contacts in the local state, run by native politicians. The union leaders, however, failed to create as many jobs for male youth after the Hill Council was formed and Darjeeling received partial autonomy from the state of West Bengal. Instead of working with plantation owners to hire more male workers, the GNLF politicians used the labour and time of male youth for their own ends. Male relatives of the plantation workers sometimes found temporary employment, if they were lucky.

Unlike other places in Asia, where kin community ties were used to contest the commodification of labour in the absence of unions (Ong 1987), in Darjeeling women were apprehensive about using such ties to mitigate workplace inequities because of the envy that existed in their communities about their paid work. Women plantation workers found that participation in the unions was useless. However, they silently hoped that the unions would do something for their sons, brothers or husbands. Women plantation workers joined their male counterparts at important political party events and public demonstrations as a show of solidarity. Women plantation workers in Darjeeling did not have to bear the brunt of 'deterritorialization' (Collins 2002) like their counterparts in Bangladesh or Mexico because their workplaces did not relocate; these workplaces did, however, present them with a situation of intense disciplining which even their struggles for justice could not deflect, as Chhaya outlines in her comments below.

Chhaya and I were neighbours in one of the plantation villages. She was illiterate and could barely sign her name. She was among the most talked-about women in the plantation because of her past labour activism. She was the leader of the Communist Party's Women's Wing, *Mahila Samity* (Women's Organization), when the unions were dominated by communists. Chhaya, now forty-eight, started as a child labourer in Sonakheti when she was ten years old. She was an active union member, and she changed parties – from the CPI(M) to the GNLF – in 1984, when the GNLF started dominating the labour unions. Though she shared the subnationalistic urge to secure Gorkhaland with other members of her plantation community and was a proud *pāhāDi*, she somehow found the preoccupation with Gorkhaland in Darjeeling's plantation community stifling.[12] Chhaya told me that she used to hide from the local GNLF men in the community and go to the CPI(M) meetings in Siliguiri and Darjeeling when the first Gorkhaland move-ment was brewing in 1986. Once the GNLF had started the movement, no other party or political opinion was tolerated.[13] In fact the situation in Darjeeling continues to be that way; many of my informants feel pressured to join the new Gorkhaland movement because of fear of violence and of becoming unpopular in their communities.[14]

Chhaya argued that there were problems in the present GNLF-dominated union. She liked unions because she expected them to provide a sense of community, a fellowship of concerned people, who shared their ideas and understood each other's workplace problems. But she did not get that from the present GNLF union. She told me that from the beginning she liked the way CPI(M) trained them to understand workplace politics. I urged Chhaya to talk more about her activism and her views on the 'union problem'.[15] The following are excerpts from Chhaya's interview, which upholds her subjective reflections about the transitions in labour union politics:

> CHHAYA: In the beginning there was no politics. But slowly problems began with our bonus and other benefits and a union was formed. Every plantation should have a union; it is an absolute necessity for our daily problems. Earlier we consulted the union in the smallest of disputes. This is why the union was important. But now there are no regular union meetings to discuss our issues. Now you see no one; they are all busy in Kurseong or Darjeeling town. Come election time, they will not let you rest in peace because they want our votes.

> DS: What did you learn from your experiences in the union when you were active?

> CHHAYA: I used to meet women who were older than me in Kurseong. Women in important positions in the Women's Wing of the Communist Party urged me to head the *Mahila Samity* in the plantation. I listened to them and learnt a lot. I used to travel to all the units in Sonakheti with some other women; we listened to each other's experiences and problems; tried to find solutions to each other's problems. I even went to Calcutta to consult senior members of the party. There was a lot of sharing and planning and a great sense of camaraderie. The party and the union worked out a system for dealing with the management.

> DS: You say that the union is a necessity. So what is the state of the present union at Sonakheti?

> CHHAYA: I was in CPI(M). During the agitation time, the older men in our locality came and explained to me that I should join the GNLF. As a Nepali, it was my duty to join our local party, so I joined. But I used to hide and go to all the CPI(M) meetings in Siliguri, Kalimpong, Kurseong and Darjeeling town. I almost did not survive once as our vehicle

was pelted on our way to Darjeeling to attend the CPI(M) meetings. Those were troubled times, but in my heart I always liked what CPI(M) taught us, although I hated the *Bongali babus*[16] in the CPI(M).

The GNLF always talked about 'Gorkhaland'. CPI(M) on the other hand emphasized rights and entitlements of the average poor workers who are not looked after well in the plantation system. GNLF is not interested in the issues of workers; they are only interested in making us understand the significance of our land and making us conscious of our identity as Nepali. Yes, I understand the significance of the land we live in; we have lived here for so long, and our forefathers toiled here. There was no doubt that 'Gorkhaland' was important for us because we need a place in India we could call our land. Technically, it was my duty to support the party of the hills that championed this cause. But that is not enough. There are other very important issues besides land. When I look deep inside my heart I do not like the principles on which GNLF operates today. I think the issue of workers' rights has taken a back seat in the plantation. Before, we used to think how to take up these issues with the plantation management; we used to strategize. Our party used to teach us how to negotiate and talk to big people in difficult situations. As small people, illiterate people, it was important for us to learn these strategies. We had friends in different plantations, we used to have important meetings and shared information about how we small people could fight and negotiate with the management. Our leaders in the CPI(M) used to ask us to think about the most important things for our life as workers and then teach us how to place it before the management. If the management did not agree then we would have to let the leaders know and they would have a meeting with the planter *sāhib*. We had to choose our issues well. Our 'company', our '*sāhib*', is like a parent; you cannot fight with them on any old issue, and you have to be judicious to further our cause. One has to learn to strategize.

Within GNLF the preoccupation with Gorkhaland stood in the way of placing workers' concerns before the management. This preoccupation with the issue of Gorkhaland is the source of all problems in Darjeeling. It has been twenty years since GNLF gained power. There are no jobs, and the youth do not know what to hope for. But I don't feel motivated to attend the present union meetings because they are not concerned about workers' rights.

More than twenty years after development of the first Gorkhaland movement in 1986 and the formation of the decentralized autonomous Darjeeling Gorkha Hill Council (DGHC) in 1989, lives of women in

Darjeeling – like Chhaya's – help us contextualize what the search for ethnic recognition and the subnational desire for a Nepali state have meant for the labour rights of women workers within the plantation community. Women cherish their desire to be respected as Nepali workers and want their state – Gorkhaland – to become a reality. Chhaya's comments, like Lachmi's, uphold the externalities of transitions in Nepali politics and the gendered historical consciousness that evolved with them. Women were well aware of the limitations of the equality-based struggles of communist labour unions in which Nepalis had to blend in and could not own their distinctiveness. This is evident in Chhaya's aversion to the Bengali party bosses of the CPI(M). Within GNLF unions, however, the language of ethnic need permeated their self-understanding to make them respect the Gorkhaland cause despite male domination. Chhaya and Lachmi are now both active members of the local GNLF, but the politics of everyday life in the plantations, and their respective negotiations against the backdrop of the ethnic pride movement, have resulted in deep subjective ruminations about the position of women and their concerns within present Nepali politics.

Conclusion

It was the summer of 2007. The mood was upbeat in a tea plantation village. The monsoons were weeks away. Women in the household had finished plucking tea leaves and completed other household chores for the day in preparation for watching *Indian Idol*. This season of *Indian Idol* was very special for the villagers because Prashant, a Nepali soldier and native boy from Darjeeling, was among the top claimants for the title, competing with talented singers from other regions of India. Prashant's significance in the moral world of Nepali women was revealed to me in a comment made by my host, *Ama* (mother of the house), while she checked on people who had come to watch TV in her house to see whether they needed pre-paid mobile phone vouchers to vote for Prashant when the TV anchors declared voting time. As we gathered in front of the TV, *Ama* told me with great excitement, 'We have to make Prashant win, we know he might not be the best singer out there but he is *our* boy, he made us proud. We have stood by our boys despite the many challenges we face every day at work and home, we have protected them always, and this time he is going to win.'

Read through the lens of my years of engagement in this community, the comment upheld a crucial aspect of the Nepali tea plantation workers' subjective feelings about their role in Nepali subnationalism in general and nurturing Nepali boys in particular, despite the intense male surveillance of their lives. *Ama*'s statement, 'this time he is going to win', helps contextualize the feelings of disappointment that permeate the subjectivities of Nepali people who failed to get a separate state, Gorkhaland, during their movement for it in the 1980s, hence the tone of determination. Further, her comment 'We have stood by our boys despite many challenges' is a reflection of the resolve of Nepali women plantation workers to support their male family and community members in a scenario where male unemployment and substance abuse had reached their height. It heightened women's desire for respectable inclusion in their 'home-grown' subnationalist movement for a separate state, hence *Ama*'s comment 'We have stood by our boys ... we have protected them', etc.

Women are the backbone of Darjeeling's economy and politics, contributing effectively to the local subnationalist politics geared towards gaining more autonomy from the state of West Bengal. They are also subjects of intense envy in the local community because of their economic opportunities. In illuminating the complex positionalities of women plantation workers I have used and extended Nancy Fraser's (1997) framework of understanding the externalities of identity-politics-based movements and their effects on broader equality-based social movements. What is remarkable in the case of Darjeeling was that a shift in union politics from a 'politics of redistribution' (workers' equality) to a 'politics of recognition' (ethnicized minority politics) intensified the neglect of workers' needs and rights, especially women workers' rights and needs (see also ibid.). However, unlike Fraser, who is very critical of identity-based 'politics of recognition', I emphasize the complexity of the latter. Politics of recognition might engender inclusive possibilities despite its silences, as I show throughout this chapter. Women plantation workers (like *Ama*) see symbolic and material value in redistribution of household monetary resources to community males, who struggle for recognition in a national polity in which they are marginalized. *Ama* had bought mobile phone vouchers for villagers from her small salary so that everyone could cast their votes for the local boy. Politics of recognition is operationalized in subnationalist feelings of respectful ethnic recognition coupled with the desire for more jobs for men when Gorkhaland is formed. Recognition politics in one place thus intertwines with demand for redistribution of power in another. This intertwining of the symbolic and the material makes politics of recognition inseparable from redistribution because one has implications for the other, especially when the nature of exploitation is a gendered or feminized labour force.

The rule of *thikā* still binds women's lives, and they suffer from a constant feeling of deprivation at the same time as they see themselves as agentive, skilled women responsible for the distinct taste and aroma of Darjeeling tea and, according to Lachmi, the smooth running of the plantation. This pride has shaped how Nepalis in Darjeeling district have conducted their everyday lives, set priorities at work and engaged in activism in the face of the massive cultural marginalization that they face in India. These practices have defined their commitments to social justice by nurturing a desire for a separate state. Women plantation workers, in their process of simultaneously constructing 'individual selves and collective identities' (Jeffrey and Basu 1997), locate themselves within competing priorities. Their practices are significant in terms of protecting a separate Nepali working-class identity, distinct from communist ideology and mainstream nationalist labour ideology, while simultaneously producing the everyday gendered discourses of subnationalism.

PāhāDi-ness is both empowering and disempowering. It provides women workers with a chance to imagine an existence in a context of respect. It is also through this empowering self-interpretation of themselves as good workers that this ethnic movement uses women's work-related practices of self-representation, their labour and influence, to push for a more masculinist political agenda within the existing struggles for Nepali autonomy. The process, I show further, marginalizes women as workers at the same time as their desire for inclusion is stoked.

Notes

1 The research for this chapter was funded by a Wenner Gren Foundation Individual Research Grant (no. 7495) and an NSF DDIG grant (no. 0612860). Special thanks to Srila Roy, Dorothy Hodgson, Leena Her and Sarasij Majumder for engaging with drafts of this chapter and their critical comments. I remain responsible for any other errors pertaining to this manuscript.

2 Early scholarship on the 'politics of recognition' concentrated on the efforts of marginalized groups or citizens within a nation to gain public recognition and prominence (Taylor 1992: 34). The formulation was used to highlight the limitations of liberal justice systems, under which people belonging to specific cultural groups were not respected or represented in public institutions. Fraser (1997), through a discussion of the 'recognition–redistribution' dilemma, challenged the contours of the liberal democratic models of justice. For her 'politics of recognition' was expressed in the 'New Social Movements', which made identity politics the centrepiece of struggles.

3 By 'subnationalism' I refer to the political and cultural struggles of Nepalis in India who face cultural marginalization within the Indian

nation. Nepali workers migrated to Darjeeling and adjoining areas in the early 1800s to work in the tea plantations of the East India Company and they have lived there ever since. They have been fighting since the 1980s for their own homeland – Gorkhaland – a separate state for them within India. The movement was spearheaded by the Gorkha National Liberation Front (GNLF), a local political party devoted to the ethnic cause of Nepalis in India. This struggle has taken various forms, but recently it has centred on the preoccupation among Nepali leaders with creating a unified Nepali identity, which I refer to in this chapter as the 'cultural politics of subnationalism' and frame as a form of 'politics of recognition', using Nancy Fraser's (1997) terminology. The first Gorkhaland movement began in the 1980s, culminating in the formation of Darjeeling Gorkha Hill Council, a semi-autonomous administrative unit within the state of West Bengal. Since 2007 a new movement has begun to revive the cause for statehood for Indian Nepalis living in Darjeeling, India.

4 The Nepali word *pāhāDi* means people belonging to the hill areas. It denotes a particular kind of place-based identity distinguishing Nepalis from people in the plains. People in Darjeeling tend to think that they are not as cunning and opportunistic as plains people.

5 Henchmen of the plantation owner, supposedly his favourite Nepali male supervisors.

6 *Partybazi* implies working for the local political party, in this case the Gorkha National Liberation Front (GNLF), which was fighting for greater cultural and political recognition for Nepalis of Indian descent

living in Darjeeling and other places in India.

7 Another name for the plantation owner. It is also spelt *Sāhib*, but in Darjeeling it is pronounced differently and hence I use *sāhib*.

8 I use *pāhāDi*-ness as an expression of Nepali or hill people's pride in India.

9 Since October 2007, Darjeeling has been under the sway of the second Gorkhaland agitation, this time led by Gorkha Janamukti Morcha (GJM), a breakaway party from the GNLF.

10 Apart from a daily wage of Rs53 ($1.28 at the time of this research) in the peak seasons of tea production, women received a bonus payment if they plucked leaves beyond the daily requirement.

11 While the wage for plantation workers is set by the central government, small adjustments are always made internally. The rates for extra tea leaves plucked in the peak season would vary; sometimes workers were also compensated for extra cleaning work if the plantation owner was generous. Festivals were also an important occasion on which to get free meals.

12 Chhaya's views about the coercive politics of GNLF are shared by many women workers, some of whom are not as articulate as Chhaya and did not share her leadership qualities. Women who were not explicitly critical of GNLF were extremely nostalgic about past union activism and the colonial period, and also complained about the rise of nepotism and the uselessness of unions in raising wages and looking after their concerns.

13 Criticizing the leaders of the 2nd Gorkhaland Movement, an opposition party leader in Darjeeling

expressed concern over the undemocratic methods of the movement's push for social justice in an English newspaper. The GJM (Gorkha Janamukti Morcha) is being accused of diverting attention away from many other problems in Darjeeling by promoting this single-issue movement. The new Gorkhaland movement, initiated in 2007, has made economic development a major issue in its propaganda.

14 Phone interview with Chintamani Rai, December 2007.

15 The phrase 'union problem' was often used in English to emphasize the dismal state of the unions in Darjeeling.

16 This refers to Bengali male leaders of the Communist Party. Nepalis have a very fraught relationship with Bengalis given their desire for autonomy from West Bengal, dominated by Bengalis. The latter also perpetuate stereotypes about Nepalis in daily interactions, just like other mainstream Indians.

References

Banerjee, N. (1991) 'The more it changes the more it is the same: women workers in export oriented industries', in N. Banerjee (ed.), *Women in a Changing Industrial Scenario*, New Delhi: Sage.

Basu, A. (1992) *Two Faces of Protest: Contrasting modes of women's activism in India*, Berkeley: University of California Press.

Bladez, L. (2002) *Why Women Protest: Women's movements in Chile*, Cambridge: Cambridge University Press.

Breman, J. (2003) *The Labouring Poor in India: Patterns of exploitation, subordination and exclusion*, Delhi: Oxford University Press.

Chari, S. (2004) *Fraternal Capital: Peasant-workers, self-made men, and globalization in provincial India*, Stanford, CA: Stanford University Press.

Chatterjee, P. (1989) 'Colonialism, nationalism and colonized women: the contest in India', *American Ethnologist*, 16(4): 622–33.

— (2001) *A Time for Tea: Women, labour, and post/colonial politics on an Indian plantation*, London: Duke University Press.

Collins, J. L. (2002) 'Deterritorialization and workplace culture', *American Ethnologist*, 29(1): 151–71.

Dasgupta, J. (1997) 'Community, authenticity, and autonomy: insurgence and institutional development in India's northeast', *Journal of Asian Studies*, 56(2): 345–70.

Elliston, D. A. (2004) 'A passion for the nation: masculinity, modernity and nationalist struggle', *American Ethnologist*, 31(4): 606–30.

Fernandes, L. (1997) *Producing Workers: The politics of gender, class and caste in the Calcutta jute mills*, Philadelphia: University of Pennsylvania Press.

Fraser, N. (1997) *Justice Interruptus: Critical reflections on the post-socialist condition*, New York: Routledge.

— (2000) 'Rethinking recognition', *New Left Review*, 3: 107–20.

Hancock, M. E. (1999) *Womanhood in the Making: Domestic ritual and public culture in urban south India*, Boulder, CO: Westview Press.

Hodgson, D. L. (2001) *Once Intrepid Warriors: Gender, ethnicity and the cultural politics of Maasai development*, Bloomington: Indiana University Press.

Jeffrey, P. and A. Basu (eds) (1997) *Appropriating Gender: Women's activism and politicized religion in south Asia*, London: Routledge.

Kohli, A. (1997) 'Can democracies accommodate ethnic nationalism? Rise and decline of self-determination movements in India', *Journal of Asian Studies*, 56(2): 325–44.

Lama, M. (1996) *Gorkhaland Movement: Quest for an identity*, Darjeeling: Nathu Press.

Leichty, M. (2002) *Suitably Modern: Making middle class culture in a new consumer society*, Princeton, NJ: Princeton University Press.

Lynch, C. (2007) *Juki Girls, Good Girls: Gender and cultural politics in Sri Lanka's global garment industry*, Ithaca, NY: Cornell University Press.

Ong, A. (1987) *Spirits of Resistance and Capitalist Discipline: Factory women in Malaysia*, Albany, NY: State University of New York Press.

Ray, R. (1999) *Fields of Protest: Women's movements in India*, Minneapolis: University of Minnesota Press.

Roy, S. (2007) 'The everyday life of the revolution: gender, violence and memory', *South Asia Research*, 27(2): 187–204.

Samanta, A. (1996) *Gorkhaland: A study in ethnic separatism*, Delhi: Khama Publishers.

Sen, D. (2009) 'From illegal to organic: Fair Trade organic tea production and women's political futures in Darjeeling, India', PhD thesis, Rutgers University, New Brunswick.

— (2011) 'Measured invisibility: *ghumauri* and the challenges of worker organizing in Darjeeling plantations', Conference paper presented at the First Association for Nepal and Himalayan Studies Conference, 28 October.

Taylor, C. (1992) *Multiculturalism and 'the Politics of Recognition': An essay by Charles Taylor*, Princeton, NJ: Princeton University Press.

7 | 'Speak to the women as the men have all gone': women's support networks in eastern Sri Lanka

REBECCA WALKER

Sitting in the shadowy darkness of another evening of power cuts in Batticaloa, Ranjini[1] turned to me and commented, 'Batticaloa is like a cemetery. Everything is dead and broken.' It was March 2007, and I was back in Batticaloa in eastern Sri Lanka after a seven-month break in the UK for my final month of research. My host family, of whom Ranjini was a member, had warned me that things had changed since my last visit and that the situation had become much worse. My return coincided with a dramatic intensification of the government's attempts to clear the LTTE (Liberation Tigers of Tamil Eelam) from the Eastern Province. What I and others did not know at that time was that this period of fighting marked the beginning of the end of the war between the Tamil Tigers and the Sri Lankan government. The offensive, which saw the LTTE routed from the east by mid-2007, then shifted its focus to the north of the island, capturing the LTTE's de facto administrative capital of Kilinochchi, in January 2009. Finally, in May 2009, after trapping the LTTE on a small strip of land along the north coast along with thousands of civilians, the government of Sri Lanka declared victory.[2] This last brutal and bloody battle brought the end to a conflict which has ravaged the island of Sri Lanka for almost three decades.

It was during the early signs of the final offensive in January 2005 that I began my fieldwork in Batticaloa, a district situated halfway down the east coast of Sri Lanka.[3] Batticaloa has been one of the most disrupted and devastated areas of the island since the conflict started in the early 1980s. Framed on either side by the sea and the lagoon, the district forms part of the northern and eastern regions of Sri Lanka that the militant group, the LTTE, drawn from the island's minority Tamil-speaking population, sought to secure and establish as a separate state, which they called Tamil Eelam.[4] With Sinhala, Tamil and Muslim populations having almost equal presence with areas of ethnic concentration, the diverse demography of eastern Sri Lanka stands in contrast to the northern province, where Tamils are the dominant group (McGilvray 2008). Marked by occupation, Batticaloa is a town that has been under the control of different military groups; the Sri Lankan army (SLA), the Indian Peace Keeping Forces (IPKF) and the LTTE. A split in the LTTE in 2004 had also led to the Tamil Makhal Viduthalai Pulikal (TMVP – Tamil People's Liberation Tigers), informally backed by government forces, challenging the military rule of the Tigers. Despite being militarily much weaker, the TMVP were successful in gaining control of Batticaloa and bordering eastern regions (HRW 2007).

A time of uncertainty

At the time of my arrival in Batticaloa in January 2005, Sri Lanka was also just coming to terms with the enormity of the tragedy of the 2004 South Asian tsunami, which on the east coast alone had taken more than three thousand lives, devastated homes and livelihoods and left thousands more displaced (WHO 2005: 1). Against the backdrop of an unravelling ceasefire, failed peace talks and a chaotic tsunami response, the political situation, which had experienced a temporary reprieve after the tsunami, was once again worsening day by day. The power cuts were a part of this – a result of shelling by the Sri Lankan army from their main camp in the centre of Batticaloa town.

Like many other places of conflict, Batticaloa represents a mosaic of intricately woven lives and histories with allegiances and opinions sutured across critical boundaries and spaces. The nature of people's mottled identity and the narrowing of spaces can be seen starkly in the way that the LTTE and other armed groups target 'traitors' based on suspicion and fear of betrayal (see Kelly and Thiranagama 2009). Although inhabitants of Batticaloa learnt to live with experiences of violence, they have had to do so in continuously threatening and unsettled environments. While men often joined an armed group, or were forced into hiding from the security forces or LTTE/TMVP, women took on the challenge of survival. Caring for their families, they had to find ways to provide for them financially and to deal with the daily realities of displacement, risk and fear. This was also within a context where Tamil women were constricted by the ties of the gendered ethnic discourse of 'the good Tamil woman' (Schrijvers 1999: 329).[5] The reality of life for women in the east was captured in the words of a Catholic priest, who told me, 'If you want to know what is happening in the east you have to speak to the women as the men have all gone.'

It is the experience of women dealing with the everyday violence which interests me in this chapter. Taking the example of an informal human rights group known as the Valkai group, composed mainly of women, I consider the ways in which women have created networks and negotiated paths across spaces of violence, fear and isolation. In Tamil 'Valkai' means 'Life', and this name was selected to reflect the group's aims, to support and protect human life. It also reflects their ethos and belief that their work should be an integral part of daily life in eastern Sri Lanka rather than a distinct and separate activity. Activities were organized around a weekly meeting when group members came together to share information and concerns about the present situation. Over twenty-three months of fieldwork, I lived and worked with members of the Valkai group, including a married couple, Anuloja and Jeevan, and their close friend, Ranjini.[6]

Focusing on the Valkai group in this chapter, I consider how the experiences of women actively working through and against violence can be understood within a framework of feminist activism and, in turn, how the boundaries of such a framework are challenged. As a group that consciously worked with feminist and activist ideas yet explicitly rejected categorization as a feminist activist group, the Valkai group bring into focus something that is unique and yet not unfamiliar in the conflict areas of Sri Lanka. They represent what I will argue is a unique stance of feminist activism in moments of conflict, and particularly at a time when it has been suggested that the mainstream women's movements in Sri Lanka have turned away from the complex work of peace and survival (De Alwis 2009: 85). In fact, just as the plight of women during conflict in Sri Lanka has been well documented, so has the demise of women's and feminist movements, which, it has been argued, have most often succumbed to the hegemony of political and militant groups. Basing her understanding on the fragmentation of women's activism, which has often been diluted by NGO-inspired projects of 'women's empowerment' and 'gender sensitization', Malathi de Alwis argues that '[t]oday, there exists no autonomous feminist peace movement in the country, and the voices of feminist peace activists are rarely heard nationally' (ibid.).

Drawing from the experiences of one of the main Valkai members, Anuloja, in this chapter I question the ways in which feminist activism has been understood. This is in order to question the boundaries that have been drawn around the work of feminists and activists which indicate a dimunition of the role of women actively engaging in opposition to militarism and war. Instead I suggest that work *is* being done by women, within and through everyday experiences of violence and fear, and its apparent invisibility and quietness are the very factors that enable it to continue. This is work that demonstrates both the impact of conflict on women and the strategies of survival, which more often than not are made possible and sustained by women. It is not only about coping and about finding safe spaces but is instead the product of a creative effort to work with what is at hand and what is possible at a given time while challenging the overall structures of militarism, state terror and denial of atrocities. The questions raised in this chapter therefore demand a broader reconceptualization of gender, violence and the activism that coheres around these ideas. I do this by first looking at how women and violence have been understood in Sri Lanka through the lens of women's groups and a critique of feminist activists. Then, taking the work of the Valkai group, I consider how it sits outside current understandings of feminist activism in Sri Lanka. In conclusion I reflect on what the Valkai group might suggest for the future of feminist activism, as understood contextually, in the moments of conflict and peace in Sri Lanka.

Women and violence in Sri Lanka

The different paths taken by women in response to the violent disfiguration of everyday life in northern and eastern Sri Lanka have frequently been approached by feminist scholars through the concept of space, which considers women relationally, within specific settings (e.g. De Alwis 1997, 2004; Schrijvers 1999; Rajasingham-Senenayake 1998, 2004). A growing body of research has transgressed conventional approaches in anthropology and development studies, for example, by considering the cross-cutting issues of war, displacement and recovery for women (Hyndman and De Alwis 2004; Ruwanpura and Humphries 2004). Such transgressions are crucial for understanding how women have been affected by multiple factors and the constraints and limitations they face in trying to rebuild lives. However, these studies have also tended to highlight the more visible and extraordinary roles played by women, and have therefore neglected the less visible daily practices of women (and men) who have worked through and against the spaces available to them.

The role of women in Sri Lanka, throughout the decades of conflict, has also raised some interesting questions about gender identity, particularly given the number of armed women combatants who have taken (not always by choice) the path of violence, and the increasing number of women as the primary income generators and heads of household.

For many, this has been encapsulated within the dichotomous 'suffering' and 'resilience' trope, in which the struggle for women, particularly Tamil-speaking women, through conflict is translated in terms of the 'empowerment' of women's lives (Coomaraswarmy 1996: 10). This is contrasted with the traditional role of the Tamil woman in which she is seen as circumscribed by gendered norms (see Thiruchandran 1999). Based on research with Tamil women in refugee camps during the 1990s, Schrijvers notes that between the two extreme images of the Tamil woman as soldier and suicide bomber on the one hand, and the poverty-stricken, dependent refugee on the other, new identities have emerged. These new identities embody what Schrijvers (1999: 307) suggests are 'ideals that come very close to the Sri Lankan feminist discourse', according to which women assert themselves in the public and the private sphere, renegotiate gender power relations and increase their autonomy and self-esteem. While Rajasingham-Senenayake (2004) deals with this debate by stressing that these new roles for women create a sense of 'ambivalent agency' in wartime situations, I suggest that this counters the realities of war in which women suffer intolerably through displacement, widowhood, sexual abuse and marginalization. It can also be argued that by taking on greater responsibilities in the community, women have became more vulnerable, by nature of their gender and bodies (Thiruchandran 1999).

Sri Lanka has a long history of women's activism and has witnessed the formation of various coalitions, organizations and fora to address women's issues. Some of these organizations and fora have been formal and structured, such as women's NGOs and local fora; others have been based on informal and therefore less visible ties of connection. In the mid-1980s the Mothers' Front (following the example of the Mothers of the Plazo de Mayo – *Madres de Plaza de Mayo* in Argentina) formed, first in the north and then the east of Sri Lanka. According to Samuel (2006), this was at a time when women were increasingly joining the ranks of 'freedom fighters' within the LTTE while simultaneously focusing on their role as mothers in response to increasing state repression. Women activists, notes Samuel, claimed that the use of the identity of motherhood was a 'necessary form of "protection" in a climate where state repression was at its height and opposition to military presence and military activity was fraught with danger' (ibid.: 27). However, despite repeated attempts to demonstrate, protest and demand the return of their children, the increasing threat and violence directed at the Mothers' Front led to its overall weakening as an organization for political change. In the end, with the breakdown of the Indo-Lanka Accord and the increased control of the LTTE, the Mothers' Front was unable to retain its political voice (ibid.: 32).[7] In contrast, De Alwis (2004) points out that the formation of a Mothers' Front in the south of the island in 1990 to protest against the 'disappearance' of their male kin during the 1987–90 uprising was more successful than its northern and eastern counterparts. Despite being founded and funded by the main opposition party at that time – the Sri Lanka Freedom Party – and therefore implicated in political patronage, the group managed to occupy 'an important space of protest at the time when feminist and human rights activists were being killed with impunity' (ibid.: 685). By forcing the political sphere to address what was represented as the non-political and natural issues of motherhood, the movement continuously 'put the political into question' (ibid.).

The fate of the northern and eastern Mothers' Fronts reflected a pattern of decreasing space for many women's organizations that attempted to challenge patriarchal norms of war and conflict and sought to replace these with ethics of dialogue, negotiation and con-sensus (De Alwis 2009; Samuel 2006: 59). There have been many other examples of the work of women and feminist groups and the simul-taneous loss of space and silencing of oppositional voices in Sri Lanka. Often the informal networks have grown out of the failures of formal organizations to adequately address the needs of the poorest, such as widows, the elderly and the landless, serving their own agendas instead (Goodhand and Hulme 1999: 27).[8] Ruwanapura notes that although a number of women's organizations and NGOs have specifically sought to support widows in the north and east of Sri Lanka, the majority of widowed heads of households have continued to face a constant battle for economic stability, privacy and physical safety.[9] Therefore women, particularly widows, have developed informal networks built up around experiences of loss and marginalization to provide support for one another in adverse situations. However, this kind of support tends to be intermittent and/or temporary and less often in monetary forms (Ruwanpura 2006; De Alwis 2002; Ruwanpura and Humphries 2004). Some of these have been formal and structured networks, e.g. women's NGOs and local fora; others have been based on informal and therefore less visible ties of connection. The Valkai group was therefore not the only group focused on human rights in Sri Lanka or in the east, nor was it the only group of women working together.

Providing a critique of feminist organizations in Sri Lanka, De Alwis suggests that many have shifted from strategies of 'refusal', which include forms of non-cooperation, civil obedience, strikes, etc., to strategies of 'request', such as signature campaigns, charters and petitions. This in turn has rendered many feminist projects often indistinguishable from projects of governance: '[b]y increasingly mobilizing strategies of request, feminist peace activists in Sri Lanka have primarily shifted to appealing to and making requests of the state' (De Alwis 2009: 6). This understanding is based on the fragmentation of women's activism, where De Alwis argues intervention has often been diluted by NGO-inspired projects of 'women's empowerment' and 'gender sensitization' (ibid.: 85). She notes the lack of an autonomous feminist peace movement and that the voices of feminist peace activists are rarely heard nationally (ibid.). She attributes this to the same groups of feminists being stretched to support the multiple campaigns on women's issues alongside the institutionalism and professionalization of feminism. The latter in particular can be recognized as a 'sticking point' for feminist organizations through co-option and codification of local organizations by larger donor organizations and development aid. While providing funding they also narrow frameworks, forcing the recipients to devise strategies of 'request'. This has been noted not only in South Asia but also as an effect on women's groups globally (Menon 2004; Cockburn 2007). However, while recognizing the critique of contemporary feminist groups, it is also important not to romanticize earlier feminist networks, for as we have seen, they struggled precisely because of their lack of support and protection, exposing women to the violence of the state (De Alwis 2009).

Therefore, between the vulnerability of the less-defined feminist networks and the overexposure and standardization of women's feminist activism as a 'profession' (Menon 2004: 219–20), we seem to have lost a sense of what can and is being done by women actively challenging violence and subordination. I suggest that it is not that such work is not being done but that the *way* in which it is carried out – as everyday strategies and tactics of negotiation and risk – transcends the categories through which feminist activism has thus far been understood. While the 'lack of visibility and voice' identified by De Alwis is palpable in the working sphere of feminist organizations and NGOs in Sri Lanka, it does not necessarily account for the networks of women (and men) in eastern Sri Lanka who are carrying out critical and vigorous work and in many ways align themselves with the feminist peace movement. These networks may not have an obvious voice and they remain largely invisible on the surface of everyday life; however, it is also these very factors which enable them to continue effectively. As the next section demonstrates, the fact that women are working against everyday claims on space by those with guns does not always reflect choice or an opportunity afforded by conflict but reflects a matter of *having* to negotiate and challenge in order to survive. Yet at the same time this is done with a consciousness of the limitations of women's movements and civil society and the failure of local and international NGOs. Moreover, it is done in accordance with the realities of conflict in Sri Lanka, where those who speak out and act openly immediately face the risk of detention or death. Therefore, in recognizing the critique of feminist activism and acknowledging the work being carried out actively by women, the questions we then need to ask are: How do we understand the role of these informal and fluid networks? How do we locate such groups in the sphere of Sri Lanka's feminist activism and, furthermore, do we need to categorize these groups in order to consider how a post-conflict Sri Lanka can move forward?

The next section of this chapter moves on to consider the formation and role of the Valkai group in eastern Sri Lanka. It is a story that cannot be told separately from the life experiences of Anuloja. As one of the founders and key figures in the Valkai group, Anuloja played a pivotal role in its shaping and direction, and her narrative is therefore a narrative of the group. While she does not claim to represent all the Valkai members, Anuloja's experiences highlight the essential role played by the group and the strategies of the women's informal support networks through the prism of everyday experiences.

Anuloja and the Valkai group

Originally from Colombo, Anuloja had married a Tamil man from Jaffna and settled in Batticaloa in 1994, when, along with Ranjini and another woman, she decided to open a branch of a women's NGO in Batticaloa. This was at a time when many families who had been displaced from the east were being forcibly repatriated. From this point Anuloja and Ranjini began their close relationship with many families, particularly the *ammas* (mothers) in villages around Batticaloa. Anuloja described how she felt a need to go to the villages where people had been left isolated and in fear and to find a space to reach out to people. She stated that the more she become involved with the *ammas* the less she felt like being part of the NGO.

> Although they did some very important work I needed to be free to make my connections with the other women. It was the women who were dealing with the daily risks – going to the camps to look for their

husbands, looking after their children and trying to provide for them. I couldn't work with programmes and funding problems, I needed to just be there with the women.

Anuloja talked about how she became involved in supporting legal work to help the relatives of Tamil detainees in Colombo prisons and also, later, in counselling for released detainees who had been severely tortured by the Sri Lankan government. She also joined a local Peace Committee (of all men) to record and document abductions, disappearances and killings in the area, and working with families whose children had been abducted by the LTTE. Meanwhile, she set about making her own connections with families too, following up on cases of child abductions, disappearances and killings and bringing together mothers of the disappeared. 'People step in and out of our journey here,' Anuloja commented as she recounted her experiences with the many different people, local and foreign, who at various times had worked alongside her, supported her activities, and often lived with her too. Many who came to visit would become part of the family and were folded into the everyday life of this Batticaloa household. From this single household, friendships and contacts extended far out across towns and villages in the east, to Colombo and areas on the south coast and up to the northern area of Sri Lanka.

The choices Anuloja made to live in the east and pursue human rights work separated her from the original social groups (defined by ethnicity and caste) of her family. She chose to follow the journeys of those directly affected by conflict and to pursue the idea of locating, shaping and creating spaces for women to connect across and through violence. The informal meetings and discussions with the wives of young men detained by the army and the mothers of children taken by the LTTE were formative experiences for Anuloja and helped her see more clearly the route she thought her life should take.

The Valkai group had formed from a series of weekly meetings organized by affected local citizens and a small number of international workers in Batticaloa and surrounding border areas. Although the group formed after the tsunami, most of the members had lived and worked in the north and east for the majority of their lives, focusing on work with torture victims, support for abused and war-affected women and advocacy work for women's and human rights groups. Family visits were mainly to the relatives of people who had been victims of violence, and were intended to offer support – emotional and practical – to the families where possible. Assistance was provided in terms of connecting women to create support networks. For example, a woman whose husband had just been killed would be connected with another widow who knew the processes of obtaining a death certificate. Or if women from the east had to go to Colombo to seek news of their husbands detained by the security forces, then Colombo-based people would receive them and provide support during their trip. This was always done on an informal basis and with careful attention to the security risks. Activities such as meetings for mothers of forcibly recruited children and tree-planting ceremonies for the families of people killed were also organized. In one instance, Anuloja accompanied a group of women whose husbands had been abducted or killed by the LTTE, to Kilinochchi, the LTTE headquarters, where they demanded information about their husbands and signed statements reporting their cases. This was an incredibly risky move on the part of the mothers and Anuloja. By challenging the LTTE in this way they were making themselves highly visible and vulnerable to a group that was well known for callously disposing of anyone who opposed or appeared to oppose its totalitarian rule. Describing the activity, Anuloja noted, '[T]he *ammas* were the focus because they were the ones leading the way. The ones who could do things. That, to us, is putting women first and being activists for women.'

Yet at the same time one of the most important messages of the Valkai group was that although it was predominantly made up of women, and it was primarily women from whom they collected information and stories, they recognized that men also suffered irrevocably through conflict. This was not just as fighters; but as grandfathers, fathers, uncles, brothers and sons. Men also grieved for their loved ones, sought out strategies to survive and imagined a different everyday. As Segal notes, until recently an understanding of men as victims of violence and facing experiences of 'bodily fragmentation and abuse' has largely been ignored (2008: 32). Lawrence (1997) points out that during the 1990s in Sri Lanka a disproportionate share of men aged between twenty and forty-five years of age lost their lives. Although this age range is the prime fighting age it does not mean that most men died fighting; Lawrence documents the simple fact that being within that age range and therefore possibly a fighter made men suspect and at risk of arbitrary arrest, torture and disappearance throughout the war. Men had to learn to minimize their movements and visibility, avoiding checkpoints and the market in order to reduce the risk of getting arrested; instead, women took on these tasks. The Valkai group did not therefore focus exclusively on women but instead took account of the different roles that men and women could play in a context of risk and violence, and acted accordingly. It was then women who succeeded in forming connections and pushing open spaces, and most often this was against boundaries set by men with guns. In this sense the story of the Valkai group is a gendered story. Yet to consider the group only in these terms is to silence a much greater vision of the Valkai group and to ignore the fact that both women and men worked in and beyond their capacities to push for change.

Feminist activism as 'active living'

To recognize these kinds of activities as part of a group process, but also beyond the mandate of most official organizations in the east, reveals how the Valkai group operated in the face of danger while existing in a fluid form that always sought to minimize risk. Where most feminist activist groups sought to highlight the plight of women and provide assistance through aid and education, the Valkai group worked fluidly with what was at hand. Members emphasized the fact that their roles were defined by the choices that they made, based on a set of practices grounded in what could be done in the present context. Where they pushed boundaries and opened spaces, they also embedded their work in the crevices of life already present, making it a form of what they termed 'active living', rather than what might be labelled 'activism' (while recognizing that activism itself is not a homogeneous term). Cues were taken from the *ammas*, the majority of whom had experienced the loss of a spouse, parent, child or other family member, and therefore had themselves spent long periods of time riding the thin edge of survival in order to endure the violence. While the group intentionally tried to create change through networking, at the same time this was done in accordance with and as an extension of the role and strategies that individuals and families across the east were already practising rather than as new forms of activism. This was what distinguished them from many of the local and international agencies in eastern Sri Lanka. For all their good intentions, many of these agencies prioritized being known and recognized for their work, reproducing the patron–client-type relationships that tend to define non-governmental work in Sri Lanka, particularly in the aftermath of the tsunami (Stirrat 2006: 11; De Silva 2008: 2). The tactics and strategies used by the Valkai group to create close networks of consolation and cooperation as 'active living' were not defined by violence, nor were they free from it; instead they fluidly moved through and around the violence that existed in everyday forms. 'Active living' therefore transcended a defined and categorized form of action, demanding a broader understanding of what we understand by activism in conflict areas.

An example of this kind of activism is illustrated by the activities organized by the Valkai group, such as meetings for mothers whose children had been forcibly recruited and tree-planting ceremonies. Focusing here on the latter activity, the idea of tree-planting developed from a desire to bring families who had lost loved ones together in a non-threatening way with a focus on life, nurturance and growth, creating a space where they could share their stories. Families that had recently 'lost' loved ones (through death, disappearances or abductions by the army, LTTE, TMVP or other armed groups) were contacted and visited and then invited to participate in the ceremonies if they so wished. During the ceremony, photographs were placed in the middle of a room surrounded by small oil lamps. Over them, the silky leaves of young coconut tree saplings bowed. One tree for each life lost. The families themselves had decided upon the idea of planting trees and had wanted coconut saplings because of their multiple uses in everyday life. The tree was to be an active and 'growing' reminder, and one that could be tended into the future. This was not a traditional way of marking death in eastern Sri Lanka, but it was one which would not be marked out as unusual in everyday village life, and for the families, in terms of their fear, this was paramount.

One of the women involved in one of the first tree-planting ceremonies was a mother called Duwatha. In August 2005 the body of a young woman who had been raped and murdered was discovered in a schoolyard in the centre of Batticaloa town. As the body, which was badly bruised and battered, hadn't been identified, it was taken to Batticaloa Teaching Hospital, awaiting someone to come forward. News of the body had spread quickly in Batticaloa, but as usual in the town when rumours start to flow and stories abound, silences also crept in and froze information at the edges. For weeks no one came forward to claim the body and eventually a hospital porter buried the young woman in an unmarked grave. A few weeks later Duwatha approached one of the women from the Valkai group who also worked for a woman's organization that had marked the death of the young woman with a silent vigil. Together with the Valkai group, Duwatha established that the body in the schoolyard was indeed her daughter.[10] Duwatha's participation in one of the tree-planting ceremonies was significant because until that point she had not spoken to anyone other than two Valkai group members about the loss of her daughter. In the ceremony, however, Duwatha found a space to momentarily let those feelings out. The shape of the ceremonies allowed those who wanted to speak the space to do so, while those who preferred to stay silent were also respected. It was only after other individuals had spoken of losing their loved ones that Duwatha started to weep in tortured sobs. Remembering those sobs, Anuloja noted that when the tears were finally able to flow Duwatha had still remained guarded and fearful – aware that the ties that currently held her in a network of support remained tense and fragile.

Ties through loss

While Anuloja's narrative cannot represent the experiences and views of all the Valkai members (and her thoughts are particular to the journey of a self-aware and courageous woman), concomitantly they demonstrate the act of finding a way to live and to imagine a future in the east. They reveal how women can find small pathways and cracks in which to manoeuvre while trying to keep below the parapet, and how the pushing of boundaries can take place in discreet private spaces as well as in more public ways. The Valkai group emerges as an extension of this idea and represents a space in itself where a group of people could come together to share experiences and needs. The group was also a catalyst in searching for cracks and gaps in the structures of control to reach others and widen the networks of trust, principally among women. While my focus here has been on the role of women, I have shown that the Valkai group itself has not intended to discount the role played by men. Instead, the experiences of the group have revealed the extent to which gender shapes Tamil-speaking communities in creating norms and conventions which can often shape the limits and possibility of actions and agency. In Batticaloa this has meant that women, while facing increasing vulnerability and violence, have become more visible in their endurance of the everyday, and in some cases have used this as a strategy to widen spaces to support others.

Although many of the women were acting out of desperation and necessity rather than choice, I suggest that the strategies they devised revealed their determination and endurance, and demonstrated their attempts to map out a path ahead despite its lack of tangible shape or form. The strategy of the Valkai group was to dwell in the spaces of vulnerability and loss, thus allowing the process of grieving to take place in spaces which were often ambiguous and tense but also intimate and new. We can relate this to Judith Butler's argument in *Precarious Life* that the fecundity of grief and loss, which by nature of their universality make 'a tenuous "we" of all of us', can create ties which can become productive in creating new forms of connectability and sociability (2004: 23). Engaging with matters of life and death, with burial, grief and mourning, in a critical analysis of the post-9/11 appropriation of grief by the USA, Butler proposes that our proclamation of loss comprises a mode of address to others wherein we reveal our vulnerability. Through enduring such loss, we initiate a new circuit of communication with others, and from this, a basis for new forms of political community can be engendered through our exposed vulnerability and dependency on one another. This idea of using our dependency on others, and mobilizing vulnerability, as a means of transcending fear and forging connections with others resonates with what we have witnessed through the ties between the Valkai group and many of the mothers (and fathers) across eastern Sri Lanka. De Alwis (2009: 90) interprets Butler's argument in terms of recognizing spaces for a different kind of politics, one that pushes the boundaries of what is ordinarily accepted as 'political'. Thus to 'interrogate the "political"' via more affectual categories such as grief, injury and suffering is also to suggest that we can find alternative paths to peace through the politics of small gestures and working with what is at hand. At the same time, however, it is important to remain aware of individual stories and needs when dealing with loss and grief. As Duwatha's experiences demonstrated, the risks and violence that each individual faces must be recognized and accounted for lest they are subsumed by a greater sense of collective loss. Furthermore, it takes contexts of where fear runs through everyday encounters to show us that the collective ties of suffering and injury are not simply cohesive and binding but are run through with ambiguity, tensions and silences.

The above example of the work of the Valkai group illustrates the importance of considering actions that lie outside the parameters of normative understanding. Shaped by ambiguous boundaries and a lack of definition, the Valkai group's attempts to push for space and support human life located it outside the framework of other collective organizations. The Valkai group posed an important challenge to how informal groups and networks have positioned themselves and been understood vis-à-vis the context of feminist activism. Fundamentally, networks such as the Valkai group do not start from or solely identify with the ideals of feminism and activism but form and shape themselves according to risk and need and the configurations of 'active living'. Exactly what the impact of the work of the Valkai group has been on everyday life and futures in eastern Sri Lanka is beyond the remit of this chapter. However, recognizing the need for further empirical investigation, I leave this challenge open to those who want to extend and deepen an understanding of what networks of women (and men) can and will do in the face of ongoing violence in ways that can lie beyond what is immediately visible.

Finally, in conclusion, I note that as I write in 2012, reflecting back on those evenings in 2007 and all that has happened in between, it is clear that an end to fighting in Sri Lanka has not brought peace. The situation in the north and east continues to be extremely volatile, and undoing the damage the final military campaign did to Sri Lanka's economy, reputation and democratic institutions will take years of considerable effort. In light of this, with the changing contexts and passage of time, the lives and stories presented in this chapter take on a new significance. While the experiences and strategies of everyday living have been explored within the context of a protracted conflict, which at the time of my fieldwork looked highly unlikely to come to an end, they now must adapt to a post-conflict context, in whatever guises that takes in eastern Sri Lanka. Therefore, in considering how women form informal networks and work towards uncertain futures, the realities of everyday violence, risk, threat and hopes take on a new urgency.

Notes

1 The names of all individuals and informants have been changed, in order to protect their identity and safety. Details about the Valkai group have also been omitted to avoid compromising the safety of members.

2 From January 2009 tens of thousands of Tamil civilians were killed, countless more wounded, and hundreds of thousands deprived of adequate food and medical care (ICG 2010). A recent UN report (2011) has implicated both the government security forces and the LTTE in serious violations of international humanitarian and human rights law, some of which could amount to war crimes and crimes against humanity.

3 This chapter draws on ethnographic fieldwork in Batticaloa, eastern Sri Lanka, over a period of twenty-two months between September 2004 and June 2006, with a further month in 2007. The research was funded by the Economic Research Council. I am grateful to Srila Roy and Malathi de Alwis for their feedback and ideas on this chapter, as well as to all my friends in Batticaloa and the Valkai group members.

4 There is a wealth of literature on the political history and everyday experiences of conflict in Sri Lanka; see Hoole et al. (1988), Spencer (1990a), Daniel (1996) and McGilvray (2008).

5 Schrijvers notes that despite the presence of counter-discourses (encouraged by women's movements and globalization), many women in Sri Lanka remain defined through their relationships with men (1999: 329).

6 The focus of this chapter does not allow me to go into the methodology of my fieldwork. Suffice to summarize this by noting that the greater part of my work was based on informal interviews and discussions with Valkai group members, as well as documentation of our daily activities (see Walker 2010).

7 Signed in 1987 between the Indian prime minister Rajiv Gandhi and Sri Lankan president J. R. Jayewardene, this accord was expected to bring an end to the conflict.

8 For a discussion on the role of civil society organizations and peace activism, see also Keenan (2003) and Orjuela (2005).

9 Widows and women-headed households are not an uncommon phenomenon in Sri Lanka (see Weerasinghe 1987; Perera 1991), and they have increased significantly because of the decimation of the male population in the north and east. The social stigma that surrounds widows in all three communities, Sinhala, Tamil and Muslim, has not made these women's tasks any easier (Rajasingham-Senenayake 1998: 10).

10 Her daughter had disappeared after being brought in for questioning by the LTTE. Although the LTTE claimed that they had let her go the same day, she had not returned home. Despite hearing about the body in the playground and even being in the hospital the very day the body was brought in, Duwatha had been too frightened to ques-

tion whether it was her daughter. Although not officially confirmed, the injuries on Duwatha's body were said to be consistent with the brutality of the security forces.

References

Butler, J. (2004) *Precarious Life: The Powers of Mourning and Violence*, London: Verso.

Cockburn, C. (2007) *From Where We Stand: War, Women's Activism and Feminist Analysis*, London: Zed Books.

Coomaraswarmy, R. (1996) 'Tiger women and the question of women's emancipation', *Pravada*, 4(9): 8–10.

Daniel, V. (1996) *Charred Lullabies: Chapters in an Anthropography of Violence*, Princeton, NJ: Princeton University Press.

De Alwis, M. (1997) 'Motherhood as a space for protest: women's political participation in contemporary Sri Lanka', in B. Amrita and P. Jeffrey (eds), *Appropriating Gender: Women's Activism and the Politicization of Religion in South Asia*, London and New York: Routledge.

— (2002) 'The changing role of women in Sri Lankan society', *Social Research: An International Quarterly of Social Sciences*, 69(3): 675–91.

— (2004) 'The "purity" of displacement and the reterritorialization of longing: Muslim IDPs in north western Sri Lanka', in W. Giles and J. Hyndman (eds), *Sites of Violence: Gender and Conflict Zones*, Berkeley, CA, and London: University of California Press.

— (2009) 'Interrogating the "political": feminist peace activism in Sri Lanka', *Feminist Review*, 91: 81–93.

De Silva, A. (2008) 'Ethnicity, politics and inequality: post-tsunami humanitarian aid delivery in Ampara District, Sri Lanka', *Disasters*, 33(2): 253–73.

Goodhand, J. and D. Hulme (1999) 'From wars to complex political emergencies: understanding conflict and peace-building in the new world disorder', *Third World Quarterly*, 20(1): 13–26.

Hoole, R., D. K. Somasundaram, K. Sritharan and R. Thiranagama (1988) *The Broken Palmyra: The Tamil Crisis in Sri Lanka – an Inside Account*, Claremont, CA: Sri Lanka Studies Institute.

HRW (Human Rights Watch) (2007) *Complicit in Crime: State Collusion in Abductions and Child Recruitment by the Karuna Group*, January 2007.19 (1), www.hrw.org/en/reports/2007/01/23/complicit-crime, accessed November 2009.

Hyndman, J. and M. de Alwis (2004) 'Bodies, shrines, and roads: violence, (im)mobility and displacement in Sri Lanka', *Gender, Place and Culture*, 11(4): 535–7.

ICG (International Crisis Group) (2010) 'War crimes in Sri Lanka', Asia Report no. 191, 17 May, www.crisisgroup.org/en/regions/asia/south-asia/sri-lanka/191-war-crimes-in-sri-lanka.aspx, accessed 13 June 2010.

Keenan, A. (2003) *Democracy in Question: Democratic Openness in a Time of Political Closure*, Stanford, CA: California University Press.

Kelly, T. and S. Thiranagama (2009) *Traitors: Suspicion, Intimacy, and the Ethics of State-building*, Pennsylvania: University of Pennsylvania Press.

Lawrence, P. (1997) 'Work of oracles, silence of terror: notes on the injury of war in eastern Sri Lanka', Unpublished PhD thesis submitted to the Faculty of the Graduate School of the University of Colorado.

McGilvray, D. B. (1982) 'Mukkuvar Vannimai: Tamil caste and matri-clan ideology in Batticaloa, Sri Lanka', in D. B. McGilvray (ed.), *Caste Ideology and Interaction*, Cambridge: Cambridge University Press, pp. 34–98.

— (2008) *Crucible of Conflict. Tamil and Muslim Society on the East Coast of Sri Lanka*, Durham, NC, and London: Duke University Press.

Menon, N. (2004) *Recovering Subversion: Feminist Politics beyond the Law*, Delhi/Chicago, IL: Permanent Black/University of Chicago Press.

Orjuela, C. (2005) 'Dilemmas of civil society aid: donors, NGOs and the quest for peace in Sri Lanka', *Peace and Democracy in South Asia*, 1(1): 1–12.

Perera, M. (1991) 'Female headed households – a special poverty group', in *Women, Poverty and Family Survival*, Colombo: CENWOR, pp. 27–64.

Rajasingham-Senenayake, D. (1998) 'After victimhood: cultural transformation and women's empowerment in war and displacement', Paper presented at the conference on Women in Conflict Zones, International Centre for Ethnic Studies (ICES), Colombo.

— (2004) 'Between victim and agent: women's agency in displacement', in P. Essed, G. Frerks and J. Schrijvers (eds), *Refugees and the Transformation of Societies: Agency, Ethics and Politics*, Oxford: Berghahn.

Ruwanpura, K. N. (2006) *Matrilineal Communities, Patriarchal Realities:*

A Feminist Nirvana Uncovered, New Delhi: Zubaan.

Ruwanpura, K. N. and J. Humphries (2004) 'Mundane heroines: conflict, ethnicity, gender, and female headship in Eastern Sri Lanka', *Feminist Economics*, 10(2): 173–205.

Samuel, K. (2006) *A Hidden History: Women's Activism for Peace in Sri Lanka 1982–2002*, Colombo: Social Scientists Association.

Schrijvers, J. (1999) 'Fighters, victims and survivors: constructions of ethnicity, gender and refugeeness among Tamils in Sri Lanka', *Journal of Refugee Studies*, 12(3).

Segal, L. (2008) 'Gender, war and militarisation: making and questioning the links', *Feminist Review*, 88: 21–35.

Spencer, J. (1990a) 'Introduction: the power of the past', in J. Spencer (ed.), *Sri Lanka: History and the Roots of Conflict*, London: Routledge.

— (1990b) 'Collective violence and everyday practice in Sri Lanka', *Modern Asian Studies*, 24(3): 603–23.

Stirrat, J. (2006) 'Competitive humanitarianism relief and the tsunami in Sri Lanka', *Anthropology Today*, 22(5): 11–16.

Tambiah, S. J. (1997) *Leveling Crowds. Ethnonationalist Conflicts and Collective Violence in South Asia*, Chicago, IL: University of Chicago Press.

Thiruchandran, S. (1999) *The Other Victims of War. Emergence of Female Headed Households in Eastern Sri Lanka*, vol. II, Colombo/New Dehli: WERC and Vikas Publishing House.

UN (United Nations) (2011) *Report of the Secretary-General's Panel of Experts on accountability with respect to the final stages of the decades-long armed conflict in Sri Lanka*, 12 April, www.un.org/News/dh/infocus/Sri_Lanka/POE_Report_Full.pdf, accessed 3 June 2011.

Walker, R. (2010) 'Violence, the everyday and the question of the ordinary', *Contemporary South Asia*, 18(1): 9–24

Weerasinghe, R. (1987) *Female-headed Households in Two Villages in Sri Lanka*, Colombo: Women's Education Centre.

WHO (World Health Organization) (2005) *Tsunami Situation Report*, 38, 22 February, www.searo.who.int/LinkFiles/Situation_Reports_NEWWHO22Feb2005.pdf, accessed 12 September 2009.

8 | Feminism in the shadow of multi-faithism: implications for South Asian women in the UK

SUKHWANT DHALIWAL AND PRAGNA PATEL[1]

Introduction

This chapter starts by noting the contemporary tendency for feminist contributions to distance themselves from an affinity with secularism. Conversely, we will describe a mismatch between the dominant arguments of feminists on religion and the current British policy context. We offer a feminist critique of the continuities within British social policy in which religious organizations have gained a great deal through the institutionalization of New Labour's faith agenda, and now from the Conservatives' communitarian ideology of the Big Society, each in turn building upon an already existing multi-faithist frame in which religious organizations, including the religious right, have long since been acknowledged as representatives, providers and mediators of ethnic minority rights. Since 11 September 2001, religion has become associated with spectacular events, but this chapter seeks to refocus the debate towards a more critical perspective on the normative shifts in policy formulations and civil society mobilizations and their implications for the everyday construction of subjects, localities and social welfare provision.

The chapter discusses the British policy slide from multiculturalism to multi-faithism, and particularly the impact of the Community Cohesion, Preventing Violent Extremism and Big Society agendas on women's services and South Asian women's rights in the UK. We argue that these have been used to justify cuts to specialist secular women's groups and simultaneously have initiated or consolidated faith-based mobilizations, especially Muslim women's organizations. Half of this chapter draws on the contemporary experience of Southall Black Sisters, an ethnic minority women's organization in West London, which successfully pursued a legal challenge against the local authority after they withdrew funding for specialist domestic violence services in the name of mainstreaming and cohesion. Southall Black Sisters went on to conduct research on faith and cohesion through in-depth interviews with South Asian women that use their centre. The final section of this chapter highlights findings from that report and is a reiteration of earlier feminist concerns about the dangers of engaging religion, of strengthening religious leaderships and uncritically reinforcing multi-faithist practice in Britain. This chapter concludes by appealing for a renewed affinity between feminist research and secular normativity.

Whither feminism: secular and co-opted or pious and fractured?

Feminist research and practice come with a motivation. Historically this motivation has been about three or four things: to carve out a space and bring through women's voices; to reveal and interrogate power relations; to unravel the gendered dimensions of discourse; and to deconstruct that which is considered natural and common sense. This can be tricky in the context of multiplicity; to reflect and be cognizant of multiple identities, confluences and intersections has always been a tall order. Feminist researchers looking at religion or secularism within the current climate have made conscious and per-haps subliminal decisions to prioritize one of two positions – either they focus on a reading of gender through the lens of 'race' or they focus on reading 'race' through the lens of gender – each leading to divergent outcomes.

Our starting point is the growth of religious mobilizations and a sense that there has been a desecularization of public policy, par-ticularly of relations between the state and ethnic minorities. This is distinctly contrary to the starting point of much of the current feminist research on religion, which stems from claims about secular imposition especially as an erasure of cultural difference. To take just one example, Nadia Fadil's (2011) fascinating piece in *Feminist Review* is clearly motivated by a desire to critique the secular normative notions of one's relationship with one's body as elaborated in the decisions of Muslim women interviewees that do not veil or decide to unveil. Where Fadil's interviewees expressly talked about wanting to challenge power and the imposition of the veil within their communities, she analysed this from an interest in not just revealing but *critiquing* the secular normative foundations of their practice.

This reproach from secularism stems from the post-'War on Terror' (rather than 9/11), wholesale transformation of the terms of academic debate, and not necessarily in a way that could have been predicted. Specifically, there has been little feminist scrutiny or anti-racist reflec-tion on religious, particularly fundamentalist, mobilizations leading up to 9/11 or in the wake of the 7/7 bombings in London. Needless to say, Guantánamo and the invasion of Iraq have been hugely significant in releasing feelings of dissociation, embarrassment and shame at US and British imperial claims to be carrying the mantle of human rights, and particularly to be the harbingers of women's and lesbian, gay, bisexual, transsexual (LGBT) equalities. Moreover, a new wave of liberal commentary mobilized feminist critiques of multiculturalism towards assimilationist ends. The same 'concerns' have been co-opted by the racist English Defence League as ammunition in their virulent attack on Muslims and Islam.[2] In some ways it is unsurprising that where feminism and secularism are being used as part of an assimilationist pressure feminists have also been defensive and turned inwards. Feminist academic interventions have been concerned to produce their own critiques of a revival of 'civilisational discourse' (Brown 2008), where cultures and religions are ordered in a hierarchical fashion according to allegations about sexual (un)freedoms and gender (in)equality. In the process, minority religions are characterized as derided and contained. Judith Butler (2008) condemned this as a 'cultural assault' on minorities.

Rosi Braidotti, Sarah Bracke and Saba Mahmood have drawn the connections between this critique of liberalism and secularism to make additional points about the limitations of a secular normative basis for feminism. In a sense they are encouraging feminists to adjust their foundational terms to embrace a new wave of religious mobilizations. These views rely on projections of (ethnic minority) religious political identities as subjugated and also as a vehicle of the dispossessed. Braidotti (2008) argues that this new wave of 'post-secular' subjectivities may be antithetical to the (original) feminist project, but to stick with those commitments might impede the possibilities for feminists to understand and embrace these developments. Saba Mahmood's (2005) work has been hugely influential and used to make the point that feminism denies its own affective dimensions when it questions the religious commitments of others. Mahmood points to the contradictions of a feminist project that was also built on passion, emotional engagement and the impulse to politicize the personal, to convert concerns into collective and public issues, and yet its tendency to disregard this where people are asserting religious political identities. Braidotti and Mahmood in particular are used widely in analyses of Muslim women's identity and to defend a range of religious claims. In similar vein, Sarah Bracke (2008) pushes for a validation of the political activities of pious women rather than what she sees as an overemphasis on their dress codes as veiled women. Moreover, in his analysis of the British state's intervention in legal determinations about the veil,

Stewart Motha (2007) draws on Mahmood and Braidotti to argue that feminism has not been able to merge the politics of autonomy and heteronomy; it simply can't cope with the simultaneity of polity and piety despite its own evolution from an affective political commitment and a critique of liberal citizenship and despite the parallel developments of Muslim women's scholarship. For Motha, absolute autonomy is unrealizable and contradicts the basis of politics itself. In the following paragraph, he summarizes the new philosophical concerns of many others, particularly with regard to the standing of the feminist subject and an emancipatory politics:

> Here the claim is that a respect for a plurality of cultural practices and normative frameworks can lead to normative paralysis in the face of practices that are harmful to women, such as polygamy, forced marriage, or genital cutting. But in an attempt to universalise the emancipated feminine subject, this feminist intervention undoes the very important negation of the abstract, autonomous liberal subject exposed by an earlier feminist critique. (Ibid.: 146)

Where critiques of the secular dimensions of feminism rely upon legal judgments and international discourse, they neglect the contestatory dimensions of local politics, not to mention the very real normative implications for women and girls.

It is our contention that religion- and faith-based organizing are increasingly being positioned as carrying the critical edge in defining new social relations and as sources of effective counter-movements against the brute reality of capitalism. In this context it is religion and forms of piety rather than questions of women's rights and sexuality which are deemed to constitute subalternity and counter-hegemony. Pious women in particular are presented as acting against imperially imposed time, posing a significant challenge to the dominant narrative where rights are assumed to be premised on a secular language and the notion of a secular public sphere.[3]

Alongside this meta-narrative, however, are national and local stories that highlight the impact of what Partha Chatterjee (2006) has referred to as 'heterogeneous time', and especially the gender implications of what Ranu Samantrai (2008) has termed the 'technologies of ethnicity'. Put simply, in the UK context, ethnic minority women have long since been subjected to different governing rationalities that especially rely on the reification and imposition of religion. These other stories, then, are of the reality of power relations in local neighbourhoods, the proactive mobilizations of the religious right and the religious dimensions of British social policy. In recent years, rather than being a victimized or marginalized force, religion has become a structuring principle for both welfare provision and community organizing. In the UK, we refer to this as a shift from multiculturalism to multi-faithism. Moreover, in terms of the production of critique, we stand by Chetan Bhatt's (1999a) assertion that this cultural episteme has enabled the suspension of ethical judgement in the consideration of religious mobilizations and their ideologies, particularly where these movements within minority communities are being subjected to racist structural discrimination and they locate their concerns within narratives about racialization. This enables religious right formations to live and thrive within spaces of left and human rights activism. In turn, women's and LGBT concerns are either marginalized or obscured from view. We take issue with the way in which a renewed focus on religious identities has been matched by a simultaneous deauthentication of secular feminist concerns by tainting these with allegations of racism and 'state co-option'.

British public policy and religious claims

The slide from multiculturalism to multi-faithism needs to be seen as the result of a double movement: of state policy from above but also as a consequence of demands from civil society actors from below. For several decades now religious political movements have been in the ascendancy and able to assert themselves in an ever-expanding ideological void, as alternatives to consumer and market-led neoliberalism on the one hand and authoritarian versions of communism on the other. The move towards greater accommodation of religion within state institutions and in the wider public culture reflects a number of political and social trends that have resulted in the increasing communalization of minority communities, where community groups are organized solely around religious identities. This process, which started in the aftermath of the Rushdie Affair, has accelerated and affected South Asian communities in particular.[4] However, its impact is wider, affecting other minorities and indeed the larger social culture, which is increasingly being characterized as Christian.

Moreover, religion constituted an important component of New Labour's political project. Cultivated while in opposition, the administration actively extended the role of religious groups in social welfare provision and regeneration policy.[5] There is significant evidence that the state apparatus at regional and local levels followed suit. In a sense, the subsequent establishment of expert bodies and the proliferation of

173

guides or briefings on religious needs replaced the kinds of cultural competence and cultural awareness training that was symptomatic of multiculturalism in the 1980s and 1990s.

Moreover, the Community Cohesion and Preventing Violent Extremism policy agendas have fashioned new pathways along which religious mobilizations now travel. Following the civil unrest in Britain's northern cities in 2001 and the 9/11 and 7/7 terrorist attacks, the UK state responded with a series of 'hard' and 'soft' measures which have had the effect of eroding secular spaces. In the guise of the 'War on Terror', the state sought to counter the threat of Islamist terrorism with draconian anti-civil-liberties measures. In response to the 2001 racial unrest, which was rooted in poverty and exclusion, not religious discrimination, the then Labour government developed a new 'cohesion' (assimilationist) and 'faith-based' approach to minorities to replace the previously more progressive, dominant ideological framework of multiculturalism, for mediation between the state and minority communities. In other words, one product of the 'War on Terror' was the state's deliberate pursuit of contradictory domestic policies in the name of cohesion – to create more moderate versions of Islam and to promote this and other religious identities within public institutions.

There is more continuity than change with the Conservative Party's Big Society agenda, in which religious groups have been assured a space. We are in that curious position now where the leaders of all three political parties have said that they are not religious but they all see religious organizations as important partners in consultation and service provision. Without any sense of irony, Baroness Warsi, the then Minister without Portfolio and co-chair of the Conservative Party, made it clear that, unlike the previous government, her party does do God.[6] The location of religion within the coalition government's agenda is particularly connected to the influence of Christian-led think tanks, which pre-election claimed to be focused on economic concerns and poverty but have actually carried a significant anti-feminist agenda, proclaiming the need to support marriage and mediation and to reduce abortion time limits. It is no mere coincidence that feminist arguments and women-centred services are being marginalized by the current government, including on the basis of claims that they are not 'objective' or impartial providers.

The consolidation of religion within public policy has particularly filtered through a series of government interventions engaging moral arguments to reconstruct 'the social'. This is not new. It started with New Labour, who distinguished themselves from the previous Conservative government by countering Margaret Thatcher's assertion that 'there is no society, only individuals and the state'. Nikolas Rose (2001) argued that the reformulated use of communitarianism towards neoliberal ends was *the* innovation of New Labour's politics. The Conservative's 'Big Society' and the Labour Party's 'Good Society', Phillip Blond's 'Red Tory' and Maurice Glasman's 'Blue Labour', are communitarian logics that overlap in their analyses in significant ways: there is a tacit acceptance that the welfare state has somehow caused political apathy and cultures of dependence; they profess to stand against the unmitigated force of neoliberalism but they also project the state as bureaucratic, as bound up in red tape; that red tape is invariably a reference to the state's regulatory function and any commitment to equalities issues. These discourses are an extension of an age-old argument that links rights-bearing individuals to cultures of neoliberalism. Within this context individual relationships with the state are seen as problematic and all forms of group affiliation are reified. Consensus politics and Aristotelian notions of the common good are privileged over and above accountable and transparent secular public institutions. Moreover, they all support rather than question the central place of religious organizations in defining 'the common good'. In state policy terms, religious groups are being granted greater leverage through the Localism Bill and the overall Big Society framework to determine access to welfare services. To understand how an anti-bureaucracy agenda that questions rather than supports the normative injunctions of equality legislation interacts with state-led support for religious organizations, one need only note that both Andrew Stunell (a former Baptist lay preacher and the current Minister for Communities and Local Government) and Eric Pickles (the Conservative Party chair and the Secretary of State for Communities and Local Government) have been hearing from religious groups such as the Jewish Leadership Council about how they need the government to cut the red tape on equalities if they are to contribute to the Big Society.[7]

Importantly, there is a subtext to these new fashionable discourses, and that is the sense that women have become too powerful. Phillip Blond says it outright in his critique of the 'bohemian' 1960s and feminism and in his push on marriage. But Maurice Glasman also implies it in the way that he organizes his argument for tradition and permanence. His recent piece in *Soundings* positions neoliberal individualism against socialist collectivism. The former is portrayed as an empowered and privileged woman while the latter is depicted as a deflated and embattled man. Curiously, religious organizations are positioned as victims and those questioning alliances with them or wary of faith-based initiatives are accused of having a problem with diversity.

In spite of Phillip Blond's claims about replacing New Labour's 'politics of values' with a 'politics of virtue', the key tendencies within debates about Good Society, Big Society, Red Tory and Blue Labour replicate New Labour's 'etho-politics', a term devised by Nikolas Rose (1999) to describe their emphasis on rectifying individual behaviour and breaking down barriers as the key focus of social policy. This logic has underpinned such innocuous policy phrases as cohesion, coexistence, social capital and social investment. These fit neatly with religious initiatives that are equally operating on the presumption of a flattening of local relations, sidestepping questions of power and shifting the emphasis to interpersonal interactions and values. But local areas are *not* flat or neutral spaces where resources are allocated in a transparent and democratic fashion. Rather they constitute local cartographies of power where the religious right have manoeuvred over time to place themselves at the heart of local alliances and systems of representation.

Local consequences for women and women's organizations

In the day-to-day work of the ethnic minority feminist organization Southall Black Sisters (SBS), they have to engage with the fact that religious organizations are increasingly filling a vacuum created by the failure of the state to give adequate support to those who are destitute, especially migrants and asylum seekers who are unable to work or claim benefits to meet essential living costs. In particular, SBS is increasingly forced to tap into the charitable traditions of such religious institutions when seeking to address the needs of abused women who have arrived in the UK under temporary spousal visas and who have been subject to horrific violence and domestic slavery, and who then escape or are abandoned by their abusers. Many of these women are destitute because of their insecure immigration status and the existence of a 'no recourse to public funds' rule, which prohibits them from accessing social housing or claiming benefits.

As a service provider, SBS is at a loss as to how to assist women in seeking protection in these circumstances, since the normal exit routes open to abused women in the wider society are not open to abused women with insecure immigration status. Although this has formed a major campaign for an adequate state response, on a day-to-day basis

SBS is often compelled to seek the assistance of churches, temples, mosques and gurdwaras to try to deal with this problem. But seeking help from religious organizations is not straightforward. It is riddled with dangers and dilemmas for the organization, particularly as these same institutions, even those that are liberal on some issues, have strong conservative values when it comes to women and the family.

These shifts have had significant consequences for all progressive struggles, but especially for those waged by minority women, whose bodies have become the battleground for the control of community representation. At the local level, we have witnessed the speed with which local authorities around the country have divested themselves of their 'race' equality departments and officers (although these also had shortcomings) and replaced them with Community Cohesion Directorates. Many also targeted long-standing so-called single identity groups (more often than not progressive and secular) for funding cuts at the same time as encouraging faith-based groups to emerge.

This dual process was vividly evident at the height of SBS's funding crisis in 2008.

In 2007, Ealing Council decided to cut funding to SBS on the grounds that specialist services for black and minority women worked against the interests of 'equality', 'diversity' and 'cohesion'. Its very name and existence was deemed to be unlawful under the Race Relations Act 1976 because the council said that it excluded white women, and the organization was therefore seen as discriminatory and divisive. Instead, in the name of 'best value' for money, the council decided to commission a borough-wide generic domestic violence service using exactly the same funds that had previously been awarded to SBS – funds critical to SBS in meeting core costs.

SBS was concerned that, if left unchallenged, Ealing Council's approach would have allowed public bodies to redefine the notion of equality in ways that stripped it of its progressive content. Equality had come to be defined by Ealing Council as the need to provide the same services for everyone. The move had been prompted by an attempt to address some resentment among the white population that it was the majority population rather than the minorities that had historically been discriminated against and 'excluded' from civic regeneration policies. The notion of equality in this sense was no longer linked to the needs of the most vulnerable and deprived, but instead viewed as reflecting the needs of the majority community. SBS feared that if unchallenged, this approach would be replicated elsewhere in the country, leading to the widespread closure of similar organizations set up to counter racism and to provide minority women with real alternatives to patriarchal community (religious- and cultural-based) mechanisms for dealing with disputes in the family. The process by which Ealing Council had arrived at its decision was also deemed to be unfair since it did not take account of the equality legislation and its own equality policies in reaching its decision.

SBS therefore brought a successful legal challenge against Ealing Council, which culminated on 18 July 2008 when, at the High Court in London, its right to exist as a secular specialist provider of domestic violence services to black and minority women was affirmed.[8]

In court, SBS submitted that Ealing Council's approach to the very concept of equality was profoundly flawed since it rejected the notion of positive action in addressing racism and would in effect disconnect the notion of equality from the need to protect those who are historically disenfranchised and discriminated against. SBS argued that the council's 'one size fits all' approach was misconstrued because it ignored unequal structural relations based on class, gender and race. It argued further that specialist services for minority women are needed for reasons to do with language difficulties and cultural and religious pressures, and also because of the need for advice and advocacy framed within a democratic and secular ethos in complex circumstances where racism and religious fundamentalism are on the rise in the UK and worldwide.

SBS also argued that Ealing Council's approach to cohesion was fundamentally wrong because it failed to recognize that, far from causing divisions, the provision of specialist services is sometimes necessary to address substantive racial and other forms of inequality, and that in turn is central to achieving a more cohesive society. It was pointed out that the SBS project was in fact an example of how cohesion is achieved organically, born out of collective struggles for human rights, and not by the imposition of ill-conceived social policies from above. SBS described how black and minority women from various national, ethnic and religious backgrounds learn to coexist in the secular space provided by SBS. In doing so, they both tolerate religious and cultural differences and at the same time challenge those religious and cultural practices that stifle their common desires and aspirations to live free from violence, abuse and other constrictions on their lives.

The irony of the situation in which SBS found itself was that at the same time that Ealing Council decided to withdraw financial assistance, it was developing and implementing a series of initiatives and a strategy on cohesion that was dominated by the need to promote greater religious literacy, interfaith networks and faith-based (largely Muslim) groups to deliver local welfare services.[9]

Ealing Council's Preventing Violent Extremism (PVE) strategy in 2008/09 also followed a similar vein – reflecting a major preoccupation with engagement with Muslims only. For example, of the £45 million made available by the previous Labour government for local authorities to tackle extremism among Muslims, Ealing Council received a total of £205,000 for 2008/09, rising to £225,000 and £286,000 for 2009/10 and 2010/11 respectively. Ealing's Preventing Violent Extremism agenda from 2008 to 2011 sought to 'gather greater understanding of the issues/concerns facing Muslim communities; provide space for greater dialogue and discussion around Muslim identity and understanding of Islamic values; provide more opportunities for engagement with the wider community through volunteering; and establish greater support networks for Muslim women'. This included the creation of Muslim women-only projects without any reference to the politics and ethos of such projects and despite the fact that there are no visible demands for such organizations.[10] In fact, local Muslim women make up the second-largest if not the largest single category of users of SBS services and have willingly engaged with the organization and demanded that the space remains secular.

We don't think Ealing is unique in this respect. The cohesion and faith-based approach is being repeated throughout the UK, and the organizations that have so far been closed or threatened with closure are secular organizations for black and ethnic migrants, secular women's refuges for black and minority women, disability groups and rape crisis centres. Many so-called moderates such as the Hindu Forum of Britain, the Hindu Council, the Muslim Council of Britain and many individual religious leaders have used the space opened up by the government's cohesion and faith agenda to put themselves forward as the 'authentic' voice of their communities and make demands which are primarily about controlling female sexuality through the maintenance of so-called family values. Their aim is to assume communal authority and leadership. The voices of women and other dissidents are silenced in the process. Many are also sympathetic to or have links to religious fundamentalist movements abroad.

The law and education system in this respect are sites that are being increasingly used by religious 'moderates' to assert control over women and children. The demand, for instance, for the state legal system to recognize the quasi-legal rulings of religious tribunals such as the Muslim Arbitration Tribunal are attempts to subvert the secular legal foundations of the law and in particular the principles of equality, universality and the indivisibility of human rights. Yet it is a demand that has gained the support of prominent judicial and other establishment figures.

A new settlement is taking place between 'faith groups' and the state in which 'faith groups' use the terrain of multiculturalism to further an authoritarian and patriarchal agenda. These groups use the language of equality and human rights while at the same time eschewing these very ideals. The result is that secular spaces and secular voices within minority communities are being squeezed out, which in turn means that fewer alternatives will be available to minority women and others given restrictions on their fundamental freedoms.

Undermining feminist projects

No proper research has been undertaken to examine in greater detail the reality of women's lives and how connected or disconnected they are to official assumptions about faith communities and faith-based services and social policy. Yet since mid-2000, there has been a proliferation of faith-based projects which seek to undermine the feminist projects and principles that groups like SBS have struggled to establish.

For instance, in July 2005 the Greater London Domestic Violence Project organized a round-table discussion on domestic violence with faith leaders from London's main religions, many of whom belonged to minority religions. But no secular feminist groups that had worked on domestic violence within minority communities were invited to be part of the discussion. The effect of this is twofold. First, it ensures that community leaderships do not have to account to their communities for their actions since they are encouraged to account only to the state and not to their own constituents. Secondly, the absence of South Asian feminists and progressive groups from such discussions serves to delegitimize feminist and secular approaches to social issues within minority communities. The event led to the publication of a report entitled *Praying for Peace*.[11] While it does contain feminist analysis of domestic violence, it also encourages partnerships between faith leaders and the 'domestic violence sector' (presumably white feminist projects only) in addressing issues of domestic violence. Unsurprisingly, the entire debate on violence against women is circumscribed within a religious framework, which by its very nature compromises progressive human rights language and principles. For example, the report utilizes religious notions of 'karma' and 'sin', which clearly act as substitutes for the feminist notions of human rights, choice and autonomy. Perhaps the most significant aspect of the report is that a contract between state and faith leaders in relation to domestic violence and abuse within minority communities is taking shape: in return for taking responsibility for domestic violence, faith leaders can expect to see domestic violence refuges and services accommodating religious identity and the development of partnership working arrangements with local faith leaders.

The overall message is clear. White feminist groups working on issues such as rape and domestic violence can continue to organize along secular lines and from time to time enjoy the support of the liberal establishment, including the Church of England. Also, individual women can retain their right to choice as to how they wish domestic violence to be addressed. Minority women who face violence and abuse, on the other hand, must be corralled within their religious identity whether or not they wish it and be represented by 'their' religious leaders, irrespective of the ideology and objectives of such leaders. A more recent and infamous example of this is the withdrawal of state funding for the Poppy Project, which largely supports minority women who are trafficked, and its reallocation to the (Christian) Salvation Army.[12]

The SBS study

SBS conducted a pilot study in 2009/10, which tried to map the impact of the shift in government policy from multiculturalism to multi-faithism under the banner of 'cohesion' on the struggles for equality for minority women.[13]

A key component of cohesion and the Big Society policies is the emphasis on the role of religious leaders and their institutions as 'effective community representatives' with whose aid the greater integration of minority communities is supposed to be achieved. The state's approach therefore privileges religion or faith, especially within minority communities, as the main basis of belonging to a community, or of expressing identity. However, the findings of the SBS study, which comprised one-to-one in-depth interviews conducted with twenty-one women from different religious backgrounds, reveals that this is a problematic assumption. This is especially pertinent because all of the women interviewed are at the forefront of personal and political struggles which seek to redefine their identities and their environment in a positive way. Instead of this being valued and used as the basis for creating a more harmonious and just society, the effect of current official cohesion and Big Society policies is to create ossified and reified religious identities which compel women and other vulnerable groups to remain at the margins of the wider society.

The SBS study found that in the face of their experiences of gender-related violence and control, the majority of women who were believers were acutely critical of tradition, culture and religion for perpetuating gender inequality and discrimination. None of the women expressed any sense of belonging to a faith-based community. The findings have blasted a hole through the assumption that those who have no access to or interaction with broader society identify with their particular faith-based communities.

All but one of the women in the study made a clear differentiation between believing and being part of a 'faith community'. All viewed religion as a matter of personal choice or belief, rather than the basis of a social identity. The majority identified themselves according to their present locality, such as Southall or London, or chose an identity based on country or region of origin, such as Kenya or India, or primarily described themselves as a woman or a mother. In fact the most significant aspect of how women chose to identify themselves was largely determined by their experiences of gender discrimination and oppression. They regarded their gender as the main basis of their identity. For many, their common humanity was also their main source of identification. This is perhaps not surprising since their daily and often harrowing experiences of violence and restrictions left many feeling stripped of their humanity. In fact, far from inspiring 'confidence and trust', faith groups evoked a range of fears about religion and faith-based organizations. The main findings are as follows:

1 Every single Hindu, Sikh and Muslim woman interviewed expressed very strong negative sentiments of mistrust in and alienation from faith-based leaderships. Much of their rejection sprang from actual experiences of seeking out help from religious leaderships in the UK or their countries of origin. Many women had in fact grown up in the Indian subcontinent where they had experienced wars, divisions, hostility and problems caused by religious identities.

2 Gender discrimination and lack of rights were other critical reasons for their rejection of separate faith-based institutions and laws in the UK. They strongly opposed religious prescriptions against women and feared abuse of power by religious leaders, including sexual harassment and exploitation, which they said was a common reality.

3 Many women made clear that they did not want to be boxed into specific official identities over which they had no control. Few

women chose to identify themselves exclusively according to any one identity, with the exception of two women. Most women located themselves along multiple axes of difference, i.e. according to age, gender, ethnicity and nationality. Religion was often not among the top three aspects of their identity that they felt most strongly about. Nor did they see identity as something fixed or reified.

4 Many adopted fluid and syncretic lifestyles and preferred to remain that way. They appeared to be negotiating on a daily basis the right to slip in and out of various cultural and religious and non-religious spaces. This involved rejecting aspects of their own cultural and religious identities which constrained their individual freedom and borrowing from other cultural and religious traditions that enabled them to cope better with their immediate problems. The women showed that they occupied spaces at the point of intersection of a number of cultural and religious traditions, including feminist traditions that they were creating for themselves. Their realities showed that their practices and traditions are syncretic and undogmatic and that it was precisely such lifestyles that created moments of happiness and were meaningful in otherwise relentlessly difficult and traumatic circumstances. One woman stated: 'Tomorrow I go to celebrate Valentine's Day. Islam says we shouldn't dance. ... I used to get awards for dancing. I love celebrating Valentine's Day. I will wear red clothes and red lipstick and get a red rose from my husband. I wear lots of make-up and perfume. I also love celebrating Christmas and Easter. These are small pieces of happiness.' All the women cherished the secular space provided by SBS, which they saw as an empowering space – a space that enables them to gain access to other essential secular state welfare and legal services, which provide the final safety net when they are at risk of serious harm or their lives. They were clear that however flawed the secular nature of the state, it did at least enable them to assert their fundamental human rights and freedoms.

5 Although many women were practising believers and attended their respective churches and temples, none was involved in the management or decision-making process of the religious institutions that they attended. None occupied positions of any note or power, nor knew of any women who did. Their involvement, if any, was confined to attending and occasionally leading the singing, or cooking and cleaning. Their lack of power also perhaps explained their scepticism about religious institutions, which many saw as corrupt, exploitative and unaccountable places.

6   Many immediately recognized that religious institutions were not simply places of religious worship but places where the politics of those who ran them dominated and where corruption was also a reality. Many talked of internal religious, class and caste divisions and discrimination, of rifts and fights between different rival factions of trustees seeking to assert their power and authority and others solely interested in financial gain. The internal lack of transparency and accountability only increased their general distrust of faith-based organizations and their scepticism regarding their ability to address their needs as women.

When asked to think of measures which would promote greater social cohesion, every single woman spoke of equality, respect and positive appreciation of difference. None asked for a greater role for religion or faith-based groups in public life. In fact, every single woman was firmly against the proliferation of faith-based schools or faith-based laws and institutions as they believed that such developments would have a divisive and detrimental impact upon future society. They wanted the state to provide welfare and legal services. One woman described boys educated in such schools as 'live bombs' ready to explode at the slightest provocation. Other women felt that such policies would increase division by encouraging competition between different religious groups. One woman felt that faith-based schools would fail in teaching the most essential lesson of the times – the lesson of humanity.

Conclusion

Many of the prominent feminist interventions on religion and secularism depend upon a discourse analysis and a political commitment to questioning secularism. At the current juncture, this is assumed to be *the* position of critique. Such interventions are motivated by important concerns – the need to challenge imperialist intentions and actions of US and European governments, the ongoing rise of racist populism, especially anti-Muslim racism, and the claims that are being made for gender equality and sexuality as sources of supremacy and standards of judgement. However, all is not as it seems. In the same way that there was a flip side to multiculturalism, there is a flip side to the War on Terror. In the current context, the local is a key site for negotiation and policy delivery. If one looks closely at local spaces and new regimes of governance one will see a number of subtexts. Multi-faithism is the order of the day, in the process turning a blind eye to the religious right and the uses it is actively making of local fora and national spaces within both state and civil society and all the pathways that run in between them. Moreover, the new communitarian discourse of Big Society and Good Society or Red Tory and Blue Labour depend upon a secure place for religious organizations. Noises may be being made about women's equality, but in practice it is not a priority. Indeed, under the current coalition government and its huge confluence with the Blue Labour agenda a new subtext is emerging which runs all the way out to local religious organizations – and that is the insinuation that women have got it too good, they are too powerful, and traditional institutions, namely religion and the family, are suffering.

Our view is that the new cohesion and faith-based approach to minorities has become a political resource used by the state and the religious right within minority populations to aid the desecularization process. The primacy given to the right to manifest religious beliefs brings with it a number of problems linked to questions of 'validity' and 'authenticity' (Dhaliwal and Patel 2006). Questions about which religious identities and demands are valid and whose opinion constitutes the 'authentic voice' are all issues that have immense implications for minority women's human rights (ibid.), particularly as religious leaders vie for control of community representation. Our struggle to retain our secular spaces, our secular voices, and to build a truly democratic secular state, has taken on a sense of urgency and desperation. But our real fear is that we can no longer be sure of our allies.

In such a context a key component of critique would be a greater affinity with secularism, to engage critically with religious expression, introducing notions of left and right to the debate, to insist on the progressive nature of secularism, not as erasure of the right to religious belief but as the only means of safeguarding multiple versions of religious belief and the right to non-belief and dissent of all hues. In these socially conservative times, we urgently need to revive the emancipatory conception of feminism as about creating and enabling *alternatives.* It is feminism's remit to question the normative implications of entire journals and conferences that are reinforcing the discourse around the common good. What does that say about the way in which critique contains an obligation to push faith-based politics, especially when this politics can be both discriminatory and gendered? What does this new confluence in thinking about 'the social' and civil society mean for South Asian and ethnic minority women more generally? Already struggling with the unfinished business of multi-faithism and their effacement as rights-bearing individuals, ethnic minority women are now being subjected to another round of religious-based local orders premised on new communitarian philosophies.

Notes

1 This chapter is a collaborative piece by Dr Sukhwant Dhaliwal, a recent PhD graduate of the Sociology Department at Goldsmiths, University of London, and Pragna Patel, the director of the UK-based ethnic minority women's organization Southall Black Sisters. The points summarized here are drawn from two sources. The first half is drawn from Sukhwant Dhaliwal's PhD thesis entitled 'Religion, moral hegemony and local cartographies of power: feminist reflections on religion and local politics', which compared inflections of religion in two London boroughs through both ethnography and forty-seven in-depth interviews with public actors, including local councillors, council officers and representatives of secular and religious organizations. The second half is based on Pragna Patel's long history of being involved with Southall Black Sisters, of leading the legal battle in their case against Ealing Council and the findings of her joint report 'Cohesion, faith and gender: a report on the impact of the cohesion and faith-based approach on black and minority women in Ealing', based on twenty-one in-depth interviews with local users of the Southall Black Sisters' centre, a particularly vulnerable and marginalized section of the population.

2 The English Defence League is a far-right organization that was formed in 2009 with a specific anti-Muslim agenda.

3 Time is considered to be imperially imposed through international discourse (the political rhetoric of speeches), public policy, decisions about international aid, legal judgments, immigration citizenship tests (with particular reference to Germany) and indeed military action. So religious women enacting their agency in the public sphere are thought to be going against the weight of all this machinery and national/international consensus-building. We are trying to argue that this is not the case in our experience because of the new multi-faithism, and we demonstrate this by considering the empirical evidence of SBS's experience.

4 The 'Rushdie Affair' refers to the divergent mobilizations in Britain in 1989 following the Ayatollah Khomeini's fatwa against Salman Rushdie for publication of his book *The Satanic Verses*, forcing the author to go into hiding. In Britain, Muslim groups organized a march at which copies of the book were burnt and called for death to Rushdie. This marked a seminal moment in the articulation of a specifically Muslim political identity. It also marked the birth of the organization Women Against Fundamentalism, which opposed the fundamentalist-led Muslim demonstration and the concurrent fascist mobilization of the British National Party.

5 The formal state recognition of faith communities dates back to the establishment of the Inner Cities Religious Council in 1992 under the Conservative Party. This continued

under New Labour, but the Office of the Deputy Prime Minister was given responsibility to work on the Supporting Communities Programme within the Neighbourhood Renewal Unit. Moreover, as soon as New Labour got into government they extended state funding (by granting voluntary aided status) to minority faith schools on the basis of parity arguments. Then the Education Act 2006 recognized religious groups in the management of Trust schools and New Labour enabled the creation of City Academies, a large number of which are now owned and managed by religious groups and leaders. A new Faith and Cohesion Unit was established and New Labour created the first central government fund to help religious groups consolidate their base. Money was then dispensed under the 2006–08 Faith Community Capacity Building Fund. Importantly, applications were encouraged from projects operating within already designated Neighbourhood Renewal Areas or boroughs with high numbers of ethnic minority residents. This is a clear indication of a government remoulding its relationship with ethnic minorities towards a multi-faith frame. This was followed by a framework for interfaith dialogue and action and then myth-busting guidance to encourage local authorities to work with religious groups.

6 See the speech given by Baroness Warsi at the Conservative Party conference in Manchester, 15 September 2010, www.conservatives. com/News/Speeches/2010/09/Sayeeda _Warsi_The_importance_of_faith_ to_life_in_Britain.aspx. Baroness Wasi is currently the Senior Minister of State at the Foreign and Com-

monwealth Office and Minister for Faith and Communities.

7 See Robyn Rosen, 'JLC advises on Big Society' *Jewish Chronicle*, 9 December 2010, www.thejc.com/ community/community-life/42326/ jlc-advises-big-society.

8 See R (Kaur & Shah) v Ealing London Borough Council & EHRC [2008] EWHC 2062 (Admin).

9 See Ealing Council (2007), *Ealing's Shared Future: Integration and Community Cohesion Strategy 2007–2011*.

10 See Ealing Council (2008), *Preventing Violent Extremism; 2008–09 Programme*.

11 See Greater London Authority, *Praying for Peace: Domestic violence and faith communities round-table report*, November 2006, legacy. london.gov.uk/gla/publications/ crime.jsp.

12 See www.guardian.co.uk/ society/2011/apr/11/eaves-housing-trafficking-salvation-army.

13 This section is drawn from the report by P. Patel and U. Sen (2011), *Cohesion, Faith and Gender: A report on the impact of the cohesion and faith based approach on black and minority women in Ealing*, published by Southall Black Sisters and Oxfam, www.southallblacksisters.org.uk/ report-requests.html.

References

Bhatt, C. (1999a) 'Lore of the homeland: Hindu nationalism and indigenist "neoracism"', in L. Back and J. Solomos (eds), *Theories of Race and Racism: A Reader*, London: Routledge.

— (1999b) 'Ethnic absolutism and the authoritarian spirit', *Theory, Culture & Society*, 16(2): 65–85.

Blond, P. (2010) *Red Tory: How left and right have broken Britain and how we can fix it*, London: Faber and Faber.

Bracke, S. (2008) 'Conjugating the modern/religious, conceptualising female religious agency: contours of a postsecular conjuncture', *Theory, Culture & Society*, 25: 51.

Braidotti, R. (2008) 'In spite of times: the postsecular turn in feminism', *Theory, Culture & Society*, 25(1).

Brown, W. (2008) *Regulating Aversion: Tolerance in the Age of Identity and Empire*, Princeton, NJ: Princeton University Press.

Butler, J. (2008) 'Sexual politics, torture and secular time', *British Journal of Sociology*, 59(1): 1–23.

Chatterjee, P. (2006) *The Politics of the Governed: Reflections on Popular Politics in Most of the World*, Leonard Hastings Schoff Lectures, New York: Columbia University Press.

Dhaliwal, S. and P. Patel (2006) *Multiculturalism in Secondary Schools: Managing Conflicting Demands*, www.workinglives. org/research-themes/racism/cre-multiculturalism-in-secondary-schools.cfm.

Fadil, N. (2011) 'Not +/- unveiling as an ethical practice', *Feminist Review*, 98: 85–109.

Glasman, M. (2010) 'Labour as radical tradition', *Soundings*, 46, Winter.

Mahmood, S. (2005) *Politics of Piety: The Islamic revival and the feminist subject*, Princeton, NJ, and Oxford: Princeton University Press.

Motha, S. (2007) 'Veiled women and the affect of religion in democracy', *Journal of Law and Society*, 34(1).

Rose, N. (1999) *Powers of Freedom: Reframing Political Thought*, Cambridge: Cambridge University Press.

— (2001) 'The politics of life itself', *Theory, Culture & Society*, 18(1).

Samantrai, R. (2008) 'Continuity or rupture? An argument for secular Britain', in J. Jakobsen and A. Pellegrini (eds), *Secularisms*, Durham, NC, and London: Duke University Press.

About the contributors

Sadaf Ahmad is associate professor of anthropology in the Department of Humanities and Social Sciences at the Lahore University of Management Sciences. She is the author of *Transforming Faith: The Story of Al-Huda and Islamic Revivalism among Urban Pakistani Women* (2009), and the editor of *Pakistani Women: Multiple Locations and Competing Narratives* (2010). Her research interests cover diverse domains, including gender-based violence, gender and religion, social movements and Pakistani cinema.

Srimati Basu is associate professor of gender and women's studies and anthropology at the University of Kentucky, presently at work on *Managing Marriage: Family Law and Family Violence in India*, an ethnographic study of lawyer-free courts, domestic violence, rape prosecutions, and mediation in the context of violence. She has written about Indian women and inheritance laws in the monograph *She Comes to Take Her Rights: Indian Women, Property and Propriety* (1999), on property, law, marriage, intimacy, violence and popular culture in various anthologies and journals, edited the *Dowry and Inheritance* volume in the Kali for Women series 'Issues in Indian Feminism', and is a contributing blogger to Ms Magazine Online.

Sukhwant Dhaliwal is a recent PhD graduate from the Sociology Department at Goldsmiths, University of London. Her thesis is entitled *Religion, Moral Hegemony and Local Cartographies of Power: Feminist Reflections on Religion and Local Politics*. She moved into academia after ten years' work in the voluntary sector for feminist organizations tackling violence against women. Since 1995 she has also been a member of the activist network Women Against Fundamentalism. Moreover, she has worked as a researcher across a number of equality strands, encompassing: racial harassment and social housing; the housing needs of black disabled people; racism and European trade unions; multiculturalism in secondary schools; trade union responses to religious identity and religious mobilizations; and the impact of the faith agenda on women.

Trishima Mitra-Kahn is an executive committee member of the Feminist and Women's Studies Association of the UK and Ireland. Her research focuses on the continuum of gendered victimization and draws upon anthropological, criminological and statistical methods. Having recently completed a postdoctoral research associateship at the Centre for Criminological Research at Keele University, she has set up, with colleagues at Sussex and Northumbria universities, a network of academics, policy-makers, third-sector organizations and journalists working on sexual violence against university students. With a regional specialism in South Asia, Trishima serves as an expert sociological witness for gender-based violence asylum cases in the UK. Apart from peer-reviewed book chapters, she has co-published in *Current Sociology* and *Policy and Politics*.

Sohela Nazneen has a PhD in development studies and an MA in gender and development from the Institute of Development Studies, University of Sussex. She is an associate professor at the Department of International Relations, University of Dhaka, and a lead researcher at the BRAC Development Institute, BRAC University. Her research mainly focuses on institutional analysis of gender, particularly in the areas of governance, and rural and urban livelihoods. Sohela's ongoing work focuses on South Asia and sub-Saharan African countries, exploring feminist movement-building in transitional contexts, gendered politics of inclusion and influence in policy processes, intimate partner violence and women's participation in Islamist movements. She has worked as an international consultant for UNDP, the Bill and Melinda Gates Foundation, and other development agencies. Her most recent publication, *Rural Livelihoods and Gender*, was a technical background paper for the Asia Pacific Human Development Report by UNDP.

Pragna Patel is a founding member of the Southall Black Sisters and Women Against Fundamentalism. She worked as a coordinator and senior case worker for SBS from 1982 to 1993, when she left to train and practise as a solicitor. In 2009 she returned to SBS as its director. She has been centrally involved in some of SBS's most important cases and campaigns on domestic violence, immigration and religious fundamentalism. She has also written extensively on race, gender and religion. Among her many publications have been: 'Citizenship: whose rights?', in *Women and Citizenship in Europe: Borders, Rights and Duties*, ed. A. Ward et al. (1992); 'The time has come … Asian women in struggle', in *Black British Feminism – a Reader*, ed. H. S. Mirza (1997);

several essays in *From Homebreakers to Jailbreakers*, ed. R. Gupta (2003); 'Faith in the state? Asian women's struggles for human rights in the UK', *Feminist Legal Studies* (2008); 'R v Zoora (Ghulam) Shah', in *Feminist Judgments from Theory to Practice*, ed. Rosemary Hunter, Clare McGlynn and Erika Rackley (2010); and (with Hannana Siddiqui) 'Shrinking secular spaces: Asian women at the intersect of race, religion and gender', in *Violence against Women in South Asian Communities*, ed. Ravi K. Thiara and Aisha K. Gill (2010).

Shirin M. Rai is professor in the Department of Politics and International Studies at the University of Warwick. She has directed a Leverhulme Trust–funded programme on Gendered Ceremony and Ritual in Parliament (2007–11). Her research interests are in gendered performance and politics, gender and political institutions, and gender and the political economy of development. She is the author of *The Gender Politics of Development* (2008) and editor of *Ceremony and Ritual in Parliament* (2010). She is also a visiting professorial fellow at the Gender Institute, London School of Economics.

Debarati Sen is assistant professor of international conflict management and anthropology at Kennesaw State University. She is a cultural and feminist anthropologist who researches the impacts of alternative trade regimes on women's community activism. Over the past several years she has conducted research in eastern India, specifically the Darjeeling district in West Bengal, on sustainable trade regimes and ethnic subnationalism. Her research and teaching endeavour to embody a strong commitment to issues of social justice from a feminist perspective.

Svati P. Shah is an assistant professor at the University of Massachusetts, Amherst, in the Department of Women's, Gender, and Sexuality Studies; she is also affiliated to the university's Department of Anthropology. Dr Shah completed her PhD in 2006 in Columbia University's joint anthropology and public health programme. Her research has focused on the intersections of political economy, sexuality, the law, space and urbanization in India.

Maheen Sultan is one of the founders of the Centre for Gender and Social Transformation at the BRAC Development Institute, BRAC University. She is a development practitioner with over twenty-five years' experience working for NGOs, donors, the UN, Grameen Bank and the Bangladeshi government in a range of capacities, from direct programme management to policy formulation. She has worked on issues of social development, poverty, civil society and community participation, and gender equality in various capacities. She has worked closely with the government in the post-Beijing Conference period on gender mainstreaming and CEDAW reporting. Maheen is also a women's rights activist and researcher. She is a member of Naripokkho, a Bangladeshi women's activist organization, and a board member of Caritas Bangladesh and Utsho Bangladesh. She is also a member of the ADB External Forum on Gender and Development. Her current research interests include women's organizing and movements and women's work and mobilizing.

Rebecca Walker is a graduate of the University of Edinburgh, where she completed her doctoral thesis in 2010. This is now forthcoming as a monograph with Manchester University Press entitled *Enduring Violence, Everyday Life and Conflict in Eastern Sri Lanka*. Her research looks at issues of violence and conflict and in particular how these affect everyday life and the kinds of support networks that emerge within everyday settings. Rebecca now holds a postdoctoral fellowship at the Centre for Indian Studies in Africa (CISA) at the University of Witwatersrand in Johannesburg. Her latest research looks at how past experiences of violence as well as present difficulties affect the ways in which communities come together and form networks in their everyday lives in Johannesburg. She is currently volunteering and researching at a women's refuge shelter in Johannesburg, which is located in what used to be the pass office of the apartheid administration in Johannesburg.

Index

contraception, 55
Convention on the Elimination of All Forms of Discrimination Against Women (CEDAW), 32, 96
Council of Islamic Ideology (Pakistan), 55
counselling of women, 73, 74, 76, 77, 78, 80
culturalization of women's issues, 6
customary dispute resolution, 72
cyberactivism: feminist, 15, 108–30; state control of, 125

Darjeeling, tea plantations, labour relations in, 131–50
Darjeeling Gorkha Hill Council, 140, 141–2, 144
Darjeeling tea, qualities of, 140
Declaration on the Elimination of Violence Against Women, 32
Delhi Prohibition of Eve Teasing Act (1988), 111
desecularization of public policy, 170
development paradigm of women's issues, 47–8
Devi, Bhanwari, 13
Did you ask for it campaign, 116, 124
difference, valuing of, 184
disappearances of people, 156, 159, 160
divorce, 67, 78, 81, 82; prevention of, 72
D'mello, Rosalyn, 118
Doezema, Jo, 37
donor funding, 47, 54, 62, 70, 89, 90, 92, 93, 95; debates about, 94; shrinkage of, 97
Doorbar network, 95, 99, 102
dowry, 80, 111; recovery of, 78
Durbar Mahila Samanwaya Committee (DMSC), 38
Duwatha, a mother, 162–3, 164

Ealing Council, 169–88
empowerment, of women, 1, 10, 13, 69, 91, 132, 147, 155, 157; economic, 89, 102; under neoliberalism, 70, 83
English Defence League (EDL), 171
environmental movements, 101
equality, definition of, 177
ethnicity, 172; in Ghorkaland movement, 141–5
etho-politics, 176
eve-teasing, 109, 111–12, 114, 117, 124

everyday life, 120; framework of discourse, 108

Facebook, use of, 101, 115, 118, 119
faith-based leaderships, distrust of, 182
faith-based schools, 184
family assistance, 73–6
family courts, 67
family law, organizing around, 66–86
family planning, 55
fear, operating on women, 117
feminism: and cyberactivism, in India, 108–30; and sex work, 27–9; dichotomies of, 60–2; in Bangladesh, 87–107; in UK, 169–88; Islamic, 6; motivations of, 170; new forms of activism, 19; perceived demise of, 1, 2, 17; post-colonial, 109; second-wave, 33–4; seen as Westernization, 6; South Asian feminisms, 4; split subjectivity of, 110; use of term, 6, 11
feminist activism, as active living, 161–3
feminist projects, undermining of, 180–1
Fight-Back organization, 118
Firoza Begum, 74–6
flash mobs, 118, 119
Fraser, Nancy, 131–2, 146
free trade agreements, and migration of labour, 35
Friedan, Betty, 124
funding *see* donor funding

Gandhi, Indira, 133
gender: as primary axis of subordination, 72; domestication of, 8; in feminist theorization, 7; issues of (integrated into academia, 98–9; relegated to post-revolution, 77); visibility of, 1
Gender and Development, 88
Gender Study Forum, 123
generational divide in feminism, 14, 97–104
generational shift in feminist movement, 88
ghettoization of women, 118
Glasman, Maurice, 175
glass wall, between state and civil society, 56–8
globalization, 3, 5, 7